D1433709

Paul Darcy Boles

Storycrafting

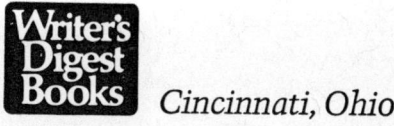 Cincinnati, Ohio

Storycrafting.
 Published by Writer's
Digest Books, 9933 Alliance Road, Cincinnati,
Ohio 45242. First edition.

Library of Congress Cataloging in Publication Data

Boles, Paul Darcy, 1916-1984
  Storycrafting.

  Includes index.
  1. Short story. I. Title.
PN3373.B62 1984 808.3'1 84-15182
ISBN 0-89879-147-2

Design by Noel Martin

For all who have helped so greatly: **Dorothy Boles**
Carol Cartaino
Nancy Dibble
Howard I. Wells III
Pat Conroy

By Paul Darcy Boles

Novels:
The Streak
The Beggars in the Sun
Glenport, Illinois
Deadline
Parton's Island
The Limner
The Mississippi Run
Glory Day

Short Stories:
A Million Guitars
I Thought You Were a Unicorn

Novella:
Night Watch

For Writers:
Storycrafting

Paul Darcy Boles

March 5, 1916–May 3, 1984

*O*nce upon an Atlanta evening, I met a man so exuberantly outrageous I knew he had to be better than good at what he did. Supreme self-confidence usually puts me off, but somehow I found myself beside the writer in the red-lined Roosevelt cape, trading thoughts on what "the ultimate short story book" might be. Not many months later, I was receiving intense, elegant letters from this same person . . . now trying to produce that very book for us.

What was he out to accomplish, Paul Darcy Boles, with that intrepid typewriter and that bold pen? What *would* a better book on story writing be? We can read the following pages and see: Someone not just widely published, but in prestigious places, giving us gentle but unwavering guidance every step of the way. Not making writing more difficult by creating an artificial universe of terms, rules, and corollaries to be mastered—but managing to make it more immediate and understandable. Not just circling at the surface muttering the same old maxims: "Dialogue lends life to a story." "Write a detailed description of each character before you start." But taking us down *in* to that interior process of which we know so little—except the beginning, poised over the paper, and the end: sentences on a sheet. Smoothly navigating that huge, hazy landscape, illuminating all the invisible acts of writing, guiding us through and making us comfortable with the complex and sometimes perplexing set of choices writing is. All the while, exulting in our wholly human urge to carve stories out of life, and building every skill we need to make those stories sing.

Paul Boles took great joy in the act of writing and the wielding of words—you could feel it in his every call and letter. And one sensed his very special pleasure in distilling a lifetime's knowledge of his craft—not only a craftsman's pride but the "deep and strange responsibility" he felt for every writing student he ever had. He was always ahead of schedule and full of excitement about this book "beating in me to be born." Thus his death, shortly after completing the last revisions, was an even greater shock.

"Writing is a form of immortality"—not until reading this finished manuscript did I fully realize what that means. Paul is alive in these pages, holding a conversation with you and me—telling us what he knows, with his own unique force and in his own inflections. His joy is alive and his craft is alive, and you can feel not just the wisdom, but the person, through the pages. Our sadness that he isn't here to see the publication of *Storycrafting* has given way to comfort in the fact that he was able to bring it to full term.

As Paul himself said:

Outside the always underestimated gifts of life and sunlight there is this fierce need for interpretation . . . The thing that starts a poem, seeds a novel, is a form of love . . . Libraries are as important as good bread, and what they hold will outlast all bread and flesh and keep pace with the dreams of those unborn. Who asks for finer compensation for work than that?

Carol Cartaino
Editor-in-Chief
Writer's Digest Books

Contents

Chapter 1

Beginnings

A history of the short story would be longer than the *Encyclopaedia Britannica*. And it would still be incomplete.

It would start with the cave men and women speaking tales of wonder to the listening tribe—bits and pieces of dreams which gave courage, entertainment, and awe.

It would go on through picture writing and the various transitions of the written word into the languages of man.

It would follow Gutenberg's invention of movable type with the saga of Eastern and Western sophistication in the story. It would take in the gilded, discursive Arabian tale, the hundreds of interlocked stories that make up the Japanese *Tale of the Genji* by Lady Murasaki, the Elizabethan broadsheet and all fairy tales, folk tales, and legends. It would trace the evolution of the story from Homer, Chaucer, and Boccaccio—and from the French *conte* with its sharp tang, and the golden tongue of the *schanochie*, the professional storyteller who walked the roads of Ireland. It would give due weight to the Yiddish story and the American Indian, the Spanish, and the Polynesian. And the tall tale in all languages. The East Indian and the African heritage of story would be fully explored.

It would come down to the day before yesterday with a hundred names and biographies of skilled storytellers who have pushed the boundaries of the art outward.

It would light up what's being done in the story today and speculate with much hemming and hawing over what will happen to it tomorrow.

It would end with the upbeat conclusion that the story has held its own through changing customs and every sort of roller-coaster market and that it's miraculously still around to delight, inform, and startle us.

All writers of the story are still storytellers sitting around the cave of the world.

What Is It?

It has as many definitions as the blind men had for their fabulous elephant.

Its bright and buoyant virtue is that it's traditionally short.

Somerset Maugham said that it must have a beginning, a middle, and an end.

But some beautiful stories are as long as young novels.

And some excellent stories have no more beginning, middle, and end than a plate of lasagna.

Its forward motion may be like the catapult, sudden and fierce and moving from *here* to *there* in a parabola of impact that hits the reader straight between the eyes.

Or it may be artfully slow, rising around the reader in a tide of sensation and revelation.

The best all-around description of it was given by Stephen Vincent Benét: "something that can be read in an hour and remembered for a lifetime."

Approaching It

Writing the marketable story can't be taught.

It can be guided.

If you have talent, your talent can be sharpened toward the making of stories which will have a fighting chance with a magazine editor. Your special fund of emotion and skill can be channeled into the story that gets the editor's attention and starts you on a published career. There is no mystery about this. There are no tricks to it.

There is a lot of work, coupled with the joy of mastering an art almost as old as time—one which many believe to be the most rewarding of any.

It starts with knowing the kind of story you want to write—choosing your stamping ground and staking it out as your own.

And the kind of story you want to write is dictated by the kind you like to read.

The richness and quality and force of your storytelling will always be reflected by your reading. This means that the more you read, the better you'll get.

It means that what you read gives you a standard to aim at—or to surpass.

It means that as you read, you pick and choose those stories you most deeply admire and can really learn from.

It means that you learn to read in a professional spirit—for instruction as well as for plain enjoyment.

You read not to imitate, but to know. You read with analysis and comprehension of the writer's problems. With sympathy, but on the deeper level of learning.

The First Experiment

Take three published stories that have impressed you. Make sure they are what you consider the best of their kind. Don't grab at random, but sit down and think before you select. Treat this experiment as though you were about to be marooned on the Dry Tortugas and were allowed the stories as your only reading matter for six months. Be completely honest—if you like a light, flippant story, don't set it aside in favor of something someone has told you is a classic. This is not a Great Story course. It's as personal as your choice of color, your built-in taste in political candidates.

These must be stories that please you. If you lean toward Tolstoy's "The Death of Ivan Ilyich," fine, but make sure that's what you really like, not something you believe you ought to appreciate because it's gathered so many layers of holy dust through the years. If it's a story nobody else has ever heard of, something you read and enjoyed and clipped out of a magazine years ago, you're getting close to the real writing *you*. If it's a story you read and loved, or had read to you, when you were a child, so much the better. The categories don't make any difference. Romance, science fiction, fantasy, something from a literary quarterly or an old *Saturday Evening Post* or *Ladies' Home Journal* or *Esquire* or *Playboy*. Something that made you laugh, made you cry, or brought you up short with a feeling of doors opening and wonder on the threshold.

When you've taken your time, sifted through many possibilities, and narrowed them down to the three winners, go into the room where you write and sit down with the stories until you can tell yourself why you enjoy them more than any others.

Isolate the reasons for their appeal to you. Be as specific as you can. "I like this, Eudora Welty's 'A Worn Path,' because it is so overwhelmingly gentle and true, so farseeing in its understanding of a single human being in a careless world, that it lifts my heart all over again every time I read it." "I picked this, Hemingway's 'The Killers,' because it is plain horror in as few words as it can be communicated, and it says something enormous to me that I'd like to say in what I write." "This story, 'Love Is Like a Nightgown,' by Sandra Masefield Scuppernong, is my idea of what a perfect love story should be."

It's not necessary that the stories be alike in surface treatment. What is important is that each has something about it that appeals to your writing self—that clicks deep inside you and gives you a reasonable idea of where you want to go with your first real story.

This experiment is the boundary test. If you let it, it can show you where you ought to be aiming. It can save you the frustration of dealing with material out of your natural range. It can give you a sense of balance and a goal.

While you're performing it, be sure not to let yourself be overwhelmed by the mastery of your models. Keeping your chin up and realizing that every Chekhov, Flaubert, and Katherine Mansfield was a fumbler at the start is necessary to your self-respect.

And your self-respect and confidence are going to be as vital to every story you write as the talent you were born with.

Don't Be a Chameleon

There is a dash of the sedulous ape in every storyteller. We take on the coloring of what we enjoy. But letting this tendency go to extremes is a waste of time and energy. If you read Ray Bradbury one day and try to write like him the next, then flit to the works of Dorothy Parker and wisecrack your way through a story, then settle down with Saroyan and do a freewheeling pastiche about Armenians, none of it will be lasting or valuable. Sincere admiration is a noble quality. But the inner you who is a serious and intelligent storycrafter can be retarded by doing all this sincere flattery.

The way to look at what you admire is in its relation to what you can do. The essence of what you are will be in your best stories. Finding out what kind of stories they are was your first step. If you want to write true-confession stories, be sure they are the best you can do. If you actually have a knack for airy humor, indulge it to the hilt. But don't be what you aren't, straining to try your hand at so many styles that you take a slapdash attitude toward storywriting itself.

Don't be a chameleon on a piece of Scotch plaid.

They burst themselves trying.

What Do You Know?

"Write what you know" is the oldest rule laid down by teachers to beginners.

Like Maugham's "beginning, middle, and end," it's useful as far as it goes.

But—Emily Dickinson spent her days and nights in the house and garden of her home in Amherst. She wrote about eternity.

The Elvish invented by J.R.R. Tolkien for his major work came from his study of ancient language roots. The hobbits, fur feet and all, walked out of his head.

Stephen Crane's *The Red Badge of Courage* was written after the Civil War by a man who had never seen one of its battles.

Joan Grant's stories of prehistory Egypt were written without deep research—you can't research the unknown—and expert Egyptologists praise them for their uncanny rightness.

Ray Bradbury's Mars is more convincing than many a story of Southern California.

Whatever pulls you to it like a secret magnet may be your story meat. Your imagination is a somewhat holy and mysterious place. You may know the place or places where you grew up as Twain knew the Mississippi. But unless they tug and twitch at you to be put in stories, you don't have to limit yourself to that kind of realism.

Your imagination is also a free-floating balloon. Like a balloon, it needs solid earth to take off from, a decent wind of urgency to take it from Point A to Point Z, a good sense of navigation to keep it from coming to grief. But if you're a born balloonist, you don't have to look longingly at the clouds while you slug away at a grounded story that never did enchant you.

Not long ago I asked six storywriting friends what they thought had been their biggest difficulty when they started.

After a few wry comments such as "Not being born rich," and considerable genial argument, the unanimous answer boiled down to, "Finding what I do best and having the sense to do it."

This didn't mean any of the writers was stuck in a formula rut. They were all still growing, and their stories ranged from absolute fantasy to romantic love to explorations into the lives of teenagers. One had been born in a military family but put his special stamp of indelible humor and distrust of the military mind and enormous family affection in everything he wrote. Another had grown up in a sheltered small community as an only child, but her work moved from the discovery of a compassionate wisdom during the integration of the South to a deft horror story with surrealistic overtones. Another had been born long after the Holocaust, had never set foot in South America or Germany, but his best work dealt with the memoirs of a Nazi doctor who had served as an officer in a death camp and was summing up his past from a South American jungle.

My first novel, actually an extended and intense short story, treated the rocketlike rise and the death in action of a racing driver on the Continental circuit in the 1930s. It was commended for its authenticity and immediacy of emotional detail. I had never seen an automobile race, never sat in a Bugatti or Maserati cockpit, never visited Europe at that time. But I wasn't faking, either. I had somehow been there. The core of the book was right. It was what I could do best then and had had the luck and the sense to find.

A strange point is that when you're nudged toward a particular story—even though it takes place in Tibet and you live in Ottumwa, Iowa—odd facts and bits of specialized information about that story keep coming to you like gifts. This isn't just the result of focused research. It's as though you'd made yourself into a receptacle to which accurate pieces of a story pattern are drawn. Every storywriter has had it happen. Hervey Allen once described an English family house he thought he'd imagined, only to receive a letter from the residents of a certain house in England asking when he had seen the rooms and how he had known certain details they thought nobody else could know.

But an idea is your own, nobody else's, only when it fits your talent and your gifts of perception. Just setting off into the blue with a vague feeling that you can write about anything at all is plain waste.

When writing not simply what you know, but what you believe you know, trust only the material that haunts you.

Thinking Story

The novel has an up and down motion. It goes in a series of wave crests and troughs. It moves with undulance. Even in the pared-down, almost bald novels of the late James M. Cain, which are restricted to action and dialogue whittled to their simplest elements, the movement is Alpine, roller-coaster, rising, falling, and rising.

The story is a straight line. The marketable story is nearly always held in tight reins of time. The time elapsed in most stories is at most a season, usually a few days or hours. Chekhov's marvelous observation, "The art of writing is the art of abbreviation," applies to the commercial story of today more than it ever did.

Abbreviation is not private code. It is the clarification of the complex. In the story large ideas are briskly implied. What is between the lines looms as largely as what appears on the page. But there can be no cryptic semaphoring, no messages held so close to the chest they're unreadable. The modern story is like the modern poem in that it relies on the reader's informed imagination much more than did the stories of Sir Walter Scott or Thomas Hardy or Robert Louis Stevenson. Today's reader simply doesn't need excessive explanation—he can see clearly when he is given a few clear-cut hints. But the modern story is not dense and it doesn't require footnote or translators. Its works may be simple in the extreme, as in Hemingway. His story vocabulary has been estimated at about eight hundred words—that of an average high school sophomore. A story's words may glitter with light and allusion, as in John Cheever and J.D. Salinger. They may be serviceable earthenware with flashes of gold, as in Scott Fitzgerald. They may be as full of fireworks as Faulkner's. But their common ground is that they are intensely readable.

The more you train yourself to think in terms of the story, the more readable your stories will be.

The Second Experiment

Study these story openings for their readability and their power to make the reader want to know what happens next. When you've finished, write three openings of your own which you feel have the same quality.

Suddenly Red Boward took his brass knuckles out of his pocket, he slipped them over his fingers, banged his right fist into his left palm and said, "I'll fight any man anytime I'm crowded."

Once upon a time, very far from England, there lived three men who loved each other so greatly that neither man nor woman could come between them.

There are times in everyone's youth when the whole sense and meaning of being young comes up like a wave and leaves in its path forever a warm, bone-deep residue of strength and rightness.

John Bell Clayton wrote the first in "The Soft Step of the Shawnee," the second is from Rudyard Kipling's "Namgay Doola," and the third is from my "The Big Beast." All of them deal with young men. They are all carefully balanced sentences filled with narrative conviction and calculated to draw the reader into the story with sympathy and a minimum of words. Clayton's opening is pure action and a picture of character. Kipling's charming use of the "Once upon a time" lays the groundwork for a legend. My statement promises a singular revelation of event and discovery.

Make your openings as memorable as you can. Get the reader's attention, but get it in a way that leads naturally to the next fact or picture you want the reader to see. An opening is a compressed emotional promise of things to come. It may be terse or leisurely, but it contains the seed of everything that will grow from it. It sets the rhythm of the story. It is not merely a dramatic hook. It is as unselfconscious as possible, sliding into the reader's mind like a voice at the shoulder.

Bad openings are those that stretch the longbow of reader credulity and can't be followed up. (" 'Hell,' said the duchess as she fell off the Leaning Tower of Pisa" is a striking opening, but hard to follow.) Weak openings are those that stroll in vaguely like actors who have forgotten their lines. "I wandered lonely as a cloud on that grand April morning, or possibly it was May because I've really forgotten the month, but then I'd been watching so many soap operas that I might have had amnesia."

What bad openings signal to the reader is blatant false confidence; what weak openings signal is confusion.

Readers don't have time to sort out what you mean. They'll believe what you say if you say it well from the start.

Write your openings over as many times as it takes to make them shapely and packed with promise.

Then begin to think about going on.

Chapter 2

Brevity

*Y*our story will stand a far better chance in today's market if it can be told in 3,000 words or less. This is ten pages, double-spaced. If this restriction bothers your sense of story values, cheer yourself up by reflecting that the Gettysburg Address is very brief and that the Song of Solomon takes up only modest space in the Bible.

The days of voluminous magazine room for short fiction are over.

Thinking in story space will encourage you to trim your story as you plan it—to leave out the fat, eliminate side trips, and hold back your self-indulgence for other pursuits.

It will cut down on characters, help to aim you in the manner of a rifle rather than a scattergun, and bring in focus what was fuzzy.

It will eliminate all the dreary padding by means of which so many former long-winded tale-tellers gave the effect of importance by loading their work with detail.

Your detail will improve simply by being vital to the story and not dragged in by the heels.

If you throw up your hands in alarm and say that these artificial boundaries stifle you, that you need room to let the story breathe, and that *Reader's Digest* condensation is a curse meant to squeeze decent prose into palatable capsules, perhaps you were a novelist all the time and shouldn't come near the story except to sneer.

But if you rise to the challenge of capturing on paper a story strong enough to compete with television, movies, and radio for the attention of the much-assaulted general reader, then you will teach yourself economy.

By doing so you will improve your writing in all other forms.

The habit of the short story is insidious.

Once you have done a good one, the prospect of the next will be doubly attractive.

If you start out in the little magazines or reviews, which vary startlingly in quality and, at their most generous, pay enough to keep a canary in seed for a week, length won't be an immediate problem. The pleasure of seeing your name in byline print will be sufficient to keep you smiling for a few days.

But if you are a born crass professional who intends to build a career by concentrating on stories, you are bound to take more than one look at your first limited-audience effort and see where it could have been cut, shaped, and doctored into something with wider appeal.

This writer has had the experience of seeing one of his best stories turned down by a national magazine at a time when they were buying every third story he wrote. In a burst of artistic madness he bypassed his agent and sent the reject to a university review. The review paid $10 for it, which was exactly what the author had received for his first published story while he was an adolescent. A week later, the large magazine reconsidered and asked to see the story again. He was forced to admit that it was now out of circulation. The difference in payment was $2,490. It was worth every penny of the larger price. The moral is that you can please God and mammon at the same time, but pleasing the dilettante can be expensive.

Each daughter and son of woman born has a little dilettante in the soul. It is the part of you that likes praise, awards *sans* cash in scrolls and plaques, the pleasure of reading aloud from your own work to a warmly receptive audience for next to nothing, and art for art's sake.

It is a good part of you to throw into the round bin beside your desk when you sit down to write.

Understanding this from the very first is important.

Understanding that you are competing on the highest level for the best story pay against experts.

Understanding that while little magazines and reviews are nice places to visit on your first few tours of duty, you don't want to live there.

And understanding that a great story may be fitted into 3,000 or even 1,500 words.

Desk Time

Few story writers can afford to devote their full time to writing. And few expect to make a living by this alone. Even successful and well-known writers of the story find themselves unable to spend eight hours a day at their desks. A maximum of four working hours is the usual storywriting stint. Many give it less time than this—knowing that the intense concentration called for by telling a story well on paper is an actual physical effort and that persisting too long at a stretch takes the edge off performance.

Nearly all the best writers of the story have, at first, sandwiched their writing time between other jobs. Dr. Anton Chekhov practiced medicine with skill on a heavy load of grateful patients and worked on his stories between rounds. Kipling turned out his first stories in India while putting out a newspaper, and learned word economy because the newspaper space in which they were first printed demanded it. Like all storywriters, they were aware that a story keeps working in the mind like wine in a vat and that the minutes while it pours out are only the end of a much longer cycle of creation.

Time at your desk is simply the visible part of the winemaking. As you train yourself to focus on the demands of today's commercial story, you will realize increasingly that what your brain has done is to take over the story while you were doing many other things—office work, work around the house, a thousand and one demanding tasks. Down there in the dark of your subconscious, the story has been forming ever since you started it moving. It has shifted and taken on layers of meaning and possibilities of action. Ideally, by the time you go to your desk, you can feel the story aching to get out, the words following your opening forming in the air before you write them.

Writing speed varies from writer to writer as widely as does painting speed among painters, composition time among composers. When a story is ready to be set down, some writers bring it out deliberately, pausing between sentences, feeling the shape and impact of each before they go on to the next. Others bring it all out in a steady rhythm of accomplishment, hardly stopping to read what they have done until the entire story is there in its first draft. Either way, there is a cadence—a feeling that the story is growing line by line, like the solid bricks of a house being laid in place. The deliberate writer may need half a dozen sessions at the desk before the first draft is done. The swift writer may take only one. There are in-between writing speeds as well—bursts of speed alternating with long minutes of waiting, thinking, allowing the story to gather itself and go on unfolding before the next words fall in place. John Steinbeck's

"The Red Pony" was written in intervals while he helped take care of his dying father.

There are countless articles around today telling the novice how the successful author clamps himself or herself to the desk for a disciplined four, six, or eight hours per day and produces x number of words. This same assurance and advice often comes from the mouths of friendly established authors addressing star-eyed groups of beginners. These Puritan word mills should be listened to with enough skeptical grains of salt to season a good ragout. There may be times when you would be much better off away from your desk, letting the story ferment and grow in power and decisiveness. A marketable short story may, when completed, be looked on as a highly commercial enterprise. But while it is in the making, it constitutes a decent mystery, and the best ones resist all production-line techniques.

Every storywriter has to discover his own speed and proceed at it and no other. Impatience has no place at the desk. If the story hasn't been thought through, *felt* through, this is the testing ground that will show you you've rushed ahead, pushing it where it should have been given more growing time, twisting it where it should have grown straight. If you've done that, shelve the story and go do something else until the kink comes out—but don't fling it aside in disgust and start another story on impulse. If you do, you'll end up, usually in the small hours of the morning, with a wastebasket full of false starts and a belly full of frustration. Stick to what you started. If it was important enough to you to conceive, it's important enough to be born.

Substance

Brevity is not brusqueness. It's the ability to say much in little because you have a precise vision of the body of your story and are excited about revealing it to as many people as possible. It's a partly intuitive but schooled knowledge of what to leave out the first time around, what to slice out in the second draft. It is knowing where you're going and having a superb time getting there.

Don't worry if you *don't* know where you're going at this point. It happens to every storywriter—especially to beginners. The seasoned professional is likely to have a notebook full of more or less sound ideas which fit her or his self-estimated capability. But many of these that looked so promising during the chimes of midnight fade away in sunlight like yesterday's moths. Sometimes the answer is to attack the typewriter or drive the pen in the hope of coming upon something that was there all the time and doesn't want to show itself until it's teased out. Sometimes a scribbled word or two, a title—"The Maine Mermaid" worked for me, although it wasn't the final title—will bring out a story full-blown.

But even eagles have lapses of vision. The temptation to plunge ahead and bluff your way into a story because you feel in good shape and the sun's out is often irresistible.

Once in a hunter's moon it works.

Generally it leads to pages of guff that might be fascinating to a psychoanalyst or your biographer, but whose only value to you is that it keeps you off the streets and may sharpen your technique. Going on the assumption that nothing is wasted—that bees nest in rotten logs and owls use abandoned barns—you can console yourself with the thought that you have once again learned how not to write a story.

But the lesson is always frustrating.

It increases the consumption of aspirin and working time.

Storywriters use plenty of the former but never have enough of the latter in this life.

In an entry in his journals Scott Fitzgerald wrote concerning a novel by John O'Hara: "He started chewing without anything in his mouth."

Fitzgerald knew what he was talking about on that score.

His rueful, confessional, and funny article called "One Hundred False Starts" is a dirge for all the stories that started off so bumptiously and petered out after six or ten or thirty pages. He called himself "one of the champion false starters of the writing profession." As usual he was too modest. Chewing without anything in your mouth is a trap you'll fall into more than once. It stems from the belief that because you enjoy the act of writing, as a race horse enjoys running in a pasture without any official starting gate in sight, you can skip the preparation time that brings a story alive before it's written.

With great luck the body and substance of a real story *may* be pinned down during this blind running.

But don't depend on it.

There's no substitute for feeling so sure of yourself as you start a story that the adrenaline of honest confidence gets into it from the first line to the last full stop.

Subject

Not long ago most of the big-circulation magazines were shackled with a host of don'ts as alarming as the guest rules of a Victorian hotel.

Stories dealing with adultery, or its suggestion, were taboo unless they were treated with the gingerly archness of well-bred gossip. Families were uniformly happy and unified, or would be by the story's end. Mom and Dad were permanent entities like strong elm trees whose arms were always spread to shade their offspring on demand. War was a necessary patriotic evil to be faced without cavil by everybody but cowards and slackers. Rights for women consisted of the ability to cook heartily at all hours, keep a house shining on a minimal budget, and serve as a jolly subservient foil for male-dominated dialogue. Poverty happened offstage to the invisible poor, and blacks officiated as smiling maids, men who came to mow the lawn, and comedians who rolled their eyes and spoke a dialect never heard on land or sea.

A surprising number of good stories slipped past the steel gates anyhow. Their authors became adept at innuendo and symbolism that said more than the story's surface, indicating the presence of monsters under the serene water.

Good taste is still in sharp demand at the high-paying magazines.

But as long as it's treated with skill and truth and a maximum of dramatic communication, anything goes.

Homosexuality and lesbianism are fit subjects for today's slick-magazine stories, and so is divorce in all its shadings. The specter of violence can be met head-on. The reasons for war, in the mass and in the individual, can be explored with strength and expertise. Women are no longer tractable dolls or lovable matrons, and men are no longer bare-fisted breadwinners without stain or blot. Children are people. Blacks suffer, bleed, speak to the point, and can take watermelon or let it alone. Stereotypes still occasionally limp into a mass-market story, but they are there as mistakenly sketched adjuncts rather than central characters. Humor is still a welcome undercurrent to realism, but not at the expense of minorities, the crippled, the retarded, the illiterate, or the dispossessed. Sorghum and treacle and double weddings in vine-covered churches don't conclude stories of imitation love enacted by puppets. Genuine affection in a story rates high with any large-magazine editor, but sentimental fakery is as unwanted as a drop in circulation.

In the teeth of all fact thousands of the stories submitted by beginning writers—and often by writers who have been at it a while—as candidates for purchase by large-scale magazines are as mired in the past as though their authors had suffered a time warp and had read nothing since the presidency of Calvin Coolidge.

A timeless story is forever timeless. The flappers of Fitzgerald, the American-history-based fantasies of Benét, the Mississippi citizens of Faulkner, don't date because they are real and fully imagined.

But a story full of echoes of a yesterday that never was is an imitation of what was never valid in the first place. It may be studded with references to current events, but it flashes to the editor the sad news that its author is stuck with a simplistic viewpoint that went out with spats and Arrow collars and should have been buried before then. It says that the author at the most exciting, terrifying, demanding era of history ever known is pushing plastic figures into position in grinning Kewpie attitudes, trying by means of carefully memorized plot rules to blow life into bad-quality cardboard.

To make your reader care about your people, *you* have to care about them. Care constantly and desperately and deep down. Care that the reader will laugh with them, hurt with them, recognize them as living flesh and next-door neighbors whose existence becomes unique through your story. If your story is placed a hundred years ago, this is equally true. If it's set in the future, the same thing holds. If a story is light, even flippant, it must still have the warmth of a reality you know is there. You have to model your people on traits and characteristics of those you love, those you deplore, catch the beat of breath in their actions, never depend on dim mirrors to reflect them cloudily.

You also have to care enough about the world around them to let it color their lives with its flaws, ugliness, and unexpected spasms of beauty.

Your ability to care, along with your need to artfully express their resonance against a background recognizable to any reader—whether in fantasy or observable fact—gives you your subjects ready-made for the best story markets.

Don't imitate anything but able craftmanship.

Don't fool around with secondhand subjects.

Be free to say anything with pride and taste, humility and insight.

The Third Experiment

Take three top-selling, brand-new copies of magazines that carry short fiction.

Spread them out and read them cover to cover. Read the covers too. Read the ads. Read the nonfiction. Soak yourself in the purpose of each magazine. Get yourself behind the scenes, imagining yourself as the publisher, the managing editor, the articles editor, fiction editor, feature editor, columnists, letters-to-the-editor editor, advertising editor, and head of the Sales Department.

Treat the fiction as if you'd bought it from each author at extremely decent prices. Get out of your own critical skin and give yourself half a dozen good reasons for buying it. Weigh it against its competition in the nonfiction. See where the lead story starts—the first one in the magazine—and why it ought to have been the lead story. Establish an underlying link between all of the stories. See if you can find a balance between them even if they seem totally different from one another in mood and approach.

Heft each story in your mind for length. Think of yourself as having written it and then hold it all in your mind as if you were about to start writing it all over again. Do this until you can actually feel yourself speaking the words in your mind before they appear on your manuscript page. Study the possible reasons why each story was titled as it is.

Frame a series of questions for each story author. Why did you open with that line of dialogue? Why did you take that little seemingly meaningless excursion in the middle, and end on a note that didn't quite seem resolved? Were you completely involved in this passage, or were you staying a few feet off to get some objectivity on it? Did you take this from something you'd seen or heard, or did it just sail into your mind at that particular point? Outside of wanting to write a sound commercial story, what incident or event in your life jogged this story into being?

Answer your questions for yourself, undefensively and with logic.

Think about your three story openings. Choose the one you like the best, set aside the others, and begin to tell the rest of the story in your head without writing a line.

Chapter 3

Eye

*B*ringing a story into the light calls for the interplay of sight, hearing, smell, touch, and taste. All the writer's sensory gifts are working at once, and they are alert to the creation of images that use every one.

Your eye works like that of a camera, moving in for a close-up and back for a long shot, inspecting minutiae as well as overall composition. It lingers on the color of a strand of hair, passes quickly over a landscape or the cement canyons of a city.

The power of visualization is a gift you either have or haven't, but in the storywriter it can be improved with steady practice. "The train went past" may be a serviceable statement, but if the train is important to your story, you can evoke it in strength with, "Then it was there alongside, the locomotive sudden as a tornado, black, huge, screaming, the whistle sounding again in two heavy blasts, cinders and smoke streaming, and the car roofs like the backbone of a dragon." The *roofs like the backbone of a dragon* is going to fix that image in the reader's eye.

A jaunty little fox terrier becomes memorable as soon as you have told us that it "tacked along like a sailboat against the wind."

Simile and metaphor are your fast friends when it comes to passing along to the reader what your eye wants the reader's to see. There have been storywriters who worked without them—John O'Hara is a notable example—but it is a little like a painter who is color-blind.

Don't overuse them. If you're good at the striking, apt, and not over-drawn metaphor, the simile that sums up much in a splash of color, save them for moments in your story when you want the reader to see very clearly what you also want to stand out. A string of similes wearies the reader because it makes the eye work too hard. A bunch of metaphors in a line is—to speak metaphorically—a bunch of boxcars passing while the reader waits. They stop the motion of the story dead as the train does traffic. Both metaphor and simile are points of color, illuminations that give the rest of the story special life by their reflection; they are not objectives by themselves, to be flaunted for their own sake.

If you don't easily see vivid correspondences in the life around you, you can teach yourself to begin looking at mundane objects for the first time—actually *seeing* their likeness to others. A bowling pin, for instance, has a marvelous shape, like a diminutive monk with a spherical stomach. A fountain pen is a spear with its point split. A small child's hand spread in the air is a wriggling starfish. On a clear soft night the full moon is a nailhead holding up the sky. If you stare into a garbage can—holding your nose meantime—the orange rinds and the wilted lettuce and the eggshells form islands of matchless color and gradations of tints which would intrigue Paul Gauguin in their Tahitian brilliance.

Nothing is actually "like" anything else. A pebble on a beach has its own integrity of being. But in the story your eye's ability to compare can bring to the reader a close approximation of what you want him to see, and since every story is, in part, a quick series of flowing impressions, it's important to use your eyes, and the reader's, to the limit of what both can take in.

Remember, always, that too much eye imagery can get arty and offputting. The stories of Katherine Mansfield that deal with her remembered childhood in New Zealand—"At the Bay" is one—are steeped in her homesickness, which is all that keeps the eye from blinking and turning away from the heaped-up images, wonderful as they are.

Yet used carefully and with judicial impact, the eye image can lift a reader with the sort of inner approval that exclaims, "Yes! That's how it is!" This touch with the reader is the real strength of the storywriter's eye.

Ear

Acute hearing is more to the storyteller than the ability to write good dialogue. It's the ability to hear what people really say between the lines.

If you take a page of Hemingway dialogue and read it aloud, you'll find that it's flat and doesn't play well. It has a tension that needs to bounce off the reader internally for its full effect. It says more inside the context of the story than it can ever say outside it. It's highly stylized, played close to the chest like a top poker hand.

What people mean and what they say is the difference between the reef under the ocean and its bland blue smile. "Yes, Charlie was always such a big spender" may mean that Charlie was the skinflint of the world. "Myra, your hair looks wonderful today" may be a compliment, but the operative word might also be "today" and the implication that Myra's hair is usually unsightly. Dialogue is never mere talk, but a way of characterization, of advancing the story and deepening it without narrative.

The way in which your ear hears is the way you'll write the story. Overtones and undertones are all-important. This applies to much more than an accurate ear for human speech.

The whistle of a train in the early morning has a distinctively different sound from its sound at noon and at dusk. The effect of music can be communicated by close approximates, by putting the reader into the mood for its genuine sound and feeling.

A good many of this writer's stories are about musicians. The job of soaking the reader in the sound is accomplished by images aimed like little solos at both the reader's eye and ear, but concentrating on the ear. Here are the opening and the first few lines of a story about the loneliness of the profession, the personal half-bitter, half-moody exploration of the self concentrated in a young man who has played all night and needs to find something to approximate his love for what he does on the stand.

Down the street in this edge of spring every leaf seemed its greenest, and the sky held the moon like a white dime on fire, looking through the sharp edges of the poplar boughs. It was the time before dawn, milky and serene, and a little used up as though all the music that had been played along the street— Rush Street, Chicago—still echoed far back in the inner ear, making an undertone for the thought and the spirit. The loud music and the soft, the bad music and the good—all of it pulsed softly now in some dim background, worked its way between the weary bones.

And a little later:

Rennie walked on, listening to the hollow but wonderfully alive sounds of his own heels on the paving—this time of morning the sound was like it was at no other time, it seemed to hold the feeling of the city in its beat. There was an afterbeat to each step, too, echoing down the surfaces of the buildings, charming the ear with its lost, dark and rhythmic bounce.

And still later, when in the first flush of morning Rennie is playing horn while a girl sings:

She said, "I know the words now," and he set the mouthpiece to his lips again. As he did so, he felt everything he was—his inmost being, the quiet center—pour itself through the trumpet. And she began to sing; her voice like a bird's, artless, and singing for the joy in the act. And as clear as a stream coming down through pines on a warm morning, with everything bright-polished and steady and also everlasting.

But a story needn't be about music or the people who make it to use the full range of sound in order to get over its complete message. Fitzgerald's "the Tap, K'Tap of ping-pong balls" sums up a lot better than any "He could hear them playing ping-pong" might do, and "the ruffling of a hen with iron wing-feathers" applied to another story of mine, plays on the reader's imagination more sufficiently than a great deal of automotive-engine-sound description could do.

Dialogue, too, is always a form of description. The use of qualifying adverbs such as "He said sternly" is necessary once in a while, but too many adverbs create a curly effect like poodles running around the page. There is a quality of delivery that can be picked up quickly and given the reader, which will tell the reader how anything is being said—if you're introducing a person whose voice is low and clipped, the reader will know from this that "I'm terribly sorry" came out that way, and you don't have to add that it was clipped and low. Voices tell an enormous amount about the people who have them, so that a voice full of sandpaper is going to speak in an entirely different manner from one that's as rich as old Burgundy. Skip the qualifiers whenever possible—lay down the manner of speaking and let the spoken words be delivered from then on with that in mind.

In straight first-person narrative—"Call me Ishmael"—the voice is going to be implicit all through the story, even though it's never described. This is where your ear comes in on all frequencies. Following are the first two paragraphs of a recent story written specifically for a particular magazine, *Rod Serling's Twilight Zone*. It's a fantasy, but I wanted my narrator, Jeb Malifee, to be a down-to-earth but imaginative man, both self-sufficient and a little ingrown, like so many of the natives I admire in Maine, and the task was to make him sound like what he is without ever saying what he looked like or going out of character.

> She was a quiet woman, the best kind. Up around the rocks nobody much goes in after Labor Day. But there she was, here into October, stroking in as if the water wasn't fit to chill a lobster. Naked, far as I could see, but for what looked like a shell necklace. Clean arms, with the shine of silver along them in the twilight and her legs scissoring nice and smooth, and no strain to it at all. A wonderful swimmer. Quiet, as I said.
>
> Sun was just going out of sight out at Bradford Point, hanging behind the old lighthouse and making it look like a black candle in the middle of the afterglow. It's a time when I always liked to be by myself on shore. The summer people—the "straphangers" we call them, and you can figure out why—are gone and the pines and the rocks just sort of turn into themselves again. The boards of the docks look bleaker and quieter. The ring of green weed around the dock pilings gets a gentle, lost light in the evening. Molly's Fish House down the line gets its slabby contented look back again. It seems to be about to fall into the sea but it never does. The smell of the water is stronger and like iodine around a scratch. Some places on the island you can stand still and hear a moose drinking from one of the creeks. It's a near-to-wintering time when the sun feels better than it will again all year.

Eye, ear, *and* nose are working with the reader there, but the ear is most concerned because the reader is listening to Jeb and judging him while he tells the story, accepting his laconic but pointed style of reminiscence. And receiving from him a series of impressions which are more believable and effective than they'd be if the story were told outside him in the third person.

Sound penetrates every good story and gives it resonance and extra echoes. The "kreef kreden kreden" of crickets—a phrase used by Robert Nathan—is straight onomatopoeia, which is the Greek word for the formation of words in imitation of natural sounds, such as *crack*, *splash*, and *bow-wow* and the "brek-a-kek-kek, co-ax, co-ax" of Aristophanes' froggy friends.

The Fourth Experiment

Before you go on reading, step into a room where people are talking and, trying to take as little part in the conversation as you can, listen. Listen to the murmuration and hesitation that precede a sentence. Hear how sentences themselves are rarely complete and how a surge of silence between words says as much as the words do. Filter out all the extraneous sounds—television and similar clatter—and try to pick out which words you'd use to sum up the gist of what is being said.

Now stand outdoors and listen to the sounds of a city, trying to separate the far-off noises from those near at hand—describing them to yourself either in onomatopoeia or approximates. "The prowling cat wail of a siren," "the wind's fingers fumbling poplar leaves," "the yoo-hoo of a mother calling children," "the slish-slish of slow traffic."

Go to the place where you write and while everything is fresh, put down in metaphor and simile, without pausing and straining for effect, everything you can of sight impressions and sound remembrance. How the talkers looked as they spoke and what stands out in your mind about them. Don't do complete descriptions. Try to catch them on the wing in impressions. Do the same with the sounds. (If you don't live in a city, use the country sounds you just heard.) Then sum up the talkers' dialogue in five or six pertinent sentences.

Let all that cool and look at it from time to time.

Thinking how you could say it better.

Nose

While we're talking about sensory stimulation in the story, let's consider the nose.

Television and movies haven't as yet, in this sense at any rate, really begun to smell on a wide and fully accepted scale. Back in the sixties, Mike Todd, trifling with the olfactory organs of potential millions, introduced a device called Smell-o-Vision; how it worked this writer has no idea, but his reference sources are unimpeachable and he can only say that he is glad it died. And in *Brave New World* Aldous Huxley projects a nauseating device which rejoices in the name of "The Feelies" and gives the benighted but delighted slaves of tomorrow substitutes for intimate human touch. Also, a good many science fiction storytellers and novelists—see Ray Bradbury's "The Veldt"—have taken for granted the future use of a complete sensual wraparound environment.

But, to date, not even Japanese technology has perfected and made universally popular the transmission of odor from television and movie screens to nasal passages. It may come about next week. If it does, or if it happens before this reaches print, you can still take satisfaction in remembering that good storywriters were there first.

Meantime the marvelous gift of the human nose is there for you to play upon in short stories.

Three samples:

> *There was a fragrance of honeysuckle along the fence and of early apples fallen in the small and unattended orchard just behind the brick Colonial house that had been built between 1825 and 1830.*

> *The store in which the Justice of the Peace's court was sitting smelled of cheese.*

> *Cautiously, as one might test the edge of a cliff before crawling outward to an eagle's nest, I smelled the air. And again the feeling of wonder and strangeness filled me, for the air was different.*

Those are very different uses of the sense of smell to evoke reader response. The first is from John Bell Clayton's story "Sunday Ice Cream," the next is the opening line of Faulkner's "Barn Burning," and the last is from my "Night Watch." Each is fitted to its special time and place and is meant to place the reader directly inside the scene, so that he or she not only sees and hears with the protagonists but exercises still a third sense to inhale the essence of the scene and enrich understanding. The reader's nostrils work as the writer's do, and when the reader's memory is touched by familiar odors—or unfamiliar ones carefully described— the reader becomes a physical participant in the story.

Clayton wanted that honeysuckle—a particularly southern scent, perfect for the mood of his story—and those early fallen apples with their slight tinge of rottenness to summon up a slow-moving Sunday in a specific section of Virginia. Faulkner wanted that general-store cheese to fill your nostrils as it fills those of the always hungry boy, Sarty Snopes, whose father is on trial for malicious arson. I wanted the beckoning, olive-laden smell of the shore to drift through the sweep port of a Roman galley and to quicken the nostrils of a rower who was resting on his oar after a storm.

There are, of course, a thousand ways to use smells in your story, and along with them goes, once more, the cautionary reminder that as in the case of simile, metaphor, and sound evocation, enough is far better than a feast—a story is not a guided tour through a fragrance factory, and the fragrances are not there to dominate but to help create the feeling of a true and whole experience.

But they are there for you to *use.* To use with an appeal to primitive alertness: "the smoky tang of flint." To use with more sophisticated nostrils: "the warm delicate hothouse puff of Chanel Number Five." To use as a reaction to raw nature: "For three seconds after the lightning, the world was pure ozone." And to use as ideal evocation of a full experience in seven words, as when Huckleberry Finn tells us: "It felt late. It even *smelt* late."

Reading a story about a grocery, a barbershop, or a tree in summer without a few illuminating words about the smell of fresh produce, the heady sharpness of bay rum, or the living smell of leaf sap is like having an important sense arbitrarily blocked off by the author.

Try never to write as though both you and the reader shared a bad cold. Think of your story as appealing to the hunting dog in everybody.

Taste

The sense of taste is connected to those of sight, sound, and smell by tiny invisible conduits which work together to create a single immediate effect—of enjoyment or revulsion or mere neutral acceptance.

"It was good" is one plain manner of describing a meal your story character has just eaten. "It was bad" is another.

And these may be serviceable and adequate methods of telling the reader what went on in somebody's mouth. If your natural storytelling style is flat and direct, there's no need to labor to describe the effects of grits and gravy on a Yankee or Midwest pot roast on a Southerner used to Brunswick stew.

But if you believe in and are able to think of the kind of color that lights up the demanding framework of a story, you may want a few analogies to strengthen "good" and "bad." Sinclair Lewis, in *Main Street* and numerous other books, seldom fails to produce a bright little series of snapshots underlining either the awfulness or the splendor of the cuisine. Hemingway is often as rhapsodic over varied Spanish dishes as his style will allow. Rex Stout's Archie, with his favorable reports on the preparation and intake of the food from Nero Wolfe's kitchen, lends firm authenticity to Wolfe's reputation as a gourmet. Certain stories revolve around food—Paul Gallico's "The Secret Ingredient" is one—and when they do, the reader usually salivates.

M.F.K. Fisher, as well as being a masterly storyteller, is a great writer about food, and her work is worth relishing not only for its excellence in other respects but for its dazzling insight into gastronomic mysteries. Writers who love food, respect it, and believe it to be a primary mover and shaker of civilization are likely to vivify the human palate in their fiction.

You are not, of course, composing a cookbook when you write a short story. A dash of salt and Tabasco—the communicated realization that what your story people eat and their reactions to what is served sometimes have direct bearing on who they are and what they are—is often enough. When Joe Christmas, the running, haunted, angry, displaced no-man of Faulkner's *Light in August*, eats cold corn bread, we know how it tastes to him. We can taste it with him. The delectable goose in "A Christmas Carol" is an elevated piece of goosehood that takes central position and soaks the revelry of the Cratchits in its juices. Your story may skip the acts of eating, tasting, entirely—it may have completely other aims—but if these happen in it, particularize; let the reader know how they sat on the tongue.

Touch

The sense of touch is another glorious gift to humanity and a constant companion of the alert writer of stories. Textures animate our lives much more than we have the ability to notice and constantly record. They consist of much more than mere harshness and softness—all gradations of tactile experience are encountered in the course of a day and night, and nerve endings are steadily caressed or assaulted by both simple and extremely complex forces. A little of this entering a story by suggestion can be splendid; too much of it can spill over into a mere sensory list of pleasure or displeasure. Like the other sensory attributes of men and women and children and animals and all of nature, when touch is kept in balance in a story, the reader recognizes it and nods in recognition; when it's insisted upon to the detriment of spirit, the story slips into self-indulgence—which is one reason why pornography for its own sake is so boring.

Waking with rough blankets around your chin and touching the floor with your bare feet while you feel an autumn sun warm them and walk over to put your hands on a cool oak windowsill constitutes a series of light enjoyable shocks which can be transferred to a short story with wholeness and great reader pleasure. Relaying the feeling of salt wind as it fills your pores, the elegant substance of new-cut wood, the almost murmurous life of human hair, the yielding toughness of the dirt in a freshly plowed field, and a hundred other experiences of the receptive and appreciating body can be done without neglect of any other story element—in balance, so that it feels right to you and to the reader and so that, by the use of artifice, you have passed along more "naturalness" than so-called naturalism would ever achieve.

As for sex, in the short story the sense of touch if kept in balance is an essential part of it—as long as it doesn't slop over into silly excess. Used sparingly, it underlines the warmth between people, between people and animals, people and seemingly inanimate objects. Instead of running on with heated descriptions of lovemaking—which are impossible to convey without honest passion running beneath them—simple suggestions are always more effective.

In Willa Cather's *A Lost Lady* there's no word that could offend a Puritan of the stripe of Cotton Mather. But there is one of the most effectively done scenes of adultery in literature, which tells us forever that Marian Forrester is an intensely desirable woman in the physical sense, as well as helping us to sympathize with her and dislike her despoilers. As in all writing, in the short story when sex is clinically handled—even in a time when anything can be said—the act of love becomes dispassionate and cold. But if it's expressed in an electric touch, shared laughter, the impress of a head in a pillow, it turns into story magic.

The Fifth Experiment

Make a list of smells that start your thoughts going backward to moving or outstanding times in your life. Hay, horses, new-cut clover. Pencil shavings and black ink in a schoolroom. Blackboard eraser dust. Sweeping compound. Milky and soupy smells in a cafeteria. Grain and feed smells. Smoke of leaf fires. Crisply ironed handkerchiefs. Old leather and faintly musty paper. Anything that reels in from the past your good or bad experiences. Brassy cartridges on a firing range. Raw pink puppy smells. The swarming sharpness of ether.

Linger on these until each brings up a living image. See if any of the images fit into the story you've been thinking toward. If they don't, keep on smelling backward and try to find a few that do.

Remember how something you really liked tasted the first time. Rhubarb pie, chocolate, a tomato off the vine, an egg cream at Schrafft's, cider sharp from a barrel, a girl's astonishingly peppermint-flavored lipstick, a man's earlobe. And how something you hated actually tasted. Castor oil, green quince, creamed carrots (if you like creamed carrots, shift this to the good side), and whatever else is taste-bud anathema to you. Work at remembering what happened around you while you were reveling in the good and recoiling from the bad. Find images for this— faces of people, backgrounds of places, shapes of a room or a landscape. Again, try to fit these, without forcing, into the story you're leaning toward.

Put your hand, palm flat, on a concrete surface. An automobile fender. A human cheek. A chair, a carpet, the bricks of a fireplace. An egg. A rough, scarred board, a smooth-planed one, a stone in a wall, the trunk of a tree. Whatever you touch, keep your eyes shut and let words form describing it quickly and rightly to anyone. Then go write them while they're new and clean, without thinking in "literary" terms at all but just trying for your own sort of accuracy.

After you've let your lists simmer awhile, think how you could improve them without borrowing from any other source or getting the least shade fancy.

The Sixth Experiment

Go back to the first experiment—to those three stories you picked so carefully for what they do to you. Does the story you're thinking about writing now have some real kinship with them? Does it, somewhere along the line, express the same personal belief, not in so many words but overall?

You're not comparing surfaces here. You're digging to find out whether you're on the inside track. Whether you're being an unconscious servant to what you think somebody else might like, or whether you're getting down to the bedrock of your storywriting self. If you feel that nobody else on earth appreciates the stories you chose as much as you do and that the story you're readying yourself to write is somehow a sister or brother under the skin to at least one of them, you're doing fine.

If you feel you've gone off at a tangent and that your story in embryo is shaky because it isn't actually yours and that it really has nothing in common with the three stories you valued above all others, scrap it. Start over, sitting still or pacing or whatever you do when you're making a life-or-death decision, and keep on digging until you have the germ of a story that's honestly close to you in every way. Then go back to the second experiment and do another opening for the new story.

Rewrite the fresh opening for readability and promise-to-the-reader until it feels, sounds, and looks good to you.

Check through the fourth experiment, the one where you listened and recorded what you heard and what the speakers and the sounds of the night told you in those quick impressions, and mull over how you can use your eye and your ear and the reader's in the story you've reaffirmed or the new one you've fought for and found as yours. Do the same with your lists of smells, taste, and touch.

Don't write another line no matter how much you want to. Make yourself walk away from the desk and consider everything you've learned so far about your storymaking self.

Chapter 4

The Wonderful Difference

*S*o far you've read about the short story as if it happened to be an art form walled in by as many rules as the fortifications of a medieval castle.

It's an art form, all right, but everyone who's written successful stories has at one time or another broken all the so-called rules.

Like a poem, a story is so close to the particular person you are—so allied to everything you represent—that it mirrors you the way a faithful portrait reflects more than features, hair color, the shapes of hands. It brings out your quiddity, your true difference from anyone else.

We are, thank God, wonderfully different one from another.

The best stories you write will project this difference in every line. And they'll emphasize it more than the novel does. A good story in sharp focus is a burning glass turned on the author as well as the people the author's writing about. Virtues are plainer, flaws are more obvious, choices are easier to see. The story is a microcosm of style—artfully arranged to look styleless. There's no such thing as a plain, easy story. If there were, its ingredients could be mixed every morning, rolled out like pie crust, baked in the afternoon, and turned out sparkling for a reader's evening meal. But the storyteller's oven is hotter than that and not always amenable to certain control. The taste of each good story tells something about its maker. Whatever its subject, it's an adventure in self-discovery. As you learn to make stories, you learn to make that taste, that individual difference, more and more pronounced.

You learn to follow your own "rules," which are likely to be much more difficult than those broad—and sometimes rightly suspect—rules for "everybody" laid down by story analysts.

No amount of analysis can tell why some stories move readers more than others. In a Sherwood Anderson story the elements seem simple, almost primitive. The reader feels that Anderson is groping toward understanding through a fog. Actually, this fog is there, created by Anderson's humility and his admission that he doesn't know the answers and needs desperately to find them. But his stories themselves are a long way from simple.

In a story by H. H. Munro—"Saki"—a sharp glitter of confidence shines from the page. Sophistication leaps to embrace and amuse the reader. It's like being at a self-conscious afternoon tea where all conversation is heightened for effect. The plot will have a sly turn, and surprise will sting from the tail of the story to overwhelm the reader with admiration for its polished economy.

In every successful commercial short story there's a touch of this human difference—the thing that somehow sets off the story from others and makes it, sometimes only during the first reading, sometimes for many successive readings, distinctive.

If you sometimes have to break a few solemn rules to be yourself in a story, and at the same time to hold the reader in a firm grip—do it.

Language

We all hear differently.

Many writers collect words, treasure them, gloat over them. They started this hoarding when they were children, while they were being read to and learning to read, and they keep on piling up word riches all their lives.

Other writers, while not indifferent to words, use them more as a carpenter builds a house with boards and nails in plain utilitarian fashion, thinking only of the final shape of the house.

A story such as Richard Connell's famous "The Most Dangerous Game" hasn't one outstanding phrase or flash of special color in it. A story like Scott Fitzgerald's "The Baby Party" is packed with glints of gold, extra flourishes that heighten its line-by-line intensity but don't detract from the final moving effect.

This is a passage from "The Most Dangerous Game":

Rainsford held his breath. The general's eyes had left the ground and were traveling inch by inch up the tree. Rainsford froze, every muscle tensed for a spring. But the sharp eyes of the hunter stopped before they reached the limb where Rainsford lay. A smile spread over his brown face. Very deliberately he blew a smoke ring into the air; then he turned his back on the tree and walked carelessly away along the trail he had come. The swish of the underbrush against his hunting boots grew fainter and fainter.

And this is the beginning of "The Baby Party":

When John Andros felt old he found solace in the thought of life continuing through his child. The dark trumpets of oblivion were less loud at the patter of his child's feet or the sound of his child's voice babbling mad non sequiturs to him over the telephone. The latter incident occurred every afternoon at three when his wife called the office from the country, and he came to look forward to it as one of the vivid minutes of his day.

"The Most Dangerous Game" is action adventure, a straight course of danger from the second Rainsford falls from a yacht, lands on an island, and meets the crazy hunter who stalks him with a gun for sport. "The Baby Party" is a revelation of the primitive protector in every man which will fight for his child if necessary.

The only point the language of one story has in common with the other is that they're both written in English.

Fitzgerald was a collector and burnisher of words.

Connell wasn't.

If your ear doesn't take in words to cherish, but simply hears them as instruments by which to get from one place to another with a minimum of fuss, you may still be an admirable maker of stories.

If you buff words on your sleeve and use them in your stories for brightness, accuracy, and the enjoyment of a reader who hears the way you do, you'll still need the sense of overall construction and balance the carpenter has.

If you have good sense from the start, you'll avoid words that might give you pleasure but that feel out of place or alien in the story and could stop the reader cold. A story is no place to exhibit the extent of your education and vocabulary. Usable story words may be out of the ordinary, but they're always alive. Unusable words seem to have been dragged in by their hair, showing off rather than working: dead obstacles. If you have a gift for what is sometimes called "poetic prose," be careful not to make the reader tired with what an editor friend of mine has called "too damned much humming." All the reader really wants you to do is get ahead with the story, and if you're a word collector who wants to give the reader an extra gift of grace as you go along, remember that it has to be done in continual action and fit into the story with ease.

If you hear words as useful weapons, no more and no less, as thousands of expert storytellers do, the overall impact of your story will be its importance, and you'll aim for that alone. It's difficult to remember any set of words from a John O'Hara story. But you remember the story as a whole, its emotional drive and what it spoke with eloquence between the lines.

It's possible that you stand somewhere between the Fitzgerald and the Connell extremes in your feeling for language. Sometimes you'll take off with a little flight of words that work compatibly to make the reader see and feel more clearly, and again sometimes you'll be driving nails. In either case, keeping the outlines of what you're making in your mind's eye is all-important to the way it comes out.

Use language as well and as sensitively as you can.

Don't let it stand in the way, but let it serve you.

The Sentence

A story is *not* putting one sentence after another.

It's a series of aimed sentences.

The opening of James Joyce's "Two Gallants" is a series of nearly protoplasmic impressions, floating like light above tepid water, breaking most of the "rules," and leaving the reader puzzled as though he had been dipped in a murky bath, yet intrigued and even entranced. Here it is:

> *The grey warm evening of August had descended upon the city and a mild warm air, a memory of summer, circulated in the streets. The streets, shuttered for the repose of Sunday, swarmed with a gaily coloured crowd. Like illumined pearls the lamps shone from the summits of their tall poles upon the living texture below which, changing shape and hue unceasingly, sent up into the warm grey evening air an unchanging, unceasing murmur.*

Reading that over, even casually, you'll be struck by an apparent laziness, a repetition of such words as "grey," "warm," an inner chiming and murmuration that sounds a bit like an elderly lady talking in her sleep. It is one long metaphor of sleepwalking, and it sets the scene as nothing else could.

There is no repetition, no incantation, only a direct series of extremely vivid pictures, all in flowing motion, in the opening paragraph of E.M. Forster's "The Story of the Siren":

Few things have been more beautiful than my notebook on the Deist Controversy as it fell downward through the waters of the Mediterranean. It dived, like a piece of black slate, but opened soon, disclosing leaves of pale green, which quivered into blue. Now it had vanished, now it was a piece of magical india-rubber stretching out to infinity, now it was a book again, but bigger than the book of all knowledge. It grew more fantastic as it reached the bottom, where a puff of sand welcomed it and obscured it from view. But it reappeared, quite sane though a little tremulous, lying decently open on its back, while unseen fingers fidgeted among its leaves.

The sentences in both of those stories are aimed at what the story wants. For all its seeming amorphousness, the Joyce story exerts a powerful mood like a rising fog in which specific people will presently be encountered. The Forster story has a sliding, plunging underwater motion which follows that lost notebook like the eye of a whimsical god and gives it specific personality—"quite sane though a little tremulous"—as it rests in sight but drowning.

Your sentences are servants of your story mood, each pulling its proper weight as it enters and makes way for the next, and each related to the other by more than the mere fact that the same person is writing them. Get and read Flannery O'Connor's "A Good Man Is Hard to Find" and notice that in its commentary on good and evil—and the fatuous helplessness of mankind when faced by pure evil—it's as succinctly told as though a lucid stream of icy air had been turned on and then off. Look up Eudora Welty's "Powerhouse" and see how the sentences jump into the skin of a black musician—Fats Waller—seeing him from the inside as a bolt of lightning might be felt.

Find Faulkner's "The Bear" and notice how his sentences smell like the big woods in Mississippi before they were razed by developers. Read Benét's "Freedom's a Hard-Bought Thing" and listen to the voice of an ex-slave talking quietly about the titanic experience of finding freedom. Take any Damon Runyon story and hear in it the stylized voice of a professional Broadway "character" speaking nasally and from a guarded mouth corner.

Good sentences pace in step with their story.

If you're writing a light story about a mother's struggle with her eight-year-old daughter who wants to enter a dubious neighborhood theater beauty contest and is asking for the ten-dollar entry fee, your sentences won't be heavy and overdramatic. They'll be humorous, straightforward, concerned. A story about a husband and wife on the verge of breaking up because he's a slipshod driver will have its contemporary pulse in every sentence, using brief description and dialogue to bring out what they're really fighting about—which may not be his driving at all. If your story is told by a young woman and concerns a radio announcer in love with his own chest tones, its sentences will be crisp, sardonic, pungent.

In ten years of reading stories by beginners, this writer has come across too many in which the sentence is regarded as a slack noose, aimlessly thrown in the hope of surrounding a story.

It's as if many people believe the act of throwing words at a page to "express themselves" was enough. As if the heaping up of any old sentences, accurate, wildly inaccurate, long, short, grammatical, or cloudily askew, was sufficient for short fiction—while the story's ghost stayed buried somewhere in that sentence welter, gasping for life.

While teaching himself to write, Hemingway slaved until he had what he called "six true sentences." Each moves like an uppercut. Each presents a complete action picture and leaves a stark mood with the reader. They were true for *him,* and they were the start of everything he would do. Here are three of them:

I have seen Peggy Joyce at 2 a.m. in a Dancing in the Rue Ca-martin quarreling with the shellac haired young Chilean who had manicured finger nails, blew a puff of cigarette smoke into her face, wrote something in a notebook, and shot himself at 3:30 the same morning. . . . I have stood on the crowded back

*platform of a seven o'clock Batignolles bus as it lurched along
the wet lamp lit street while men who were going home to supper never looked up from their newspapers as we passed Notre
Dame grey and dripping in the rain .... I have watched two Sene-
galese soldiers in the dim light of the snake house of the Jardin
des Plantes teasing the King Cobra who swayed and tightened in
tense erect rage as one of the little brown men crouched and
feinted at him with his red fez.*

Aim your sentences.

Cut them out of the cloth—coarse tweed, linen, watered silk—you
want your story to wear.

It's not hard.

If you stiffen up and go cold in your center when you think about aiming a sentence, look on it as malleable, fluid, subject to your will. The
poor thing needs your direction. It wants to say as much as it can for the
story you have in mind. It's waiting to be modeled into kindness, curt-
ness, flexible grace, gleaming steel. It asks to be fitted into your story—
to be part of the ambience. Give it a nudge here and there until it's part of
the crowd, feels at home. If it opens your story on too high a note, tone it
down. If it's flabby, make it work until its muscles show. If it's just a
wrong sentence and belongs in some other story you may write later, set
it aside with a good word.

All good sentences are organic, belonging in their stories as cherries
grown in the same orchard have the same family taste.

In most stories you'll want to keep the sentences short. The attention
span of the reader of marketable short stories varies from the flick of an
eyelash to the dart of a lizard. Most readers aren't familiar with the long,
looping, and wonderfully prolix sentences of Proust, and Faulkner even
at his most intense and grand makes them itchy. They're conditioned to
television, in which images flitting by keep the eye in a steady state of
daze and semistupor. By asking them to read a story you're taxing them
with the job of cooperating with you. Brief sentences insult nobody's intelligence. Nor do they have to be in baby talk to be immediately comprehended. Maupassant's stories, even in so-so translations, clip along
with the eagerness of horses heading for a stable. He was the short storywriter most in demand in his time. He's not in favor with critics today,
but critics don't read popular magazines.

Saying Enough

In any group of friends or casual acquaintances there's somebody you're careful not to ask questions because you'll get windy answers.

The long, exhaustive explanation with numerous backings and fillings is a social plague.

You like the person who, when you put a question about health, answers, "Tolerable," and moves on to greener fields.

You suffer when someone asked the same sociable question goes into medical detail fascinating only to the subject and to doctors.

When you address your pencil, pen, typewriter, or word processor, remember that egocentric soul. Tell yourself, "I will not be long-winded."

However imperative the mood of storytelling which may be on you, the temptation to make yourself into a cataract rather than a fresh, tight stream will be equally there. You can save yourself extra hours of editing grief by building a few dams in your mind at the start. This doesn't mean that you'll "write short" for the sake of shortness alone, or leave out anything vital that you'll have to insert later with a shoehorn.

It means you'll write in a controlled state of mind, conscious with part of yourself that the market won't stand for self-indulgent excess, and caring enough about your story to make it occupy a tidy space at full strength.

Kipling said he never "wrote short"—that he'd tried it and found the story weakened by too much vigilance. His way with a story—and it was quite a way—was to drift until it was ready, then to let it come out, then to set it aside—sometimes for months, in a few cases for years—and, at intervals, have at it with black India ink and a brush, until he'd cut out everything extraneous and the story spun like a top in righteous balance.

Saying enough is as necessary as not saying too much.

Skimping during the composition of a story is slow death. Stopping after every sentence for arduous stock-taking, asking yourself, "Did I need that?" instead of "What comes next?" is a strong indication that you haven't spent enough time testing the story before you began it, that you're not yet involved enough to know, emotionally, where you're going, and that you're making a formidable mountain out of the process of creation when you should be skipping along the hills.

Knowing emotionally where you're going is different from knowing mentally where you're going.

Fitzgerald—who should be quoted, daily, by every working storywriter as a matter of habit—said that *all good writing is swimming underwater and holding your breath.*

Some splendid writers of the story never know just what they want to say until they've said it. They visualize well, but they shun mapping everything out because they're aware of the dangers of cut-and-dried conclusions. They may make outlines, but these are usually sketchy enough to merely touch the nub of the story, yet let it leap and breathe in its own freedom as it moves onto the paper. They've learned that a real story often resists too much conscious guidance—that like a Zen parable, it can nearly tell itself, and that it often insists on this.

They know that if they're true to their own emotional wisdom, they'll write clearly, including everything needful to make the story comprehensible and convincing to any reader. They've learned that if they trust the wisdom, what the story says will imply more than is there, and nothing essential will be left out.

They know that such swimming underwater is the most fun in the world, and that while it's being accomplished, easier than talking about it can ever be.

Make whatever experiments you feel like doing at the end of this chapter.

If you've read it with reasonable enlightenment, a few should occur to you.

Chapter 5

Who Speaks?

*T*hat question is one that Ben Hibbs, editor in chief, used to scribble in the margins of the galleys of *Saturday Evening Post* stories.

He wanted to know which character, in the middle of a patch of dialogue, was delivering a particular line.

The remedy was simply to write in, "Joe said" or "Milly said," so the reader wouldn't be forced to retrace a finger through the dialogue thicket to keep track of who was talking.

Hibbs wanted it done as a courtesy to the reader—an easement of the eye and the mind.

He was quite right. There's no excuse for offering the reader anything but clarity in a story. Puzzles exist to be solved on the puzzle pages and are labeled as such.

But the phrase "Who speaks?" goes deeper into a story than the simple indication of who says what.

It brings up the matter of viewpoint. And that quiet two-syllable word is treated as a bugaboo by many beginning storywriters. Sometimes it gets to be a hurdle on which knees are brutally skinned. There are dozens of rules and theories surrounding it, some of them as esoteric and complex as theories about outer space.

Forget all you've ever heard, read, or guessed about viewpoint.

Think of it as your Line of Sight on a story—as the way *you* are telling it, or telling it *through* someone else.

In the foreword to his *Collected Tales* A. E. Coppard, a master of the story on a level with Chekhov, pointed out that the relationship of the short story to the novel amounts to zero. He underlined the truth that the story, which we now call the folktale, was there before writing, let alone printing, was discovered. And he maintained that the nearer the modern short story comes to being spoken to you—rather than read at you—the better it is. Then he added that the most effective stories are plotted through the mind or consciousness of *only one of your characters*. (He also stressed, wisely, that a literary principle is a guide, not a dictatorship.)

There are only three basic Lines of Sight in telling a story. One of them will be right for your story.

There's Third Person. "It was a rainy spring morning when Jannikin Ballard set off to seek his fortune."

This is you, the writer, writing *about* Jannikin Ballard. You'll stick with him throughout the story. You may give the reader his thoughts, his reactions, and you may tell what the people he meets look like and what they say, but you will never, at peril of losing your reader and your mind, start dipping into the thoughts and reactions of anybody else but Jannikin. The Third Person Line of Sight is much more free than it looks. It gives you room for adequate picture painting: "Jannikin sniffed the watery air of the highroad, taking it in great gusts through his long and humorous nose, and noting that just ahead of him, straddling the muddy ruts from ditch to ditch, stood a giant about eleven feet tall, picking his teeth with the shoulder bone of a sheep." If at this point you should be inspired to go on: "The giant's name was Bumbersnill, and he was thinking about stuffing Jannikin in his pocket and taking him home to his mother for Mother's Day," you will have snatched the story away from Jannikin, scattered it all over the place, and caused yourself no end of approaching headaches. If you stay close as a saddle burr to Jannikin and have *him* do the thinking, you're all right: "Jannikin stopped, doffed his hat, and said, 'Good morning, Bumbersnill,' reflecting as he did so that Bumbersnill had the wistful but crafty appearance of a creature who wished to stuff Jannikin into his pocket and take him home to his mother for Mother's Day."

In a novel you may have room and the inclination to use more than one Line of Sight. Faulkner's *As I Lay Dying* uses the thoughts, interior monologues, and author-painted insights of fourteen people. Kenneth Fearing's *The Big Clock* shifts its Lines of Sight from chapter to chapter. But a story is projectilelike in form, and if you begin jumping about from one sight line to another in it, the projectile wobbles and the reader develops vertigo. So will you.

It's Jannikin's story—not the giant's, not that of the rabbits and dragons and maidens in distress he'll encounter along the way. And, peculiarly, it becomes more and more your story as you adhere to Jannikin's sight line. It grows in a straight course from you through the perceptions of your central character, turning into a virtuous and immensely useful limitation as it travels, keeping you honest and the reader happy. Any Line of Sight is a focusing instrument. The one you pick depends on which way you decide your story can best be delivered.

More "Who Speaks?"

Your second possible Line of Sight is the First Person Whole.

Sometimes it's called First Person Major.

But since that conjures up the image of a red-faced military man with wax on his moustache, let's designate it as First Person Whole. The *Whole* means that the entire self of the narrator is concerned in the story he or she is telling; that its big moments belong to this narrator and nobody else; and that the First Person voice becomes a skillful instrument in the use of atmosphere, shadings of speech, and ways of reaching the reader which the Third Person Line of Sight can't handle.

Jessamyn West's "Up a Tree," Eudora Welty's "Why I Live at the P.O.," Truman Capote's "A Christmas Memory," Poe's "The Fall of the House of Usher," Benét's "By the Waters of Babylon," Sherwood Anderson's "The Egg," and J. D. Salinger's "Raise High the Roof Beam, Carpenters" are all told, very differently, in First Person Whole. What happens in each story changes the narrator's life directly; and even though Anderson is telling *about* his father, Capote *about* a favorite loving relative, and Salinger *about* a brother who doesn't enter the story at first hand, all of the events in each story work on the narrator, who keeps the center of the stage. A First Person Whole narrator is considerably more than a concerned bystander. He or she is in the middle.

"I, Jannikin Ballard, met Bumbersnill the giant just one minute after I'd left home on that wet April morning to seek, as they say, my fortune."

You may find First Person Whole palatable to yourself and as easy as lemon pie to serve the reader. Its great danger isn't that it's hard to deliver, but that it's a temptation to overindulgence; it calls for an excellent ear, acutely aware of the perils of saying too much, and for firm willpower that keeps the words in character, and the knowledge that the form can very easily slip into glibness—sloppiness. Not strangely—because it sounds and looks so simple—a lot of starting writers leap into First Person Whole with a joyous shout, a where-has-this-been-all-my-life feeling, telling themselves that all they have to do is write a personal letter to the public and that God will guide them to the homestretch.

But First Person Whole isn't merely confessional. It's very close to the bone, and it nearly always conceals more art than Third Person shows. It has the plain disadvantage—which can also serve as a beautiful challenge—of barring you, the Seeing Eye and Cocked Ear in the center of events, from knowing what's going on in another part of the story forest. For instance, in the Third Person Line of Sight you can write, "While Jannikin, having handily discouraged the giant with his ready wit, loped through the drying buttercups of the meadow, little did he realize that the village toward which he headed was under magical siege. For at that very moment the Enchanter from the North had taken it over from cow byre to castle."

Jannikin doesn't have ESP or an operable crystal ball. In First Person Whole he's limited to seeing, hearing, feeling, and talking about what happens immediately around him. He can *speculate* about what may be happening in other places. But it would be more than a little cheap and tricky to have him receive a telegram—possibly delivered by a gopher—which informed him about the machinations of the Enchanter from the North. It's only fair to the reader to plan the narrative so that its First Person Whole narrator doesn't have to depend on coincidence, sleight of hand, or pure miracle to reveal to him or her those events the reader needs to know.

If you choose First Person Whole for your story's Line of Sight, remember that you're inside another brain (not necessarily your own) and another body (also not your own), seeing through other eyes, using another voice. You're depicting from inside out, not standing off a fraction of an inch or a foot or a yard in space. You don't have a bird's-eye or a worm's-eye view. You know what your narrator sounds like as though you heard the speaker in your head and simply set down what was said. There are cases—Anderson's "The Egg" is one; Capote's "A Christmas Memory" is another—where the narrator's voice is, more or less truly, the actual voice of the author; both Capote and Anderson speak as if they're merely passing along stories they lived in. But who is it who tells us about wild-eyed Roderick and Madeline Usher and their doomed piece of real estate? Not Edgar Allan Poe, but the luckless narrator Poe elected to relay to us this umbrageous and woeful adventure. Again, in "Why I Live at the P.O."—an intensely and wonderfully funny exploration, in the choice words of its protagonist, of one woman's adventures in persecution mania carried to rare heights—we're not hearing Eudora Welty, but the result of her great art.

Margery Finn Brown's "In the Forests of Riga the Beasts Are Very Wild Indeed" is narrated in First Person Whole, without the woman who is speaking doing much but moving from room to room, but it is so closely and sympathetically spoken that its internal action—that of a witty and noble lady driven to madness—becomes more gripping than a hundred James Bond shoot-outs.

Your Line of Sight in First Person Whole can be intriguingly conversational or raised to the voltage of a high-tension wire. It can be as easygoing, sunny, and deft in turns of speech as Huck Finn; as soaked with fear as the voice of the narrator in Maupassant's "The Horla"; as civilized, perceptive, and enchantingly detailed as E. M. Forster's aforementioned "The Story of the Siren." It can't be *loose*. The "I" who is telling your story has to be in charge all the way, as a lion tamer is in control from the moment of stepping into the cage—and perhaps even more appositely, as a magician is in charge of the audience while the illusion is achieved.

In its right place we'll go into the risks and benefits of using the First Person Whole in various dialects and word coloring.

Right now, look at this second Line of Sight with gratefulness—and decent caution.

And More

Your third potential Line of Sight is the First Person Offset.

It's been classified in some quarters as First Person Minor. But because it isn't *minor* by any stretch of the imagination, and because offsetting the shape of the story is exactly what it does, calling it by a better name can't hurt.

Your First Person Offset narrator stands on the edge of the story, a greatly interested observer and commentator:

"Yes, I knew Jannikin Ballard. Before he set off to find his fortune he used to come bothering around my blacksmith shop all the time, putting his smart long-nosed face in at the door and asking, 'May I have a few fresh coals for my fire, Brother Birdsell?' "

This narrator is privy to events he's heard about, seen from far off or happened on close-up, and he's pieced them together in a neat package whose full importance he may or may not understand. He's a conduit, a happenstance relayer of information in a way the First Person Whole narrator, to whom the story has happened, could never be. He has some of the characteristics of the inveterate yarn spinner whose curiosity about human nature is unslakable—he's objective in a slightly untrustworthy manner. Through him are filtered the odds and ends of a story whose deeper meaning may escape him, but which he allows the reader to grasp while he stays on the periphery of understanding. He, or she, is a gossip—and sometimes a complete innocent, like a child trying to explain in its own terms a battle which shook the earth.

Ring Lardner's "Haircut" is an ideal piece of First Person Offset storytelling. It is narrated by a small-town barber whose command of language is as barren—and as perfectly heard and written—as all of Lardner's savagely accurate vocal portraits. In the course of cutting a customer's hair, the barber tells about a local practical joker and his favorite butt—a retarded young man. Through the barber's cruel and manifestly approving words as he describes the artful joker, the reader gets a dark picture of a full-time sadist, and at the same time sees the young man as a mute, inglorious, and pitiable figure struggling against terrible odds. When, almost casually, but with certain relish, the barber reveals how the good-citizen joker was "accidentally" killed, the reader—who is, in effect, the customer in the barber chair, hearing the story between snips of the scissors—knows as surely as if he had been on the spot that the blighted young man did the killing. And he is quietly glad about it. The barber, on the other hand, will obviously never make this connection—he is the perfect, bland channel through whose insensitivity the *real* story has come out.

There are, obviously, other ways in which "Haircut" could have been told. But it's highly doubtful that any other could have been this effective. The barber's blindness to the long pain and stifled agony of the young man is an essential part of the texture of the narrative. Using Third Person to tell the story would have taken it too far from the immediacy of the barber's words, muffling the rawness of his speech. Using First Person Whole—putting the barber in the core of the story—would have wrenched it to another plane, on which what the barber saw and experienced at first hand would have been far less powerful than his recital of what he *thought* had gone on. First Person Offset used Lardner's greatest gift—his ability to separate what people say from what they think they say—at its best.

Your First Person Offset narrator may be in the story to a small extent, but he or she is always in essence a bystander... not always brainy, nor always in full command of "facts." But he or she makes the "facts" add up to more than is actually said. In "A Rose for Emily," Faulkner's gradually unfolding story of Miss Emily Grierson's ghoulish pride in, revenge on, and triumph over her unfortunate lover at whose side she slept long after he had turned to bones and dust, the narrator is merely a shadowy editorial "we"—but the presence of this much-removed First Person Offset narrator can be felt throughout, saving the worst and final revelation for the last, brooding over the infinite strength of the past to shape women and men.

Handling First Person Offset, you're working closer to Third Person than you are to First Person Whole. Here your speaker, your teller of the tale, may seem unconscious of the general effect—such rare narrators as the "we" of "A Rose for Emily" are uncommon—but there need not be a limit to the speaker's fund of knowledge; anything can be touched upon in time, space, simultaneous occurrence. First Person Offset stays with the story line but remains on one side of it. It flanks a story, sneaks up on it, maintains its status as an interested nonparticipant.

Drawn too far toward the story's center, the First Person Offset speaker talks too much. "Let me tell you about my wife and what *she* thought of this Jannikin fellow." Your First Person Offset narrator's job is not to editorialize at length, not even if she or he is a born blowhard. It's just to suggest, to stay a little puzzled, while allowing the reader to see the whole game from invisible bleachers. At the end of a successful First Person Offset story the narrator may well be in doubt—but the reader is always enlightened.

Suggestion

This isn't an experiment.

If you haven't read all the stories mentioned in this chapter, try to beg, borrow, buy, or find them somewhere, and relish them as you study them.

And—this is still a suggestion—root around in current magazines for

First Person Whole and First Person Offset stories.

Consider the nature of your talent and the keenness of your ear. Ask yourself if you feel more comfortable with Third Person than you do with First Person Whole or First Person Offset, and try to pin down why. Think about which Line of Sight your now tested-and-true story opening has taken—and if you'd be more sure of yourself by taking another. Give this a chance—try to see and hear your story in a different sight line.

Which way speaks best in your head and in your story?

Juggle them awhile.

Make a few self-to-self suggestions of your own.

Chapter 6

Here and Now

*T*hird person, first person whole, and first person offset can all be used
in the present tense.

"Jannikin sniffs the watery air of the highroad."

"I sniff the highroad's watery air."

"From my blacksmith shop I watch Jannikin's long nose wrinkle as he
sniffs the air."

Present tense is the here and now, happening under the reader's eyes.
It can sustain a whole story in any Line of Sight. It etches a story more
slowly and deeply into the reader's consciousness than the past tense
can do, and its motion is correspondingly a bit snaillike and deliberate.
This is from a story called "A Few Words About the Arabian Oryx," in
which I wanted to build up, stroke by stroke, the feeling of baffled agony
in a young man whose small brother, angered at a trivial family dispute,
has run away from home:

> *Now, on Old Rushing Drive, as we leave the populous section
> and approach the bridge (somehow it looks gloomy and roman-
> tic, a place Edgar Allan Poe might have doted on), I slow up and
> come to a stop beside the gray and fawn stone of the bridge. Len-
> nie and I hop out and gaze down into the fast-moving, twinkling
> water. There's the shred of an old boat, its sail crumpled and
> torn and dirty, nosed into the bank. There are old breakfast food
> boxes and other trash. I cup my hands around the sides of my
> mouth and call up through the scrub oaks and the pines, "T.W.!
> Ohhhhhhhhhh, T.W.!"*
>
> *The noise beats against the stone of the bridge and seems to be
> swallowed beneath it. There aren't any other people around here
> right now. A couple of birds seem to swim from bough to bough*

of the bigger oaks, downstream. I put my hands on the stone of the bridge, and it's cold. I call and call. Lennie joins me. There's the feeling that neither of us wants to stop calling because we know when we do, all we'll get back is that echo, that mocking reverberation. We shake our heads at each other and I say, "Wait a minute." I slither down the bank as fast as I can around the end of the bridge. I stick my head under it where it's so dark I can't see anything for a second or two; then I can make out bits of things—the stonework above my head flashing in a prismatic dazzle, a watery shaking—and here I yell for T.W. again. Nothing comes back but my own voice, magnified and yet lost. There is nobody there. I scrounge back up the bank and get in the car. Lennie says, "Next, that way," curving her arm to the south.

The present tense, with its emphasis on each separate second and its feeling of time closely examined, was the right tense for that story, in which time hangs nearly suspended. With other stories the present tense would have served as an inconvenient anchor, holding up the flow of immediate action.

The present tense can pose a special problem when it comes to ending a story. If you've used first person whole throughout—as the story quoted above does—when you approach the end you're faced by a time-change enigma. You must keep the reader believing you're still in the story as its chief character, explainer, and narrator, but you have to do this in a way that doesn't remove the illusion that you're talking and not writing. I got around this in the "Arabian Oryx" case by beginning the last section with:

Now it's night and everything has been settled. It becomes an anecdote to be told for years in family annals...

and so on, to the end. This worked, but it was an uncomfortable moment of transition, something to be skated over quickly. Moments such as this can make you wish you hadn't chosen the present tense in the first place. But if the advantages of the here-and-now tense overbalance everything else, and it works better for your story than any other approach can work, use it and rejoice in it.

Be as steady as the North Star in keeping to one Line of Sight throughout your story. Shifting around from one to another is like offering an art patron a Paul Klee or a Georges Braque when an N. C. Wyeth painting was expected. Experimental stories may have their place in the advancement of the story as a great and unique vehicle for human enchantment, but that place generally isn't in the pages of a magazine whose editors are willing to pay you well for your work. And with very rare exceptions, changing your Line of Sight in midstory isn't going to improve it—it is only going to show that you're whimsical, ornery, or extremely myopic.

The Wrestlers

Whatever Line of Sight you're weighing for possible use in your story, and whatever opening you've come up with at this point, there needs to be something wrestling under its words.

The science of isometrics deals with pitting one set of muscles against another in the same body. In the body of a good short story something of the same action takes place.

Sometimes this process is called conflict—but what goes on is actually not a pitched and obvious battle, and it shouldn't be confused with the idea of cowboys and Indians, Minutemen against Redcoats. "Conflict" is merely the primitive surface word for the underlying element that stiffens and suffuses and permeates a solid story.

The word "struggle" comes closer to characterizing what really goes on here. It doesn't have to take place between antipathetically opposed individuals. The ground of war is often located in only one person—and this person can be made real and fascinating because the reader is conscious of the full intensity of the unseen warfare inside him or her.

In the first story William Saroyan ever had published, "The Daring Young Man on the Flying Trapeze," there is a titanic struggle.

All of it happens inside the nameless young man of the title. All of it centers in his graceful, sad, deft, and yet deeply angry realization of his human meaninglessness in a world where all he can do is starve to death. In the course of his last hours of life the people he meets are seen to be uncaring and wrapped in their own shells of imperception, fearful of their depression-shaky jobs, blind occupants of a beautiful earth. His own thoughts soar like falcons, whisper like lovers in the dark, and at the last he admires the perfection of a United States copper penny, thinking that a child might appreciate it—and he turns his face to the sky and dies.

But before he dies the wrestlers in him have made the story burn and burst with meaning. It is about death, and it is marvelously alive. It's alive because it brings out, with complete accuracy, the wrestling inside the young Saroyan. When he wrote it, he was a long way from dying—though never far from hunger—and he became the story's doomed poet, using quick, bright words to build himself a combined obituary, requiem and good-bye song.

He got twenty-five dollars for it from Whit and Hallie Burnett's *Story* magazine. And he got overnight fame, which he immediately fanned with a healthy belief in himself. He was this writer's friend; the symbol of the wrestlers is his. It came from a conversation, one green afternoon, when, wanting to needle him a little, I asked him if he could tell me the most important thing his stories, novels, plays and essays and poems did. Without pausing to think, he said, "Wrestle."

If he were still breathing, an action which he confidently expected to be performing at any given point in the next hundred years, he would not mind my adding that every worthy, and cash-worthy, story both wrestles and reveals.

Revelation

In simplistic stories the wrestling goes on in plain sight. It can be spotted by the most indifferent reader at a distance of thirty paces. It contains "bad" people who are labeled as such in the equivalent of black letter Gothic, and "good" people who, however adult and knowing their dialogue may be, are cut from the same true-blue bolts of cloth as Tom Swift, Nancy Drew, and for that matter, Dick Tracy.

In the past such stories filled a need for clearly defined and uncomplicated heroes and heroines in a kind of mythology which served as both escape and reader glorification. The reader puts himself or herself in the place of the star—Tarzan, James Bond, and the thousand offshoots of their breed—and conquers the fiends. Some quality of perseverance and ingenuity, American know-how or British doggedness—or plain blind luck and the arrival of a squad of hypothetical marines—brings about the reward. The wicked are punished. The "good" man gets the girl, the "good" girl achieves nuptial bliss or its romantic and fulfilling equivalent. There is no real interplay of wrestling under the surface, no real suggestion of the monsters and saints latent in the human psyche. A spate of novels in this impeccable traditon goes straight on flooding the market as you read, "romantic" novels in all categories, "spy" and "end of the world" novels which are either done with art and fidelity to humankind—as in the case of the books of John Le Carré—or ground out as if the mills of the gods had slipped a gear and human behavior were observable only through a spectrum of obvious good and evil.

But in the short story of today such treatment, seen in the framework of a short story which magnifies every word, can bore the epidermis off the reader. For with the wrestling limited to visible action and the dispensation of just desserts, there's no room or chance for revelation.

By keeping the wrestling down in the depths, it's always possible in the commercial short story to create real people, who are neither big winners nor large losers, but who change in the passage of the story enough to undergo a genuine revelation, which may not even be mentioned in the words of the story, but which is palpably there.

In one of this writer's stories, neither typical nor atypical of his manufactory, a seller of honey who operates a roadside stand in the North Georgia mountains is asked by a wealthy automobile maker to sell him his old and rare automobile for a price that would ease the mountain man's existence and brighten his family's.

The mountain man, Journey—I didn't give him a last name—understands, as the story unfolds, what a treasure he has in the old red automobile. His understanding goes beyond avarice and gloating, mounting into mysticism. He becomes aware that this antique automobile, handed down by his father, sets him apart from others in the close-knit isolated community; he sees that because it has been esteemed by the outside world as valuable, it has turned into his own legend—like another man's cherished long rifle, still another's "magical" walking staff. So with much sorrow and internal sweating he turns down the tempting offer. And when he has done so, and wheels to stare at his wife, he suddenly sees that she feels exactly as he does; that he has triumphed by keeping his legend beyond price.

In the story the wealthy would-be purchaser isn't a villain; he is only a catalyst. At the story's end the reader feels mildly sorry for him—but gloriously glad for Journey's intact pride and for Journey's inchoate defense of that pride and truth. Taking into account the threads of honey-selling and automotive lore that run through the story, its title was a natural: "Sweet Chariot."

The wrestling in it is almost hidden—concentrated in Journey himself, revealed to the reader merely in suggestion, and never shown to his friends, his wife, or the hopeful would-be buyer.

The more the wrestling is kept locked between the lines of your story, the more powerfully will what is revealed at the end affect your reader.

Good and evil are not black and white, but forces impossible to separate and label with convenient tags—and it is the tremendous understanding of this hard fact that informs and lends shattering strength to Shirley Jackson's celebrated story "The Lottery." Its muscles are fathoms deep; we do not see the westling, or actually know what is really going on, until the last few lines. Mrs. Bill Hutchinson, Tessie, gathers with the rest of the townspeople in the village square, where a formal ritual—which we're told is also practiced in other towns—is going on. In Shirley Jackson's skilled, underplayed prose—which tells just enough, but never puts up signposts—the reader feels a nervous, growing awareness of something wrong, of an immense terror underlying the sunny day with its commonplace, even gently humorous talk. And when, finally, Tessie's name is drawn in the lottery, and her friends and children and husband are on her to stone her to death, we have a feeling of absolute loss and horror, which has been prepared for in every quiet sentence—but which, all the same, is cumulatively more terrible because of the very reality and humanity of Tessie's killers; we feel we have touched the true core of violence in mankind, more truly than we might have done by poring over a library full of criminal statistics.

Sometimes the end result of the buried wrestling, the revelation, is itself concealed—concealed, but not muffled, still there for the reader to see, hear, and feel in all its story power.

"Alive and Real," by Jessamyn West, takes place on a Sunday morning in California in the suburban quiet of the Johnsons' flourishing orange ranch. On this morning Meredith Johnson wants to listen to a radio broadcast of the Bikini bomb test. But he leaves the radio to go outside because his wife asks him to see what their children and a neighbor's are up to. She believes the children have been acting a little mysteriously. Meredith goes out and strolls along the rows of trees—then, hearing the children chanting, he creeps up on them. He discovers that they are worshiping a cardboard figure of Satan hung from a eucalyptus. In his blind revulsion, and on pure impulse, and while their heads and bodies are bowed in the dust, Meredith steps in behind the cardboard figure, so that when they look up again the children will see through its eyeholes his eyes, and so that at least for a moment they will be petrified with fear.

That is almost all of the story. But we *know* why Meredith did what he had to. We can feel his loathing of evil as if it were a shock wave from the far-off Pacific island, and we can somehow hear those children screaming for a long time after the story is over. Wrestling of a primordial kind is going on under the words; and the revelation doesn't have to be spelled out or underlined.

In most of today's commercial stories such underground wrestling is expected by your reader. It may be found on many levels—in a sunny, breezy story whose apparent aim is plain entertainment, and in a story whose shape is more obviously serious. Few readers know why they anticipate its presence, but nearly all of them will feel subtly disappointed, even cheated, if it's not there. A story whose "moral" is telegraphed, trumpeted, and laid out like the components of an advertising campaign is bound to overshoot its mark because its revelation, what it *means*, or what its author thinks it means, has moved ahead of its value as a story; the art of letting the reader see, hear, and feel for himself or herself has been bypassed.

Wrestling, leading to stunning revelation, is always there in the best and most durable stories of the past. Chekhov's story "Rothchild's Fiddle" appears, on the surface, as plotless and without real point as a gentle, rambling anecdote relayed over several glasses of vodka in a Russian tavern. It concerns the restricted life of a man named Yakov, a feckless and disappointed fellow who, we're told, lived beside a river—which, Chekhov also tells us, was "a respectable river, and by no means contemptible." We learn that Yakov was a decent performer on the fiddle, that he grumbled considerably over his ill luck, and that no doubt as a result of this sour attitude, he treated his wife abominably, blaming her, in part, for his wasted days and nights and his lack of rubles. And at the end of the story Chekhov springs his wonderful trap—he opens his hand to show the diamond shining in the center of his palm. In no more than a dozen lines, with sure economy and an almost laconic precision, he mentions everything that Yakov could have done to create a marvelous career; that he could have traveled from country house to country house, making money by fiddling for parties; that he could have fished in the river for happy profit, that he could have acted as a bargeman, that he and his wife could have reveled in the gifts of this amazing river.

In one great flash we see that the river is life—and that Yakov is Everyman. And that those simple words "a respectable river, and by no means contemptible" have taken on timeless meaning. For this is wrestling in the short story carried to its highest power, so that what has been said will go on revealing itself as long as there are women and men and children to read.

The Meeting

As soon as wrestling has evolved into revelation, your story is over. This doesn't simply mean that you've kept a variant of the O. Henry trick ending in reserve until the last. It means that the reader has been given a clear look at a change which the wrestling has brought about, and that it's time to stop. You, the author, have wrestled within *yourself* to understand your people, and to make the reader understand them as they grappled with themselves or with others, and now that the lightning of change, or sometimes even the flicker of possible change, has been shown, the story must stand on its own. A meeting has been achieved. Nothing may have been permanently solved—but something has been apprehended.

The reader knows more than he did when he read your first line. He has been informed; as wrestling met revelation, he was present at the meeting, and the rest, as Hamlet said, is silence. One extra word can spoil it.

In first stories especially, the temptation is to run on past the story's natural stop—to embroider slightly, to give one last parting sentence or so as a good-bye, a rounding off and farewell. This is an orator's impulse. Good storytellers learn early to suppress it. In another place we'll go into the endings of stories, their problems and their pleasures, but for now just remember that the best stories stop when their wrestling stops and a little light has been shed on the reasons for it. They don't stop with a big bang or a trailing whimper; they stop for the excellent reason that they are finished.

The Seventh Experiment

What's the real struggle going on in the chief person or persons of your story? Don't try, as yet, to define it. Dip for it. Ask yourself if you, faced by the same problem and set of circumstances, could work through to a solution to which you'd been blind at the start.

In asking yourself this, all sorts of false solutions will present themselves. Many of these will be illogical and inorganic—coming in the shape of gods from a machine, rich uncles, generous aunts, who float down out of the blue and cut through your story dilemma and dower your people with deliriously impossible endings. Turn your back on these solutions and consider your people as *people*, not Snow Whites and Rose Reds and Prince Charmings. Keep on dipping, penetrating as many layers of yourself as you can to find out what actually goes on in those depths.

Avoid pinning down any real discovery at this point. What you want to know is why the wrestling is happening, not who wins or who loses.

See if there might be, under the fabric of your hard-won story opening, a strong suggestion of struggle. You've tested it for readability and promise; now check it for implications of true wrestling. As you started to tell the rest of it in your head, did it seem to move toward inner battle?

If you're inclined to think of yourself as a tough-minded, pragmatic individual, try to understand the wrestlers in your story as subject to the winds of chance, not mere projections of your iron-willed self.

If, on the other hand, you're cheerful and sanguine by nature, try to see them as genuine enemies, groping for fair or unfair advantage, dirty and determined players in a very serious game.

Keep on dipping for a time, until, without fooling yourself, you've caught at least a few glimpses of what will be going on under the surface of your story. Then, to avoid schizophrenia, go do something else—while holding the story alive and warm and well in the back of your mind.

Chapter 7

Getting into Plot

P lot is a word as frightening and alien to many beginning writers as *syntax* is to a rock lyricist.

It's a scarifying word because it smacks of something mechanical that holds a story in place like braces around imperfect teeth. It also sounds like a mysterious invention that may, if you know how to operate it, shoot out a short story when the right buttons are pushed—or, if you happen to push the wrong ones, produce a piece of yesterday's newspaper or the *Congressional Record*.

Actually, plot machines of one sort and another have been on the market for years. They are advertised in the back pages of enthusiastic little magazines, along with plausible plans for making millions by breeding guinea pigs and prospecting for uranium in the backyard.

The oddest of these labor-saving devices was an instrument called "Plotto." It was a flat wheel with little windows around it, which was affixed by a navel button to various other wheels. When all these were spun together, on the principle of roulette, various themes and situations were juxtaposed in the windows, leaving the baffled user to stare at them—like a movie producer locked in a bank vault, with many reels of film and no projector.

But all Plot has ever meant is *What Happens First* and then *What Happens After That.*

Here, with reservations, is the fairly shapely skeleton of a Plot. (The reservations are expressed because this writer seldom makes outlines of anything, preferring to let a story seethe and boil inside until he is forced to write it to get rid of it and simultaneously to surprise himself with it. He knows that this outline will undergo drastic changes as it reaches the form of a story, and he is equally sure that its second draft may bear only a cousinly relationship to the first. He doesn't want to mislead any reader into believing that a story outline can be anything but a rough and crudely imagined map of unexplored country—often more useful as a goad than as any kind of reliable tour guide. He has known writers who made handsome outlines, and who stuck to them, but he has always felt some lack of richness in the stories that come out of them. The writers were kind to their mothers, paid their income taxes on time, and were all-round exemplary citizens, but they seemed to mistake outlines for passionate dedication. And with this out of the way, here is the structural libretto:)

A young man who has published one novel which received critical appreciation but did not sell wonderfully has been invited to have dinner with a world-famous poet. The poet, highly influential in literary circles, has asked the young man to bring along the galleys of his second novel and has intimated that if he likes it as well as he did the first one, he will give it a good review—in a newspaper whose book review section is read by more book-buyers and booksellers than any other in the nation. As he enters the hotel where the great poet is staying, and where he is entertaining his retinue, the young man encounters a very pleasant girl. It is a windy spring night, with birds blown about the sky and April penetrating the spirit of man and even the canyons of a great city. The girl has a sheaf of poems held haphazardly under one arm. One of the sheets is caught by a gust and whirls away. He captures it for her, and in their ensuing talk he learns that she is here to see the great poet too. The poet has been writer in residence at a Maine college attended by the girl, and he has encouraged her to show him more of her work.

I don't know the young man at this juncture—this is one of the troubles with an outline which concentrates on Plot alone—but I feel that I shall know him better than a brother by the time we have lived together awhile, and I feel that already he disapproves; not of the girl, but of the poet having invited her to the romantic hotel on this night; I also feel at this point that the hotel is the Plaza, and I can see it glimmering in the background. I also, without going into it much more deeply as yet, feel that the great poet is a bossy lecher who uses people like paper napkins and that the young man knows it and is uneasy about it, although he is hardly prudish by inclination and has spent a good deal of time, and lost a little unreclaimable blood and joy, in Vietnam. I think the young man sits down for a minute with the girl, and speaks, however allusively, of these things, and finds out in the process that the girl is fully aware of the great poet's well-publicized frailties and is willing to take her chances for the sake of her poems.

I think the next scene takes place at the poet's table, where, surrounded by acolytes of the particular parochial variety which Mr. Hemingway once referred to as "worms in a bottle," the great poet takes immediate possession of the girl's arm and continues a diatribe he had started before they came in, concerning the flaws in the work of all living poets with the exception of his own. And I believe that at the conclusion of this brilliantly suggested if rather one-sided speech he throws a Plaza key on the table and invites the girl to run on up and make herself comfortable, in the manner of an established pasha making certain of his companion for the night.

At this point I am sure that the young man, while causing no outward fuss to speak of, is staring earnestly at the girl, hoping that she will throw the key back at the great poet; inflicting at least slight bodily damage, before she walks out; and I am also sure that he is, for a good reason, thinking of times in Vietnam when children of five, six, and seven years of age watched their homes and parents being firebombed without lifting a hand to protect themselves or even finding themselves able to speak in protest. The uses of power, and the acceptance of power by the mild and the hopeful innocent, is one of the issues at stake here, although there are others not usually examined in the popular short story. This doesn't mean that they can't be; nothing is taboo, and this is going to be an entertaining story with built-in guts. I am now getting a slight feeling of its surface, working my way downward; I am almost as angry and baffled as the young man.

And I feel, with him, a sense of vast loss when the girl picks up the key. Like him, I find myself unable to follow her as, compliantly, like a piece of April transplanted to this place, she drifts on out of the room. I next find myself occupying the limited, brooding, angry space of the young man as he listens to the worshipful small talk buzz around him, and as he reflects on the fact, which has been mentioned earlier, that the great poet has a fetish of keeping only the original of his famous manuscripts, never making copies, and that he has brought with him to the hotel a new manuscript, a series of poems on which he has labored for the past ten years. In the *persona* of the young man, I have decided now that I, too, will presently leave—but not before I have walked to the end of the table and given the great poet a good one on the point of the jaw, not severe enough to fracture, but strong enough to make certain I shall never need to ask him a favor again.

Well into the skin of the young man, I am about to retrieve my brief-case with the galleys still in it and make my only possible, perhaps futile but necessary, gesture and exit, when the girl returns. She is just sudden-ly there, floating along, standing at the elbow of the great poet. She has the crisp delighted look of a child fresh from the bath, and indeed she an-nounces happily to the great poet that she has had a shower, and thanks him for the chance to freshen up after her long bus trip from Maine, and drops the key back upon the table. She also remarks, with polite grace-fulness, that she has taken advantage of the chance to read over his mag-nificent manuscript, that she finds it, from her own necessarily young and awkward and lower plane of appreciation, superb—and (even more casually) that since it felt a trifle stuffy in the suite, she managed to open a window, upon which a number of manuscript pages were snatched away by an April draft over Manhattan... but, she says confidently, she is sure the great poet is an essentially wise man and that he has really taken the trouble to make copies.

She then goes out of the hotel for good, while I, wrapped in the young man's flesh and with sudden delight in my bones, get up and follow her, and catch up with her, leaving behind a smitten void in which the great poet is for once in his voluble self-advertising life unable to speak, and learning through the young man's ears that she actually opened no win-dow, lost no irreplaceable manuscript. Why, I tell myself, this is in effect a happy ending—even a Boy Meets, Loses and Gets Girl ending, if you want to look at it that way. But if I didn't feel it was much more, I wouldn't have started the outline in the first place.

Going Beneath Plot

Those bones already have a modicum of flesh on them, and in several ways the story is ready to write. As yet there are no names for the central characters, so I shall remedy this lack right now with three: for the great poet, Hamilton Ferris, a name possessed of resonant dignity with over-tones of hammy emotionalism; for the girl, Amelia Sammons, because Amelia is a stout New England name like Emily and Tracy; and for the young man, Grady Calman, because it's an intermediate name and could be an offshoot of any ethnic root.

There is a lot I don't know yet about Grady and Amelia; I want Grady to be unattached, living somewhere in Greenwich Village, an isolated and somewhat sardonic spirit but not at all removed from the heat and salt of existence; since he was in Vietnam about thirteen years ago, and this is a contemporary story, this would make him about thirty-three or -four years old. Amelia is around twenty-four, ten years younger but hardly, because of her sympathies and instincts, sharply removed from Grady's generation. Hamilton Ferris is in his ageless fifties, with a façade like an overgrown child and the rapacious gentility of a killer whale.

Before I sit down to write the story, which will be done in the course of this book, and printed here, I need to go farther under the felt and lively surface to explore more than merely What Happens. At the outset, I'm deeply aware that the weather has its primary importance to the story; without the mischievous April air scurrying around the cornices of buildings and snatching hats and sheets of paper with poems written on them, Amelia could talk about opening all the windows she wanted to and the authenticity of possibility would be flattened and dulled; with it, it becomes an actor in the story, perfectly capable of whisking ten years of Hamilton Ferris's imperishable lines away like ticker tape thrown in a Fifth Avenue parade. Then, besides the weather, there is the point about Ferris's proud and foolish habit of retaining only his original manuscipt; this cannot be blatantly presented, but it has to be worked very naturally into the body of the story and it needs to be impressed upon the reader as early as possible.

All this will have to be done with all the artifice I can summon; the process of making a story appear inevitable is, itself, a highly artificial one, and it often consists of working a kind of legerdemain which palms the ace while allowing the reader to believe all the cards are in full sight. Then too, there is the moment of misdirection in the story, when Amelia appears to be amenable and meek and trots off to the lair of the dragon with the suite key in her hand like a good little slave girl. Pure emotion will have to carry this; Grady's anger cannot be directed at her, but almost wholly at Ferris, for his use of his reputation and influence as a bludgeon to drive her into his bed.

And last, there's the large query of what Line of Sight to take. As I got into the so-called outline, I favored First Person Whole; yet there are big dangers here, not the smallest of which is falling into the trap of talking more like a man with an axe to grind than a man caught in an untenable, baffling situation. So at this point I shall reserve judgment on Line of Sight, continuing to test First Person Whole, Third Person, and even First Person Offset in my skull before I even think about starting off.

In the days when H. L. Mencken and George Jean Nathan were producing the original *Vanity Fair*, they uttered strictures against any story that dealt with writers, painters, sculptors, or musicians. This is a story about three writers, and it is meant to be just that because this is a book to be read by writers. It is a completely commercial story with a serious and solid center. It may come off whole and shining in the first draft or it may be an example of how first ideas and illusions are altered for the better on their way to market.

What, Then, *Is* Plot?

We know what it isn't; it isn't a wheel, a contraption in which buttons are pushed so that stories may be emitted, or a fixed set of rules chiseled in stone.

Nor is it necessarily the result of a laborious outline in which each second of the story is traced to account for its emotional peaks and the amount of suspenseful adrenaline it carries in every sentence.

It is, much more authentically, you—you in the process of walking around the people in your story until you start to see them as if you had known them for a hundred years and had just begun to recognize their special qualities, with emotional sympathy that plunges to find the wrestling in each of them and starts to explore it in dramatic terms.

It is you, making a story grow like a strong vine from the ground of character.

Where It Starts

Like Jonah in the whale's stomach, Plot crouches in the dark.

It begins in you with small flashes of memory.

Battered by all known varieties of current news every day of the week, you have often thought, "*That* could be a take-off point for a story," or "*That* might be a splendid springboard into this mysterious thing called Plot."

And so it might—but only if it complemented your own chemistry, joined forces with your own emotion, and was somehow touched by your own memory which started your imagination moving along exciting paths.

Years ago a capable short story maker named Tess Slesinger wrote a story which she called, aptly, "A Life in the Day of a Writer." In it, quick flashes of remembrance, need, and desire pass through the mind of one articulate person in a progression like chain lightning. By the end of the story the reader has experienced a lifetime of fact and fancy. Yet the story is successful, not diffuse; from it the reader obtains the calm feeling that out of this jungle of images will come a unified story with what can, at least roughly, be labeled a Plot—What Happens First and What Happens After That.

Like everything else about a short story, Plot is sensed before it can be touched. It's the residue of feeling that stays with you after a host of capering impersonators representing themselves as Plots have appeared, grimaced awhile, and been rejected. Recognizing an authentic Plot, one that fits your capability and temperament, is the equivalent of discovering a perfect shell which has been washed up on a beach after a storm. Holding your breath, bending over it, observing it with suspicion and hope from all angles, you finally see that it's yours—that its contours, convolutions, shape, and shading are right, and when you pick it up and put it to your ear, it has a deeply personal roar.

There are exceptions—this writer has sometimes dreamed the endings of stories, in the best color, and discovered upon waking that all he needed to do was to lead up to those endings while preserving the full emotion of the dream—but as a general rule Plots don't come ready-made but move in like separate shadows that take on brilliance and depth as they form. When you've been writing stories for a time, Plots will sometimes loom up smiling and whole, and even after you've inspected them with the attitude of an amateur at a racetrack being offered a sure thing by a flashily dressed stranger, they'll *still* be whole and attractive. This will come about as a possible reward for much previous groping, or perhaps because the muse of short stories likes you that day; it isn't anything on whose strength you should open a new bank account.

A genuine commercial short story Plot operates on a great many levels—moral, emotional, aesthetic, primitive, sophisticated. Its thrust is accompanied by your belief that you can do it more justice than anyone else now writing on earth could. You are writing to justify your faith in it. In one of his journals Scott Fitzgerald underlines the necessity of making an Eskimo realize the importance of a trip to Cartier's. To a short story maker that doesn't sound ridiculous at all. Plot is the anteroom of your story workshop, but it's in that room that the fires are heated and the passions pointed and prepared. Your Plot must be yours alone, able to bear with firm grace the charge of emotion you bring to it—able to say what you wanted to say without bending, twisting, or falling apart. Plot is never merely an *idea*, but a consummated pledge of faithfulness to that idea, a substance already right and rounded and done before the first word of the story falls into place.

The Brimming Pitcher

What we loosely term ideas leading through labyrinthine ways to Plots come from deep inside us and are overlaid with outside events that have moved us, stirred us, made us laugh, and have become part of us. The most dazzling excursion into a possible future—pigeonholed as fantasy or science fiction—and the most down-to-earth adventure of a woman waiting for her lover both start that way. They have to, because their origin is lodged in their makers.

On one plane our creating selves are and always will be limited to where and when we were born and to what we gather as we go along—to what Alfred North Whitehead called our "withness."

But whatever accident of birth, luck, and circumstance seems to restrict the writer of stories, this same accident frees the writer to explore his or her sacrosanct and inimitable territory.

In this manner the writer of stories possesses an endlessly filling pitcher of material—the pure elixir of Plot. It's like the pitcher of Greek legend, which was enchanted by a god in disguise. Rewarding an elderly couple who had done him a favor, he caused their pitcher to keep brimming over, no matter how much was poured out of it.

Your brimming pitcher is like nobody else's.

Use it. Use your memories, convictions, knowledge, artfulness, honesty, and aberrations to go down after the best stories in you.

The Eighth Experiment

Stroll around your story plot. Study it with narrow eyes and critical objectivity. If it has a rococo touch—if there appears, already, to be too much detail in it, too many possible sideshows—clear them away. If it still seems amorphous, merely a fuzzy far-in-the-distance suggestion of two or three characters thrown together, start focusing on just one of the people and ask what is making this person tick.

When you think you know, begin plumbing the depths of your other protagonists. You may well find that you have imagined a straw doll for your more real people to react to. For instance, at this point I am beginning to be dubious of Hamilton Ferris—isn't he just a stock villain, for all his overlay of fame and power? Isn't there something in him, the same thing that enabled him to *be* a truly great poet, which could dictate how he reacts to Amelia's announcement of having lost the manuscript pages, and redeem him—in spite of his surface gloss—and change the story's ending, surprising me as well as the reader? I am beginning to think there is. It is this I must dig for, and find. I have to be true to everyone in this story, and not simply push anyone into position.

So do you, as you plan your story.

And now let's move a little farther along this curious pathway of Plot.

Chapter 8

Farther into Plot

*A*t this point it is necessary, even vital, to say, once and for all, that a literally recorded incident is not a short story. It may be the jumping-off point for a tremendous story, the jogger-of-the-mind that nudges you into the creation of a full-blown and wonderfully rich adventure. But by itself it's a puny, unclothed, shivering little faker, proving that life does not imitate art but furnishes only scrappy hints of what art can be.

The self-righteous cry of the beginning writer who has labored to produce one of these story mice: "But it's true, it's all true, that's the way it really happened!" is always painful to hear. Such defenses indicate a belief in the struggling writer that faithful reporting of trivia is tantamount to actual plot. Because what is relayed has actually happened, either to the narrator or within his or her hearing, it has taken on an aura of holiness. But a short story is an artful lie which has turned into a powerful truth in the telling; it is never the limited transcription of factual accuracy. If I step off the curb this morning and narrowly escape being wiped out by a frenzied eighty-year-old lady at the controls of a Yamaha motorcycle, that is going to alarm me and give me cause to reflect on my own mortality; I would not dream of hurrying back to my desk, transcribing the incident with full fidelity, and calling the result a short story. After my mixture of shock and amusement had settled a trifle, I might start considering the elderly demonic rider as a possible source of a story, like the irritant grain of sand which begins slowly, producing a pearl in the oyster's flesh; but chances are strong that the end result would have little to do with what really happened. By the time the story was finished, the motorcycle might have become an Allis-Chalmers tractor, its driver a twenty-five-year-old farm woman in Iowa, the locale a field of floury corn somewhere northeast of Shenandoah, and the elements of the story so drastically changed from its inception that even its author was not quite sure where it all started.

Use *what really happened* as a springboard, not a crutch. Recall its emotional impact as completely as you can, but don't depend on its "realistic" background as a substitute for Plot. What happens to you at firsthand—or at carefully observed secondhand—is not important to the reader; what happens inside the story which grows from it and changes and takes on its own distinctive life is the soul of good fiction.

What Is "Formula" Plot?

Formula Plot is, in essence, the manipulation of a story to please the reader rather than to let the reader discover something. The word "please" in this case refers to stroking the reader's aesthetic sense as well as appealing to his sentimental side. So a story about a gravedigger, a story appearing, let's say, in a university-sponsored review or some other little magazine of excellent academic credentials, a story unremittingly gray and totally grim in its final effect, may receive high praise for its starkness and sense of "reality," but remain as formularized as the story of a poor young man who, by adhering to the principles of Horatio Alger grit and honesty, becomes the president of a powerful corporation or perhaps the United States. Shades of gray, of doubt, are missing in the genuine formula story. As I mentioned in a former chapter, it was once acceptable in most large-circulation magazines—and on its reversed level, that of the ironic meaninglessness of existence, it is still found in high-toned quarterlies, along with reams of criticism dealing with the use of the ampersand by William Blake, which solidify their professorial authors' grip on tenure.

One paramount purpose of this book is to help you along the craggy path toward the making of stories capable of being sold. For these your best-paying markets will always be the "popular" magazines—whose editorial philosophies you don't have to agree with to write for them. Although in a broad sense the use of "formula" in the novel often leads to wealth and glory, this is not true of today's commercial short story. The editors of the magazines which print it are aware that "popular" sentiment is a shaky concept on which to build a public and that life in this part of the twentieth century has changed so rapidly and vastly that sheer storytelling integrity and craftsmanship are the only basic ingredients by which to hold readers of fiction. Their best short fiction reflects the world—both imaginatively and fantastically, and sometimes with far more fidelity then the fiction we easily call "literary."

Stories that fit into a particular genre—mystery, romance, Western, science fiction, fantasy—are not necessarily formula stories. They may be pigeonholed under a single heading, but their individual treatment, the art and viewpoint of their authors, is the reason why they are purchased and published. Their actual entertainment value is considerably higher than that of the more simplistic and frequently crudely arranged "happy ending" or "snappy twist" stories enjoyed by our forebears, in which it didn't matter a great deal if the mechanics of manipulation showed through, as long as everything came out all right. Today's superior short stories explore the writer *and* the reader to discover and reveal new territory on ancient ground—they are not content to echo past successes. A good attitude toward your own storymaking aim is that of the late Wallace Stevens, in one of his finest poems:

"I do not see things as they are,"
sang the man with the blue guitar.

The Plot Notebook

Splendid storywriters keep notebooks. In them pothooks and curlicues and apparently meaningless notations about random phenomena serve as embryonic story material. One of the tantalizing entries in Scott Fitzgerald's journals is: "The Dancer Who Found She Could Fly." I wish he had written the story.

Other writers, equally accomplished, couldn't use a notebook if it came gift-wrapped with their initials in gold on the morocco binding. The idea of using a notebook offends some seventh sense of story creation in them; they believe that simply by owning one, they might insult or keep at a distance the benevolent muse of all stories. They are superstitious, and instead of relying on jots and titles of possibilities, they cultivate all-embracing memories.

This writer does both—he keeps a series of dog-eared hardly legible notebooks, in which it is alarmingly difficult to decipher anything, and at the same time he utilizes a memory which is like a ragbag of loose information and emotion, but, in conjunction with a notebook, can be stirred into action and produce that ephemeral, important—and intensely shy—germ of a real story.

Stories may come to you in one hasty package, as if delivered when you least expect it by ghostly bystanders whose intelligence quotient is none too high, and who are likely to forget a vital part of the gift, which you will have to figure out for yourself in good time. In sifting and categorizing the workable from the useless, it's safe to depend only on the note that *moves* you—that suddenly starts to take on shape and meaning and doesn't merely sit there like a fried egg. All ideas are not inspirational for all writers; what is bad or meaningless to me may be clothed in glittering raiment to you, and what you look upon as hopeless may turn into my love-child. In a shabby notebook which looks as though it had been salvaged from the schoolbag of a backward child, I find a dim and awkward scribble: "Kids build boat in basement. Take to suburban lake. Damned thing sinks. Sympathetic older brother's girl laughs at kids. He finds girl who doesn't laugh."

Behind this less than nucleus for a story, I can suddenly visualize the powerful ambience of a village, Glen Ellyn, Illinois, in high summer, and the appearance, complete with marshy grass, of a little artificial lake, Lake Glen, and the stricken look on the face of my brother, Joe, and his friend, both about nine years old, as the great craft they have so laboriously, tongue-chewingly constructed bubbles to a watery grave. So much for the incident; by itself, it is nothing. But now I see and hear a ravishingly popular girl with an especially bland and infuriating laugh, as she observes me and my younger friends trudging to the waterside with help and encouragement. And I feel a balance coming about—a revelation in its purest form—as I see what this girl, whom I have ardently pursued for at least four of my sixteen years, really is: a spirit of fashionable scorn for dreams and holy endeavor, a lovely killer of the truth. I *feel* this, and I feel and hear the presence of another girl, who knows the importance of the project, as she arrives to say just the right things to the children, assuring them that the next boat will float. It is not a simple story at all. It will have a quiet and risible surface. Beneath it will be wrestling for all it's worth.

The story is finally called "A Verray Parfit Gentil Knight," with a bow to Geoffrey Chaucer, and it is right for me from start to finish; it begins:

*On this fine Saturday in green June my small brother Ben and
his friend Alison Grandine stopped building the boat they'd been
working on for six months. They just stopped building it; there
wasn't anything more they could do to it.*

I set it aside to cool off, knowing that it will take a little rearrangement
of phrases here and there to bring it up to what I really want; in a day or
two I come back to it and rewrite it, and send it off with the absolute
knowledge that it will be bought and paid for in excellent cash; and the
fact is, I have known this since I looked into the notebook and found the
puny-looking suggestion. Many stories will not come out with this
wholeness, but will have to be nursed, coddled, hammered, and sweated
into existence. But the notebook, supplemented by my memory and
aided by my imagination which counterpoised the two girls, has done its
work in this case. The incident has grown into the sort of story only I can
write; it may not be one somebody else would want to write; but it is
wholly mine.

You recognize your story when it is yours—when you snick a finger-
nail against its substance and hear it ring. In the constant search for
what is yours, you'll make many notes, some of which will be of no good
at all to you, even though they seemed to have predestined value at the
time. But I am not sure that even those are entirely lost. There is a detri-
tus of emotion and purpose which carries over from year to year in a storyteller's life, so that in the end the question of what was useful and
what wasn't comes down to the old and unanswerable question, "But
who wakes the bugler?"

The only real point is to keep the bugle sounding, again and again.

The Organic Resolution and the
Dirigible Ending

In the story I have somewhat reluctantly but with enthusiasm outlined
in the last chapter, the one about three writers in a book for writers,
there will be, however it comes out and however deeply the character of
the famous poet is probed, an organic resolution—which is to say that
the ending will grow, with logic as well as surprise, out of what has gone
before. I shall make sure that the Plaza Hotel does not experience a fire
which is extinguished by my pro-tem hero so that he can also save the

girl, Amelia, from a fate ostensibly worse than death. For one thing, although it is a chancy, breezy evening, I haven't prepared the reader for melodrama—for another, I do not believe that having her sleep with the great if reprehensibly amoral man is nearly as bad as fooling the reader, and myself, by dragging in what insurance adjustors call an Act of God at the last moment. The problem in this story is actually deeper and more perennial than that of the possibility of accident.

There are great stories in which a violent event is the fulcrum on which the story itself swings; Joseph Conrad's "Typhoon" is one, and "The Short Happy Life of Francis Macomber" is another. "Christ in Concrete," by Pietro Di Donato, has to do with the collapse of a concrete form upon an Italian construction man, detailing in horrific and searing vividness his last seconds before needless death; Ambrose Bierce's "An Occurrence at Owl Creek Bridge" is violence itself. In those stories the atmosphere is charged with darkness from the start, and we expect shattering results. Something must happen in a story, something must matter; but the most subtle and small events can convey large meanings; T.S. Eliot's "Fear in a handful of dust" applies to many of the strongest stories we have. A superb story of violent internal wrestling can be produced without showing any visible change an onlooker inside the story could see.

Yet there is a tendency of beginning writers to go for melodrama and situational clichés when a story gets out of their control and they don't know what to do with it—and particularly, how to end it. This is the Heavenly Syndrome; it is a calling upon fate to slap affairs into dramatic condition. Its most superb example came about in a story done by the student of a friend of mine; in it the writer takes a group of religious fetishists to a lofty hill under the guidance of their acting messiah, in the communal belief that the end of the world is very near. The writer didn't like any of the possible conclusions that occurred to him. So the writer dropped a dirigible on everyone, killing the lot. While I am willing to admit that there is some more or less satisfactory ironic principle at work here, I am also prone to break down in helpless laughter at the divine beauty of the ending. It comes literally out of the blue; it is the god in the machine carried to its ultimate conclusion, with a grand and sweeping disregard for any law of probability or any reader's getting-around sense.

Of course, the writer may protest vigorously, such things *do* happen; we *are* at the mercy of the uncontrollable, so why isn't this a valid story?

My answer is that when organic content goes out the window, chaos enters; and the good short story is one of mankind's oldest props against chaos. The temptation to play God may breed effective dictators, but it can result in terrible short stories.

With all your mother wit and native imagination, avoid the Dirigible Ending.

Mood in Plot

A story can be soaked and sustained in mood and end with the revelation the mood has promised, but still within it will be a thread of action classifiable as Plot. In A. E. Coppard's "Adam and Eve and Pinch Me," we are introduced to a man who, on a perfect English summer day, finds that he has slipped out of his ordinary body and attained invisibility along with diamond-sharp perception of the present and the future. His name is given as Jaffa Coding. He floats in and out of his house, encounters his children—of whom there seems to be one more than there were in his recollection—and after a series of exhilarating adventures in this extraterrestrial self, comes upon his wife in dalliance with a handsome stranger, which enrages him. The story is highly "poetic" in the best sense, which means it works without letting its mysticism get in the way. Then Jaffa slips back into the self he has occupied before this adventure, and finds that *he* was the stranger who was making love to his wife, and that his name is Gilbert Cannister. The story is a floating wonder, like a bubble blown for sheer joy—yet its Plot is there, and it has to do with Gilbert's intense and growing realization of his other self, his alter ego, and his increasing, bursting sense of his luck in being alive. This story, by the way, has no perceptible beginning, no discernible middle, and its end is simply there because it is over. But a Plot is there, with revelation in its conclusion.

Conrad Aiken's "Silent Snow, Secret Snow" is a study in the inexorable advance of schizophrenia in one boy's mind, coupled with his secret alliance with the cold, the snow, the need to draw into the walled kingdom of himself; the story penetrates with great sympathy and easy strength the inner yearning toward withdrawal from life, and the mood of the snow, the whispering whiteness, permeates it from the first scene to the last, in which he is lost to his family and the known world. And this *is* the Plot; a line of motion spiraling inward from the surface until it leads to full revelation of a deeply felt tragedy.

Paul Gallico's "Flight" is the story of a barnstorming parachutist who uses for his parachute a pair of batlike wire and leather wings. His mood of adventure and elemental delight in giving himself to the air is paramount; it is a highly impressionistic story, which has a skin of sentiment over it like the skin on a chocolate pudding, but which holds, beneath, something of the lure of the skies we feel in the legend of Icarus. The Plot is the suspense created in the reader over whether this half man, half creature of the air will live or crash and die.

All Plot depends on somehow knowing—not always by obvious or easily identifiable methods—where you are going in your story. It exists beneath the story's mood as a compelling force driving the reader from sentence to sentence, a bar of invisible steel holding the story together. There has never been any such thing as a plotless story. The "slice of life" story must have a kind of revelation as its goal, more than a mere recital of events in mind, or it becomes a purposeless sociological discourse which might better be expressed in an essay.

Splitting Plot Hairs

A favorite and—to this writer—futile classroom pursuit, often employed by harassed instructors of writing skills, is the breaking down of Plot into comfortably tagged and labeled sections.

For instance, a story with O. Henry overtones, dealing with a haughty, rich, corrupt broker who juggles figures in order to put his idealistic and clean-cut nephew out of business, but who ends up by putting *himself* out of business, would be called a "Biter Bit" story. Such stories, in which the wheels of justice are invariably adjusted to bring about the downfall of the obviously wicked and the uplift of the deserving, are still bought and published in hundreds of variations—but unless they are superlatively handled, with characterization as important as the hoary old Plot line, they are very likely to end up in an editor's *out* basket. The splitting of hairs over Plot leads to a sort of false enthusiasm in the beginning story writer—a conviction that if he or she pushes this ancient button, adhering to a formula that has worked for many, the story will automatically be an outstanding salable "Biter Bit" success. And there's the concomitant danger that the writer may become bogged down in this sort of half-creative sleight of hand for the rest of his or her writing life, bypassing all the opportunities for learning more about the inner self from which the best stories rise.

Plot is what *you believe in* as a plausible series of actions which justify your story characters' truth. It cannot be imposed from outside, or the people about whom you're writing will refuse to come alive. This hard truth has always applied to the making of the best and most marketable stories. It is a fact to which many so-called teachers of the short story remain blind throughout their hair-splitting and analyzing careers. When you find yourself embroiled in laborious analytic discussions about the various sorts of Plot, complete with labels and handy charts about "structure," it's high time to get out of that class and concentrate on what you know, in your writing bones, will be the right story for your people to move around in; otherwise, you will coast around in theory for a long and perhaps fatal time. The distinct difference between a professional writer of short stories and a gifted dilettante is the professional's ability to separate all literary theory, of any kind, from his working, writing self and to look at the story as a living organic gift which he, and only he, can write for profit, pleasure, and the great joy of coming as close as possible to his inward vision.

Structure

You've probably heard—because it's an easy analogy—that structure is a bridge that the writer builds to carry the reader across a hypothetical span—say from Brooklyn to Manhattan or from one flank of the Thames or the Amazon to the other. It actually is a little like that, and it does serve to give the reader a ride in a Toyota or a Rolls-Royce from one point in time and space to another.

But if considered in terms of girders and suspension cables, these comparisons can scare a starting story writer to death in the middle of an exemplary sentence.

Structure *is* Plot: it is merely What Happens First and What Happens Next under another name. There is no perfect Plot, and there is no perfect structure—no single benchmark everyone can aim for. Classifying celebrated stories as if there were a norm every writer could follow is a habit of teachers and of commentators on the story—a habit it is easy to slide into. Flaubert's "A Simple Heart" is a magnificent act of faith in story form. It has been praised for its ideal structure since the art of the short story began being submitted by eager assessors for microscopic examination. It deals with the life, death, and the actual taking up to heaven—at least in her pure-souled imagination—of a woman of all work named Félicité, who had few rewards on earth and certainly deserved all she had earned in the afterlife. The story's detail, in good translations, is stunningly effective and cumulative, so that by the time we reach the end we are inclined to believe firmly in the presence of saints on earth. It is a story you do not wish to forget, but to cherish because it has expanded your existence. But to analyze it for structure and Plot is an exercise in stripping the petals from a rose in order to discover its secret of growth. You are less wise at the end of such analysis than you were when you merely read the story and sensed its intense mystery.

There is also the point that you may vastly prefer a so-called lesser story, because it comes closer to your own experience and strikes more sympathetic chords in your special talent. Structure and Plot will be in it too, the one actually interchangeable with the other; and you might profit much more deeply from making your own mental observations, drawing your own conclusions, from this "inferior" but effective story than you would by listening to a soaring series of lectures about Flaubert's masterpiece.

To separate structure from Plot and to think about them as if they were different—as the pieces of a bridge are made of different varieties and tensile strengths of metal—is to split apart the unity and wholeness of a story in your consciousness and to end up with your own work fractured.

If, then, you like a fluffy—but neatly rounded—story in a good woman's magazine, a story which has the texture of warm thistledown and is well told, you're not abasing yourself, but getting down to your own built-in needs, when you study it for what goes on in terms of Plot.

If you're more moved and excited by a story that cuts deeper and brings more blood, go down into it—not to label it as any particular *sort* of story, but to see precisely why you respond to it as you do. Plot, complementing character, will have a major part in what you discover. This is not so much *analysis* as it is self-discovery combined with enlightenment.

And if, while you read this, you've been scouring up the short stories of every kind of writer—the great, the near great, and the vibrantly competent—you're in good shape and your sense of structure is going to be all right, no matter if you know it's there or not.

Should the passion for splitting hairs overtake you, read four or five rule-heavy treatises on the short story in quick succession, so that this will purge your system—leaving the story you've been thinking about without any shaggy theories hanging around it.

Remember that there are very few Necessary Tactics displayed in any good short story. The ones you've been asked to think about so far are those of viewpoint, the aimed sentence, your sensory gifts, and Plot, which is the blood sister or brother of structure.

These Necessary Tactics will be joined by a few others as we go along. None of them has changed for a thousand years. They were there to be used by the cave people in telling the tale, just as they were used by Anatole France in his day and by Salinger and Cheever and Updike in ours.

A Not So Idle Suggestion

First stories can, like Christmas geese, be packed with too much stuffing. There is sometimes a pressing need to get everything in, to make a story overflow its space by holding more than it comfortably can. The old and pleasantly ribald anecdote about the *Reader's Digest* editor who wanted a tale which would be All Things to All Men, and came up with the man who assaulted a bear in an iron lung for the FBI and found God, is a good case in point. So is the apocryphal story sometimes called "Lincoln's Doctor's Wife's Dog," which was wonderfully calculated to please everybody, but which would be too much for mortal readers to accept.

So look around your story for too much obvious meaning. Meaning in a story is not injected with a hypodermic needle, but issues from it after it has been written. It's highly doubtful that Aesop ever said to himself, "Now I shall produce a profound fable upon the subject of Envy, and I think I'll call this one 'The Fox and the Grapes.' " Meaning lurks inside a story, between the lines; it is not always completely clear to the writer while it is being written, or for that matter afterward. He or she leaves it to perceptive readers to interpret for themselves.

Keep yourself lean and uncluttered and able to make your people wrestle as they must.

Chapter 9

Dialogue

*J*n the Fourth Experiment you found that talk isn't story dialogue. When you listened to people chatting away, you heard odds and ends of sentences that were like scraps of meaning which the ear assembled into some kind of sense. And sometimes you heard mere code words indicating considerably more than was really spoken. Talk is for the most part vocal shorthand. When it turns formal, it becomes speechmaking—the richly confident sentences of a politician reading from a teleprompter, the sales pitch rolling past the bright teeth of a barker.

Great conversationalists do sometimes speak in intricate and perfectly grammatical sentences. Henry James did; and in his last novels, which he dictated, you can hear the rise and fall of an earnest and probing voice expressing its owner's need to get at the tiniest nuance of every meaning. But there are very few conversationalists of that stamp left in a world increasingly concerned with speed of statement—with general meaning rather than specific truth.

Remember that you are creating dialogue for your story in the most flexible and ever-changing language ever known. *American* isn't quite English, and it never was. It has a fierier undertone, a quicker delivery. This may be why the short story came into its own in the United States; it was always inclined to be a bit regal and diffuse in England.

What you'll use, at its best, as dialogue in your story is an *approximation* of talk. You'll bring it over onto the page with the sound and strength of the original. But as you do this, you'll cut away the extra wordage, and you'll straighten out human shorthand communication so that it's clear to the reader.

You'll make sure the sound of a human voice fills this dialogue, framing it with believability which is produced by the inner tone of the writing. "Inner tone" means what you hear as you write. And a lot of it is dependent on what goes on around the dialogue. If you take any one or all of those stories you most admire, and block out the narrative to leave only the isolated lines of dialogue, you'll find—except in cases where the dialogue dominates and *is* the inner tone—that the dialogue has become puzzling; it no longer has a background, an anchor, a home.

Very often a beginning writer says, "But I know I'm good at dialogue. It's what I do best. I can start out with a couple of people talking and fill up pages before I know it."

But what are these talk sentences talking about? What are they telling the reader? What do they say about the character of the talkers, the struggle under the talk? Are they dialogue in a real story, or are they chit-chat?

A barker's frenetic spiel and a senator's windy filibuster—not unlike each other in quality—aren't dialogue either. Neither is a stream-of-consciousness river along the lines of Molly Bloom's spate at the close of *Ulysses*; it's a dreamlike rendering of half-conscious memory at full gallop.

Real dialogue is shaped, balanced, and trimmed to fit the exact contours of the story it graces. One word too much of it and the story will slip out of motion like a gyroscopic top jumping the string. One word too little and the story will have a vacancy in it, a space that needs filling and irritates the reader, not because he knows it should be there, but because he senses that he has been cheated.

This is dialogue with all the inner tone of surrounding description and explanatory action stripped away from it. It's from Herman Melville's "Bartleby the Scrivener."

> "Bartleby!"
> "Bartleby."
> "Bartleby."
> "Go to the next room, and tell Nippers to come to me."
> "I prefer not to."
> "Very good, Bartleby."

By themselves those oddments of talk dangle in the air without any attachment to life. Their umbilical cords are cut and their relevance is in doubt. But placed back in context with the full inner tone of the story, and emerging from it, they become loaded with meaning, illustrating both the implacable will of the mysterious clerk, Bartleby, and the baffled doggedness of his employer. They are transformed into dialogue.

> "Bartleby!"
> No answer.
> "Bartleby," in a louder tone.
> No answer.
> "Bartleby," I roared.
> LIke a very ghost, agreeably to the laws of magical invocation, at the third summons, he appeared at the entrance of his hermitage.
> "Go to the next room, and tell Nippers to come to me."
> "I prefer not to," he respectfully and slowly said, and mildly disappeared.
> "Very good, Bartleby," said I, in a quiet sort of serenely severe self-possessed tone, intimating the unalterable purpose of some terrible retribution very close at hand. At the moment I half intended something of the kind. But upon the whole, as it was drawing towards my dinner-hour, I thought it best to put on my hat and walk home for the day, suffering much from perplexity and distress of mind.

Throughout this marvelous story, Bartleby's "I prefer not to" is repeated at judicious, impressive intervals, until it is a drumbeat dominating the narrative, a phrase that is true dialogue carried to great heights. It speaks the theme of Bartleby's resistance to Things As They Are, his willingness to die rather than to obey humdrum orders. It brings out the entire inner tone of the background, complementing all of Melville's necessary qualifiers (he *respectfully* and *slowly* said and *mildly* disappeared), which in this case are adverbs used unusually well and not simply curly decorations.

Dialogue's Country Cousin

If Melville had endowed the mystic Bartleby with a southern background, Bartleby might have said something like, "Ah prefer not to, suh." This would have given Bartleby distinctive regional identity, but it wouldn't have helped the power of the story; and it might well have weakened it.

Dialect is dialogue's country cousin. Used with care and a light hand, it can deepen dialogue. It's also a trap that even the most keen-eared writers can fall into. The fact that their ears are well tuned is itself a lure—a temptation to reproduce, intact, the nuances and shadings of dialect. In the nineteenth century the broad popular humor of such dialect entertainers as Josh Billings and Petroleum V. Nasby—names famous in their time—made readers roll on the floor. Today, reading them is a little like trying to decipher jokes told in a completely alien tongue by the inhabitants of another planet.

Joel Chandler Harris's Uncle Remus is a faithful representation of the dialect narrator, admirably reproduced on paper and deservedly popular with generations of admirers. But Uncle Remus is hard for today's children to read, not because of any lack of skill in the narrative, but because the children's eyes are constantly baffled by the look of the dialect on the page. In *Huckleberry Finn* Mark Twain walked around this trap with neatness and enormous skill. He used many dialects, but he used them by suggesting them instead of spelling them out. They are distilled and cleansed of phonetic stumbling blocks. As a result, the narrative is always as sharp as horseradish—not quaint, but biting and clear.

Western, eastern, southern, and northern speech has a sharply distinctive number of differences—and these differences possess special shadings from one state area to another: a Georgia accent is not the same in Savannah as it is in Atlanta; a Chicago accent isn't that of a native of downstate Illinois. But when these differences are too specifically underlined in a story, the reader is diverted from the story's flow into a backwater of dialect specialties—and the total impact of the story is blunted.

William Faulkner had a superb ear for the rural speech of Mississippi. In his *Flags in the Dust*, a novel published years after his death from the original manuscript which had earlier been cut to the bone and retitled *Sartoris*, the opening paragraph is in dialect as perfectly rendered as any in the history of letters. But it's spoiled for many readers by the very faithfulness of its duplication:

Old man Falls roared: "Cunnel was settin' thar in his cheer, his sock feet propped on the po'ch railin', smokin' this hyer very pipe. Old Louvinia was settin' on the steps, shellin' a bowl of peas fer supper. And a feller was glad to git even peas sometimes,

*in them days. And you was settin' back agin' the post. They
wa'nt nobody else thar 'cep yo' aunt, the one 'fo' Miss Jenny
come. Cunnel had sont them two gals to Memphis to yo' gran-
'pappy when he fust went away. You was 'bout half-grown, I
reckon. How old was you then, Bayard?"*

That is perfectly heard and perfectly set down. But inside it there are sets
of reader blocks; small mountains the eye has to climb before the ear can
become tuned to old man Falls's voice. In his later stories and novels
Faulkner avoided these obstructions. Now and then, in dialect, he
would omit a *g* or use "fer" instead of "for," but in the main he depended
on the *rhythm of the speaker's voice* and the singing quality of the
speech to sustain regional dialogue and soliloquy. You can find the same
dependence on rhythm and cadence, rather than spelled-out dialect, in
the work of many other storytellers—when Isaac Bashevis Singer uses a
First Person Whole narrator to convey the sound of native Yiddish, the
words come to the reader not merely through the eye but in the back of
the mind, where they strike the right note without stopping to shape the
impact of individual word sounds.

Even such a minor indication of dialect as the dropping of a *g* can be a
mistake when it gives an overquaint impression of the speaker. For instance, it's better to write, "Ain't nothing going to stop me but a cyclone," than to write, "Ain't nothin' goin' to stop me but a cyclone."
The first sentence causes the reader to assume that the *g*'s would be
dropped and allows the reader's eye to travel on without a pause; the second one is a trifle more laborious and gives the effect of self-conscious-
ness. Both are better than writing, "Theer h'ain't nawthin' gwi' ter stop
me but a sigh-clone," which causes the reader to work much too hard
and is likely to give him or her a slight headache.

Fidelity to the actual sound and phonetic representation of speech
may be a virtue in the collector of Americana, but it can be a picky bore
in the short story.

In everyone's life there are aural memories of good storytelling voices
from many regions. When this writer starts a certain kind of narrative,
he hears his grandfather's phrasing, the tone of his delivery, and familiar
regional usages such as "Finer than frog hair" or "Weather's clear as a
bell." This sort of remembering can add salt and fragrance to dialogue.
The trap to be skirted lies in trying to pin it down so accurately it be-

comes a curio instead of a living echo and a contribution to the story being told.

When you use dialect, use it from firsthand memory. If you pick it up from somebody else's work, it will have a slightly off-key, artificial ring—that of a player piano as contrasted to a concert grand Steinway. When you've heard it yourself, you're as close to the real sound as you can get, and you'll be able to use it with authority. And as you use it, stay wide awake to the danger of phonetic pitfalls.

Dialect has infinite gradations, some of them easily identifiable, others so subtle they can be detected only by extraordinarily acute ears. A great many phrases aren't classifiable as dialect, but are, all the same, peculiar to a region, a time, and to educational and economic roots.

A small example of such phraseology is the tendency of an Ivy League alumnus to say "fraternity" while the graduate of a midwestern college or university would say "frat."

Social distinctions of speech can be overdone. John O'Hara claimed that no woman who has gone past the eighth grade calls a fifty-cent piece a half a dollar. This sweeping generalization gave O'Hara satisfaction and confidence that his own work was in tune with its background, although I doubt that it is true. But the point is that his writing ear and heart were in the right place, and that as a result his dialogue is never tinny but gives the illusion of complete authenticity.

Dialogue's Poor Relation

Today's catch phrase is tomorrow's dodo. Nothing dates as swiftly as current slang. Even the excellent word "cool" used to express an aloof, above-the-battle, grace-under-pressure attitude cools off in a hurry. In a monumental and deeply entertaining work, H. L. Mencken collected myriad slang phrases which have entered our language to give it pungency and breeziness, but aside from the sparing use of slang in suggested rather than straight form, you'll find very little of it in the best stories.

For one whose earlier novels and stories popularized and gave body to the word "flapper," Scott Fitzgerald used a minimum of slang in his work. His references to "running it out," "petting," and the like stand up now because they are surrounded by excellent timeless prose. In his unfinished novel, *The Last Tycoon*, his First Person Offset narrator, Cecilia Brady, refers to a meeting of movie scriptwriters, supervisors, and the doomed head of the studio, Monroe Stahr, as "taking up this new theme in turn like hepcats in a swing band and going to town with it." The words *hepcats, swing* band, and *going to town* sum up the slang of the time, but they are also jarring when read today—tiny flaws in a diamond. The story has already been beautifully placed in its time. The borrowed phrases date—because they are ephemeral, they stand out of the prose like small onions in a Tiffany pearl necklace.

Slang dealing with various occupations—especially jazz, the stage, and many businesses which speak a kind of corporate Choctaw in place of English—is usually about two years ahead of its adaptation and adoption by the public. Criminal slang has changed continually since its invention in England, France, and Italy as thieves' cant to outwit the police. What is in vogue at this second will be stale tomorrow. If you really need slang of any kind to animate a contemporary story, be sure it means what you want it to. It can be embarrassingly fluid. (In jazz "bad" can mean "great"—and by the time this is published, it can have lost that inside meaning.) In all slang ordinary words take on slippery connotations. If you use slang, use it carefully so it won't stick its tongue out at you or cause some reader in the year two thousand five hundred to wonder what your story people were talking about.

She Said, Said She

Said may be the most useful word in any story ever written. As an unobtrusive companion for dialogue, it sits there on the page without drawing attention to itself, working like a faithful draft horse and in its simplicity taking the place of all manner of feverish substitutes. Followed by a judicious adverb, its meaning can be changed with great flexibility to fit the demands of mood.

"You're looking well," she said icily tells the reader about the speaker's tone and gives a wholly different effect from *"You're looking well," she said warmly.* If the writer has already established the speaker's character, the adverb may be omitted to the story's advantage. In identifying speakers in dialogue, an unadorned *said* preceded or followed by the speaker's name is preferable to the lavish use of adverbs. And skipping the adverb altogether by substituting a short descriptive phrase is often a good idea. *"You're looking well," she said, her voice uncaring.*

In certain stories *said* becomes part of the story's inner rhythm. It furnishes a counterpoint for the talk, and leaving it out can make the flow of talk seem stilted. This is a passage from a story of this writer's "Swinger," in which although the *saids* could have been eliminated by using bits of character description to identify the speakers, their use in the story is justified by the way they chime into the storytelling music:

> *Jim stretched and hoisted his belt up a trifle. Standing arrow-straight, in his white shirt and white pants in the moonlight, he said, "I bet that vine's still there."*
>
> *"Could be," Hal said.*
>
> *Carla, trying to smooth her hair down, said, "What's this about a vine you keep gabbing about? Ouch, I've got a snarl."*
>
> *"Here," Cricket said. "I'll comb it out for you." She stood beside the slightly taller Carla, tugging a comb through the long light hair. Head bent, Carla said, "Do we have to shinny up some stupid vine after we've climbed this terrible thing here?"*
>
> *Hal said, and it sounded loud in the moonlight, "We don't have to. It's—it's sort of optional."*

As a general principle, tag lines following dialogue shouldn't draw attention to themselves, distracting attention from the dialogue to which they're appended. And this is where the modest *said* is worth its weight in platinum. It is also strong in its own right. There have been theorists of the story who claim it can be eliminated entirely, but their stories seem somehow to have been wrung dry of juice.

Of course *said* is not a completely all-purpose tag line, and this writer isn't advocating it as such. The words *asked* and *answered* are eminently serviceable, and so are other tag lines not interchangeable with *said*. A good overall rule by which to test a verb describing how dialogue is spoken is this: Does it pull away from the story, attempting to show off on its own, distracting the reader? If it does, it's the result of straining too hard for effect—a sideshow rather than an integral working story part. *"Well," asserted Tom, "this is certainly a strong beverage, Father!" "Yes," responded his father, "it's gunpowder tea."* Bad Victorian writing—as opposed to the great amount of good Victorian work—was peppered with such verb qualifiers; it is as though the word *said* had to be avoided on pain of excommunication from some exclusive club, and strange substitutes came into constant play. The habit lingers in some beginning writers.

And there are, naturally, alternative ways of handling dialogue. Unless an inner rhythm demands it, not every line of dialogue needs to be tagged. This is especially true when only two people are talking:

> *Albert walked to the window. "Snowing again. If everybody in the city went out and scooped up one handful of snow and brought it in and let it melt in the kitchen sink—"*
>
> *Susan laughed. "They'd have cold hands and it would still be eight feet deep by morning."*

When tags are necessary, using them in every third or fourth line is usually enough to prevent confusion. This is not a hard-and-fast rule—sometimes in the heat of writing you'll find yourself so firmly possessed of several people's voices that each gains complete distinction on the page, and to use tag lines would only be to hang needless signposts around. In a story containing a fast and furious argument extra tag lines can slow its intrinsic action. The matter is, finally, one of your own writing intuition and final judgment—and of remembering that dialogue is complemented and caressed by *said* and that by one route or another the reader must know who is doing the saying.

So use *said* with joy, grace, and gratefulness for its presence, as you go toward the next experiment and we think about Dialogue as the mouth, voice, and soul of Character.

Chapter 10

The Sound of Character

*H*ow a character in a story sounds isn't always directly indicated. A story told in First Person Whole Line of Sight bears the weight of its sound, that of a human voice, all the way through. But this can be done without description—the voice itself, what it chooses to say and not to say, builds a picture of the speaker in the reader's mind...sometimes a picture far more vivid than any amount of graphic surface exposition could produce.

> *At six o'clock they threw me off the bus. Maybe because I'd started this little fight with this big drunk just outside Amarillo. He kept talking about my long hair. And asking why I wasn't in the army, and how he bet I never bothered to vote. I tried shutting up as long as I could—watching the brown country shuttle past and the tumbleweeds blow in the dust. They looked like the skeletons of fat elves. But he kept pulling me away from the window. And when he got a hand on my guitar and gave the strings a snap, I shoved him off. Not hard. I didn't want to hurt anybody. If the old lady in front of us—she looked as if she'd been scared young and never stopped expecting to be—hadn't yelled and made the driver stop, I'd have gone on into town. And I'd never have met Cally Mae Rivers. So I guess I should thank the old lady. Or even the drunk.*

That narrator—who just walked into this book out of a story not yet written—isn't described except by a touch of indirection. We know he has long hair, that he's a guitarist. Yet the tone of his voice carries a descriptive coloring that identifies him for the reader at once. The reader feels that he's young, observant, isolated but gentle by nature, and tolerant to a degree. There is also a sense of loneliness and lone-wolf quiet about him. This picture is made of the words he speaks and the way he speaks them.

Genuine description of character comes from inside—not merely from whatever picture strokes the writer uses to bring people alive in a kind of artist's sketch. It works from the center outward; in this case it works through a seemingly offhand soliloquy which is actually the beginning of a story that has already brought in the story's first elements—the weather, the place, the motion of what is to come. It is also, in this same case, a First Person Whole story—the teller is in the center.

It suffuses the story with a presence.

The same sense of presence—the actual sound of character—is used in a First Person Offset story such as Stephen Vincent Benét's "Johnny Pye and the Fool-Killer." The voice of the narrator is anonymous. It isn't exactly the author's, but it has the ring of the past about it and a storytelling grip that gathers us in its hands and doesn't let us go:

> *You don't hear so much about the Fool-Killer these days, but when Johnny Pye was a boy there was a good deal of talk about him. Some said he was one kind of person, and some said another, but most people agreed that he came around fairly regular. Or, it seemed so to Johnny Pye. But then, Johnny was an adopted child, which is, maybe, why he took it so hard.*

The character of Johnny Pye is stepping out of those seemingly simple words as they fall on the ear—and their reception by the ear is as important as their shape to the eye. And this is the beginning of a Third Person story, "Wet Night in Westmont," in which I wanted to keep back certain attributes of character and at the same time to steep the reader in exactly what the returning soldier was feeling and thinking by showing what went on around him as he stepped off a train into his suburban village:

> *At six fifteen Nick got down from the train, swinging off onto the dark gravel which made the same snapping noise under his soles that he remembered. The evening was already washed with gray, a soft rain falling; through this the lights of the town on either side of the tracks were like lights in a nocturne; the earth might have been steeped in gray tea. The rain fell persistently; you*

could tell it would last all night. He walked along beside the weary-looking, battered cars of the train which came from Chicago six times a day; then he turned right, and crossed the tracks. A gentle clanging told a few waiting motorists that the gates were down; the gates glimmered, too, through rain, their black-and-white cross-barred paint as familiar to him as his hands, his bag, his uniform.

There is a little chant, a little repetition of "gray" and "rain" going on in that opening passage—it is both a visual and a tactile paragraph. The sound of character beating through your story will often be close to a painter's constant color sense, but it will also be extremely tonal. You don't have to analyze it to feel that it's there. It's the insight you've developed into your chief character, or characters, coming alive in the resonance of words. *Actual* dialogue as spoken by the people of your story is important, too, but it stems from this other, all-embracing overtone; it is how you hear and see and feel your story unfolding in a clear progression, in clear rhythm.

Dialogue As a Framework

What I'm speaking of here—just to make it a shade more clear—is the point that spoken dialogue is subsidiary to a deeper, encompassing framework of author-reader communication which starts with the first line and continues through to your story's end. This, too, may be classified as a kind of dialogue—it's as though it creates the holding atmosphere in which your people act and speak. It is your framework, the stamping ground of your story. In a sense, then, no matter what Line of Sight you've chosen for your story—and this is as true of Third Person as it is of the other methods—you're constantly engaged in a larger author-to-reader dialogue, which is consistent in its special music. Your music may be spare and simple; it may be rich with over- and undertones that echo after the story is done; in any event, it cups and contains what you, the writer, say to the reader as well as what your people say to each other.

This is one of the most difficult points of writing the short story to explain. It is true of the novel as well, but in the story it is an absolute necessity. While a novel, as I mentioned a little while back, may change viewpoints, stray from a central thread of Plot and return by many paths, and use a rising and falling narrative to reach its goal, a story travels like a bee to a bee tree; its framework is the same in texture and impact at every juncture, and what begins as comedy cannot fly off into tragedy or use inorganic means to achieve an obviously forced effect.

A short story is not a natural effort. The apparent common sound and almost plebeian ring of the conversational sentences beginning "Johnny Pye and the Fool-Killer" are the results of a highly selective poet's ear using the folktale on which to base a kind of American legend; the crisp, controlled march of any story by Somerset Maugham is the result of extreme sophistication using simple words to create a framework of believable event. Again, this does not call for special analysis; only for your recognition. Sometimes when you feel right about an opening you will know that the full dialogue framework of your story has been established and that a green light inside you flashes *Go*. At other times, no matter how carefully you have considered all the aspects of your people, how deeply you have plumbed them for the reasons they are wrestling, the opening will seem out of key with your real internal purpose. Then all you can do is to keep on trying, fiddling and walking in circles until the key sounds clearly again. With practice you will always know when this happens. The trick is to keep from fooling yourself, from telling yourself it has happened when it hasn't, and from wasting time by forcing yourself to go ahead with something whose beginning wasn't right for you and your story in the first place.

I have hesitated to bring up this matter of Dialogue as Framework because it makes the writing of a story sound laborious in the extreme, like attempting to build a castle from steam and slippery seaweed. It isn't like that at all. It is as solid a job as you could find if you searched the world over; its elements, which are universal, are tangible and touchable. It is *work*, but if you are a writer and determined to succeed in bringing out the finest stories in you for hard commercial profit, it will never seem anything but pleasure. Even on days when you haven't touched what you know is there, you will have discovered new truths about yourself and how you can more successfully speak to a reader and make that reader listen.

The Ninth Experiment

Take three of the people you have been thinking about for your story—your central character and a couple of others who might be interacting with this person.

Ignore your present magnificent opening. Set it aside and try to see a scene further along in the story, one whose outlines are at least fairly clear in your imagination. When you have done this, write the scene as if your central character were someone entirely different from the person you first visualized. (For instance, if I were doing this in the story about the three writers, I would now make Grady Calman a scheming, somewhat offensive climber in the field of the arts, a man of little talent with a penchant for buttering up those who might help him.) Change his or her appearance, attitude, and sense of values. Reverse his or her characters—turn them inside out. Do the same thing to the subordinate characters who deal with your chief person. (In the three writers story Hamilton would become a benevolent friendly spirit without any designs on Amelia Sammons, and she would turn into a rapacious young woman intent on securing his goodwill by any means whatsoever.) When you have made yourself do all this, possibly against your will and your natural sympathies, carry on with the scene for about a page—make the people talk to one another in their new skins, wrestle for far different reasons than those they started out with in your mind.

Notice that what you feel about them—alienation, distaste, discomfort—begins to change as you speak through them and allow them to speak for themselves. Notice how the sound of character enters to give them validity—both in what they say and in the framework you give them to say it in. Use all three Lines of Sight for this experiment—do it in Third Person, First Person Whole, and First Person Offset. When you've done as much in each Line of Sight as you can at one sitting, study the results. What you have before you are the people of an entirely strange story, bearing the same names as those you started out with but changing the whole thrust and impact of your original idea and Plot. Yet your power of making character has somehow grown as you worked with them. And your sense of dialogue framework—of what surrounds them and is closely related to them, as opposed to mere chitchat—has grown as well.

Scrap the lot and return to your original sense of the character of your chief person and of the others in your story, which should have deepened and become firmer in the meantime.

Stage and Screen Dialogue versus Story Dialogue

A popular misconception is that stage, screen, story, and novel dialogue are interchangeable.

They are kissing cousins, but there the resemblance stops dead.

With the exception of the work of most Elizabethan playwrights and of those such as Christopher Fry, who have borrowed or adapted their singing lines for blank-verse drama, nearly all successful play dialogue reads choppily and baldly—it just doesn't stand by itself as something you want to memorize and carry around with you for inward illumination. In the fourth experiment, when you stood quietly by and listened to what people were saying, with all its disconnected opinion and sentiment expressed in segments, what you were hearing was Everyday Talk. The playwright raises Everyday Talk to a high level of stage and screen efficiency; but it depends on the art of acting for its full impact. Before it can be raised to tragedy, comedy, farce, or whatever its purpose may be, it has to be filtered through an interpreter, whose skill takes over in all manner of shading and nuance. As it does in the story, every spoken word counts—but the actor is there to express it, to voice it as capably as possible.

In the short story—and in the novel to a more diffuse extent—*you* are all the actors, the whole working cast. (You are also the set designer, the director, the lighting engineer, the producer, the original hypercritical audience sitting coldly through the rehearsals.) Any hamminess, phoniness, slips in timing and judgment come from you. Your choice of setting is crucial. How do you choose a good setting? What makes one place better than another for a story to happen in? (If I transferred the background of the three writers story from the Plaza to a small snobbish restaurant, this would change the story enough to influence both the dialogue framework *and* the actual dialogue. I chose the Plaza because it had the right, almost classically imposing feeling for a command performance rendezvous manipulated by Hamilton Ferris—and because I'm familiar enough with it to feel the surrounding. Your setting doesn't need to be liberally described. You can mention one or two elements in the setting that suggest all the rest. As mentioned before, it *has* to be a windy spring evening for the story about the writers—because the whirling, whimsical breeze is going to be built into a primary point of the story. But I don't need to describe the silver and crystal on the Ferris table or the epaulettes on the shoulders of the doorman's uniform. Or, for that matter, the doorman. Selectivity as well as brevity is part of the storywriter's craft. Kipling once said about a particular story that he painted the background, in the opening paragraphs, as hard and bright as a public-house sign, and let the rest of it tell itself against that brilliant sense of place.)

The reason good plays—and certainly all outstanding movie scripts—generally don't "read well" to the eye, but can play like houses on fire, is that the playwright is soaked in a feeling for the medium. He or she hears actors and actresses delivering the lines as they are written—and takes for granted a director's interpretation of elements which are invisible on the page. Creative collusion is already going on outside the consciousness of the usual reader. In this manner, theater, screen, and radio drama are even more artificial than is the short story or the novel, in that they presuppose the presences of middlemen to bring them all the way alive—while the making of fiction is done by one person speaking directly to another, with all the artifice centered in the author.

But reading plays to study their dialogue is a splendid idea for any beginning or even seasoned writer of stories. Doing it, you'll find that after you have jumped over the obstacles presented by the dialogue standing there by itself and looking lonesome, you'll begin to fill in the empty spaces with your own imagination. You'll see your own versions of the people as they move around the stage of your mind, and you'll understand why the apparent bleakness of some sentences is enriched by a powerful sense of personality and continuity. And it's the hope and belief of this writer that you'll also understand, even more fully than you have to this point, the sound of what I have called Dialogue Framework—the weight and depth of the writer offering a unique insight into the Sound of Character.

Another Suggestion

Look up a short story called "The Monkey's Paw," by W. W. Jacobs. It's been reprinted in many story anthologies, both hardcover and paperback, and it shouldn't be hard to track down. It is a terrifying story, based on the ancient assumption that the granting of three wishes can be a gift concealing very sharp teeth. It is told with warm and quiet skill, each detail comfortable and almost snug, with no bloody striving for dismal bloodbath effects. As a result, what happens has an inevitable ring which is horrible and lasting as well as honestly compassionate. It is a great example of the permanently honorable commercial story.

Now, after you've read it and enjoyed it, find the one-act play made from it—a play which is surefire in its effect, a war horse in repertory theater. This too is available in many one-act play anthologies in bookstores and libraries. Read it, and first of all, see how the dialogue has been cut—bitten down to essentials. And how, in the absence of Jacobs's softly gripping narrative, the dialogue has to work harder, standing by itself, shorn of descriptive character touches. The change has robbed it of reader intimacy; its character has to be inserted by the actors, the director, the trappings of the stage. The warm quick vibrancy of storytelling on the page is gone, and another sort of storytelling has come about—a more public sort, at a distance from the author and his reader control.

A good story is never "stagy" in this way. Its Third Person or First Person Whole or Offset narrator voice is its heart. Its Dialogue Framework is its overall truth—the force on which all the spoken dialogue and the flavor of the story depend.

You'll find stories that *are* stagy—mixtures of play, news story, film script, opera libretto. Sometimes they're presented as new art forms— "stories in journalism." For narrative some of them use stage directions, and for the sound of character the headline and the camera eye. But in the depth of a real story there is an older enchantment, with the character as persistent as the beating of a pulse, and its people wrestling below the action, and the most hard-to-please reader recognizing this at every step.

The Golden Differences

No good story is ever completely new. But all good stories are as fresh as though the form had just been invented.

The distinctions briefly outlined in chapter 7, which will make your story different from anyone else's—and are the results of chromosomes, genes, environment, and reactions to environment too complex to trace—can be seen in any modern commercial published story. If the magazines you leafed through looking for three stories to consider as criteria included *The New Yorker*, you probably saw stories by Anne Beattie, Donald Barthelme, Peter Taylor; in older issues were John Cheever, J. D. Salinger, Irwin Shaw, John O'Hara, Eudora Welty, Sylvia Townsend Warner. Aside from a careful feeling for word values and perhaps a subdued but compelling conviction of taste—a refusal to shout—the stories were startlingly unlike one another in method, approach, viewpoints of existence. New story voices are constantly sounding; and they sound with the fullest possible true tone of their authors. (In the all too few stories of Breece D'J Pancake—he took over the middle initials from a printer's error—who died at twenty-six, you'll find still another fresh voice; not a new *story* as such, but fresh ones, as urgent as messages from a newly discovered planet.)

Any story by Kay Boyle, any one of the half stories, half-poeticized experiences of E. E. Cummings's *The Enormous Room*, any story out of Ireland by Benedict Kiely or Mary Lavin or Liam O'Flaherty, will be as varied in mood, substance, and manner as though their makers had been born in different worlds. But beneath them is the wrestling, and permeating them is the character of their authors working through their people, and all through each is the storyteller's devotion to his trade.

They use universal standards of *reaching*.

They do more than relay talk, more than move—they relay talk with a purpose and move with a goal, and their grave or comic concerns are seen and heard inside their authors as clearly as possible.

And this ability to reach in your own way, without imitating anyone, represents your own golden difference—your storytelling stock in trade.

Your Dialogue Framework may start out tentatively—a tune on a penny whistle—but with work and continued confidence it can turn into a strong personal melody.

And at this point still more needs to be said about the Sound of Dialogue and the character it lights up. So let's look for a minute at the virtues of reading your own work out loud, and the good things and the bad that can come from it.

Chapter 11

The Critical Voice

*F*arther along in this book, after the first draft of your story is finished, you'll be urged to read it aloud—with yourself as the only audience. This should, if possible, be accomplished in a room whose door
is shut. Talking to yourself is often misinterpreted by those who over-
hear it. Max Beerbohm, in an essay on Swinburne, writes of hearing the
aging poet hum like a cloud of swarming bees on a summer afternoon as
he tried out for his own rapturous ear the cadence of a new poem.

If you are not especially gifted at soulful declamation, that's all to the
good. If you are—if your speaking and reading voice happens to be touched with velvet—you'll have to be a little careful. People who read well
before an audience are likely to make their own work sound considerably better than it is. Without meaning to mislead anyone, they can take
a fairly dull narrative, one full of holes and bulges, and by inflection fill
the holes with gold and smooth out the lumps. These people are inclined
to read well in private, too—and naturally enough, when it comes to
their own productions, they give everything they have. Unfortunately,
this sometimes convinces them that what they have written is un-
changeable and has been sent from heaven to delight mankind just as it
stands.

What such gifted elocutionists forget is that editors read with their
eyes, not in rich dramatic voices. And that the sound of character passes
through the reader's eyes before it can echo around inside.

Awkward phrasing, limp dialogue, fuzziness in characterization, easy
clichés and the substitution of loose rhetoric for tight emotion all stand
exposed for what they are under the quick (and eternally hopeful) gaze of
the editorial eyes. Every mistake is stripped mother naked. This writer,
who ordinarily reads well out loud, with expression and respect for the
sound and impact of each sentence, has, through the years, learned to

cultivate a private reading voice which is a cross between a whisper and an expressionless croak—as though he were a battered top sergeant murmuring the contents of an idiotic marching order from an addled first lieutenant. This causes the words of a first-draft story to emerge without any false glory attached to them—and to come out starkly, minus gilding, in a stern critical voice. It helps. It puts the first draft in cold perspective.

So when it comes time to read over your original story draft, do it cautiously, with the eye as well as with the glottal self. If necessary, whisper it hoarsely. Imagine yourself as a mechanical reading apparatus with no connection to human emotion. Above all, avoid sounding like a TV newscaster who enunciates everything that passes before his or her light-glazed eyes to give it "word value."

After all, these are your words you're weighing. They deserve the most acute, flat-toned criticism you can give them.

Character Outside and Inside

The voice of character from inside your story is *felt* by the reader. The impact of character from outside is *seen*. They work together so closely, with such interlocked alliance, that the reader actually can't mark where one stops and the other takes over. And now and again, they overlap. Here they are both in action, with no pauses in the story for minute and detailed description. The story opening is from this writer's "The Somewhere Music."

> *Luke woke up at twelve-thirty. He had enjoyed a beautiful dream: he was running happily through long, green-golden pastures that slanted down to a welcoming woodland. In the joyous trees of the wood, he heard music. It was eminently satisfying music which he felt, in the dream, he had heard before. The horns and the reeds were in the right places; the piano came in quietly, perfectly, and dominated the theme of this splendid music. It was a piano played with such delight that it made him laugh aloud. When his eyes opened, Luke was smiling. He lay for half a minute, the smile gradually leaving his face to be replaced by something shadowy and strange.*

The reader knows from *inside* that Luke is either a practicing musician or a man seriously affected by certain music. From *outside*, as the last sentence with its "shadowy and strange" changes the mood, the reader understands that Luke, waking, is faced with a problem—possibly one calling for a decision, possibly a crisis—that contrasts with the ideal of his fine dream. The undercurrent of "the somewhere music" has been established—the longed-for and attainable beauty, as opposed to the waking substance of Luke's life. Incidentally, the title wasn't established before the story was written, but grew out of it.

The reader is also aware—has been allowed to guess—that Luke's great passion is the piano. His appreciation of it in his dream is strong enough to make this plausible. The reader is being handed, a little at a time, *inward* and *outward* facts about Luke, and these are braided together; but until the end of the story all the facts will not be offered; until the last few sentences, the reader won't understand what event has changed his future forever. This final information is purposely withheld, not with the idea of creating an O. Henry snip-snap ending, but because it will cause everything that has gone before it to coalesce in a sort of resonance like a final chord in music that explains and underlines all previous passages.

When, a little later in the story, Luke is on the telephone, waiting for a friend's father to call that friend to the phone, the reader moves *inside* him, then *outside* again, in a fusion of remembrance which has enough detail to bring out his affection for his family and to point to a moment in the past which, when the story is over, will have double meaning for the reader.

Luke waited, looking out the window again. One of the trees near the window had a circular wooden bench built around it. Luke remembered a summer, perhaps three years ago, when his Grandfather Marston, his father's father, had been visiting them. He was quite an old man then, walking with a cane all around the yard. He had sat on that bench, sun falling on his leathery, dark-spotted hands and into his eyes, and he had seemed content to listen to the sounds of the day. One afternoon that summer, Luke's father had come home early from the office and Luke, his mother, his father and old Mr. Marston had gathered on the

*bench under the tree. Luke had sat next to the old gentleman,
who was wearing a soft bronze sweater even though it was a
warm day. On Luke's other side, his mother had sat, wearing a
yellow silk dress, her dark hair vivid and shining, her eyes
bright. Luke's father had taken the picture. It had come out well;
Luke remembered how, in the photograph, you could tell that he
and his mother were somehow related. It was something about
the eyes and the way they held their heads. Luke's mother had
said to his father, looking at the photograph, "Too bad we didn't
get somebody else to take it, then you could have been in it too."*

That offhand observation by Luke's mother will lead directly to the
seemingly simple but deeply important revelation at the story's end. It
will underscore it; make it echo. For Luke's mother and father are being
divorced, and he has learned this the night before the story begins.
Throughout the story this is implied, but not stated; it gives Luke's vision of his home, his seemingly permanent stability of environment, a
new and moving background, a wholly different light; he is looking at
apparently small, taken-for-granted objects that have gained vast importance in his seventeen-year-old experience, and are lost. Characterization cuts from outside to inside, then outside again, swiftly, quietly. As
he moves around the house—his mother and father have gone out on
this Saturday, his father golfing, his mother at a movie with a friend—he
considers going up to the attic, then merely reconstructs it in his sharpened memory.

*Everything would be warm up there, the trapped heat still and
dry. There were four or five trunks nobody looked into much
anymore. There were toys that hadn't been given to the Salvation
Army because they were too badly broken, old sleds, old photograph albums, old letters, stacks of magazines. And a bushel basket full of flint arrowheads from Grandfather Marston's farm.
Luke's father had brought them back after the funeral. They
smelled dark and earthy as if they'd lain in the ground so long
they could never smell any other way. But once they had been
new and sharp and used to kill real game.*

At certain points the outside character blends with the inside; at others it rebounds from familiar, known objects as these take on value and attain meaning they have never had for Luke before this day.

Character seen completely from *outside* may be used directly in any story, in the form of straight description. If it goes on too long, staying on the surface like an alert waterbug, it is likely to make a reader stir with impatience instead of simply being caught up in the pleasure of seeing. The reader should be reminded that something important is going on inside the story's narrator or its main character—not merely be treated to expert descriptive sentences. Here, in a story called "Citizen Bonaparte," by Alexandre Dumas, is character seen entirely from the outside by the author; the motion of the story has been stopped like an interrupted clock to allow the author to insert a descriptive vignette:

> *He was about twenty-three or -four, with an olive complexion, somewhat lighter at the temples and forehead. His straight black hair was parted in the middle and fell down below his ears. His eagle eye, straight nose and strong chin and lower jaw, increasing in size as it approached his ears, left no doubt as to the trend of his abilities. He was a man of war, belonging to the race of conquerors. Seen thus, and lighted in this way, his face looked like a bronze medallion. He was so thin that all the bones in his face were plainly discernible.*

We know that this is an acceptable version of Napoleon; but we also feel that we are not being allowed to decide for ourselves, but *ordered* to see him as "belonging to the race of conquerors." The intrusion of the author with this skilled job of paintwork removes the subject from consideration as a human being in a story and makes him into a posing statue. It has no relation to what an observant narrator might ordinarily see and feel about the young Bonaparte; it is a piece of highly colored biography shifted into a short story. It stays outside the story's flow, static and fixed; there's a tendency when finishing it, to murmur what used to be appended to the summaries of magazine serials: *Now go on with the story.*

The elder Dumas, who could be a great storyteller indeed when he set his whole mind to it, could get by with this in his day. In your day you can't. In spite of the point that teachers of composition, fondly looking for talent in their students, enthuse over just such isolated descriptions, anything that turns off the sound of character by staying outside it is going to turn off the reader as well. This is precisely what frustrated guides to the making of short stories mean when, in moments of rude emphasis, they pound their desks and shout, "Don't *tell! Show!*"

Showing—inside and outside—means weaving the exterior of character with its interior and doing it while the story keeps on running like a shady river or an insidious brook. Telling sets up a dam in that water motion. Showing Napoleon in the context of a story's steady movement isn't difficult. It could be done through the viewpoint of a humanly observant bystander and narrator; let's call this man Lieutenant Barras and allow him to have his say:

> When I looked up in the softly lamplit tent all I could see was his jawline, big as an ostrich egg, and those fanatical eyes glinting. I thought how my father had cautioned me never to trust Corsicans, but there was something about this thin one that made me think of toy soldiers coming to life—an underfed Julius Caesar in a dingy uniform. I wished to God he'd sit down, not just stand there.

I believe Lieutenant Barras. I like his mildly skeptical attitude concerning warlike posture, and through him I can suddenly see Napoleon as I never could in the Dumas genre-painting.

Of course depicting character from outside is necessary, to a degree, in all short stories; but unless this is interspersed with inside glimpses which, in their turn, tell about the wresting which is the point of the story, they merely bark a series of commands to the eye: "Now see this! Take my word for it! Don't trust your intelligence and intuition!"

Mixed with what is transpiring inside your people, character from outside is acceptable to the reader's eye and ear; it becomes an unobtrusive compliment to the reader's sensibility. Presented by itself and allowed to dominate, it turns into an egregious chatelaine nudging the reader in the ribs while he or she is steered through an art gallery—from which, no matter how colorful the pictures, the reader will soon escape to avoid further bruises.

In fact, mingling outside character with the essential inside is what Mark Twain was getting at when he said, "Don't say 'the old lady screamed.' Bring her on and let her scream."

The Tenth Experiment

Using Dumas Pére's bit of stagecraft which I quoted in the last section, rewrite it from the viewpoint of a sensible young woman who is meeting Napoleon for the first time. Use First Person Whole, and be as sardonic or as straightforward as you wish. Drop a little dialogue into the encounter; make the young woman and the world-shaker argue with force. Keep outside character interacting with inside, not allowing description to speak for itself without corresponding inward response.

Now, look carefully at your story plot again, as you did in the Eighth Experiment. By this time you have an idea of the sentences which will follow your arduously conceived opening. Test these sentences for their outside or inside character. Do they stand there, in your brain or on the paper, disconnected from any inwardness that has gone before or will come after? If they do, rewrite them—looking from inside out, as if you were gazing outward through a convenient knothole in your main character and telling the story from there. If they were right the first time—if they combined outside and inside character—rejoice. To be sure of all this, read your opening and a couple of the sentences that follow it out loud—in a low, ineloquent, critical, and expressionless voice.

Outside and Inside Character in Dialogue

There are all sorts of ways to make dialogue reflect inside character—even when the dialogue seems to come entirely from outside. In "The Somewhere Music" Luke never refers to what is really troubling him, the event that has turned his world upside down, until the very end of the story—and then it is done offhandedly, with the restriction of making his best friend and fellow band musician, Jick, promise that Jick won't say anything about it to anyone else. His reticence at discussing this or actually thinking about it—as if, if he didn't think about it, it might go away like an imagined wound—is part of the strength of the story. It is what is roughly known as a "mood story"—one so closely attached to the environment of its chief character that the background itself becomes a sentient force. But the story might have been done in a series of encounters with Luke's friends, in a way that emphasized the same bittersweetness and step-by-step revelation of loss. And this could have been accomplished without *apparent* communication of inside character:

> *Luke leaned on the marble soda fountain counter. Jackson was polishing tall glasses, using a clean soft napkin as Doc Phillips insisted his summer help do. Luke said, "I think I might leave town for a while."*
>
> *Jackson's eyebrows went up. In a voice less skeptical than his usual furry tenor, he said, "That's the first time you ever sounded like you meant it. Have a fight at home or something?"*
>
> *"No," Luke said, "I was just wondering if you had some ideas about places to go. Where somebody my age could get a job playing piano—you know."*
>
> *Jackson's hand stopped buffing a spotless glass. "You'd leave your band? Get out completely?"*
>
> *"That's right," Luke said. "Look—I can't tell you why. I just need some thoughts about where to go. Away from here."*

On the surface this is all outside character. In reality it is inside character brought out through dialogue. It performs what the other method of storytelling does by a different route; but it accomplishes this in the Third person Line of Sight at a slightly greater distance from Luke, allowing the reader to sense his quiet desperation by what he says and how he says it. All of Hemingway's short stories use this dialogue tension, building inside character as it is heard on the outside, with the wrestling pressed far down—in them the reader learns, as if without the author's full permission, just what is going on, and its importance, by the sound of the human voice under stress.

The method of storytelling used in the original published version of "The Somewhere Music" is more congenial, appealing, and flexible to most writers—I am one—than is the Hemingway approach. This is, in part, because Hemingway almost patented a style, which, although it is marvelously strong, is also restrictive; it leaves out more varieties of human experience than it includes. And unless it is accompanied by a depth charge of emotion peculiar to the Hemingway temperament, it either falls on its face or leaves an uneasy feeling of *déjà-vu* with the reader.

Being *yourself* in your story—by whatever devious and artfully artificial roads it takes you to become this amazing creature—is much more important than sounding, or "reading," like anyone else. If you set out in your story to depict inside character by means of dialogue encounters alone, be sure, to put it bluntly, that you cling to your own guts as you do so; if you stray from this self-to-self pledge, you are likely to create bluster. Bluster is unsureness, masquerading as confidence, in the outside character of the person you're writing about. When it appears, it tells the reader—between the lines and in many other recognizable ways—that you have substituted your story idea of a human being for the genuine one the reader wanted to meet and know in a commercial story.

Make the seen and the unseen elements of character work together, using your powers of observation and your own fund of emotion with simultaneous vigilance. Let the inside and the outside of your people work as they do in life. You are not creating life in a short story, but you are blowing a semblance of it onto the page; you are reflecting it as closely as you can. You will never have to fret about bluster if you do this with faithfulness—or whether or not you're "like" Hemingway, Tolstoy, or Gene Stratton Porter.

Chapter 12

Wet and Dry

*W*e're not through with Character.

As a writer of short stories, you will never be finished with it. If, in the teeth of story-market fluctuation and the suspicion that with far less effort you could easily become president of a multinational corporation, you still intend to make a reasonable living from this craft and art, you will keep in mind, each working minute, that Character in Action is your d'Artagnan sword—your shining weapon.

No matter how good you may be at devising plots or how many story situations float into your head in any given hour; no matter how deft you may be at juggling words to amuse your friends and confound your enemies, the point remains that unless you respect and revere the creation of Character, you might as well settle for becoming the world's best copywriter, rather than a fashioner of good stories worth honest cash.

To the end of his striving days, Scott Fitzgerald went on reminding himself that *Action is Character*. These are the last words of his notes for the completion of *The Last Tycoon*.

There are, very broadly, two kinds of character drawing in the short story. There's the sort you've looked at in the last chapter, dealing with Luke as he came awake and grasped at the tag ends of a dream—a story in which Luke was shown to the reader from both inside and outside. And there's the sort in which, by offering a sample of what might have been, I let Luke's wrestling appear only in his dialogue with a friend in the drugstore.

The usual marketable story is of the first kind. It has a glitter on top, like a well-polished apple. It has a delectable aura. It contains words that bounce and leap: the *long, green-golden pastures;* the *joyous trees of the wood*. Lively adjectives stir the sentences; strong action verbs—*dominated the theme of this splendid music*—move the eye along. It may be read with visual appreciation as well as heard with pleasure. You see the sentences as waves breaking before you, while you hear the words lap on the shores of your consciousness. The reader's eye is somewhat charmed, and so is her or his latent aesthetic sense—even if she or he doesn't know exactly why and even if a television set is droning on in the same room.

This is the Wet story—but not in any demeaning designation. It is the story whose juices can be felt in its prose.

The other sort of story—in which prose, as such, is secondary to the effect of deep forces moving to the surface in dialogue and merely glinting through narrative—is the Dry one. In it Character is kept down and under, showing through at guarded intervals—sometimes revealing only the barest hints as to the state of mind, the condition of soul, of the character. Kafka's "Metamorphosis," like his other stories and novels, is agonizingly *dry*. In it an unassuming young man named Gregor Samsa wakens one morning to discover that he has turned into a strange, appalling insect. The texture of the story is matter-of-fact, spare, logical—there is no open irony, no flash of the storyteller's brush at any point. But the story has the persuasive physical tug of an undertow—we are pulled into it whether or not we want to be. As Vladimir Nabokov has pointed out, in his wonderful lecture about this story, we are not told what *kind* of insect Gregor has become (Mr. Nabokov insists that it cannot be a beetle, and that calling it one is an error of translation) because the author has expended no word painting on definition. Yet Gregor's Character and that of his family and neighbors seep up strongly through the nearly arid surface. The reader is forced to grope after it—moving through a mystery, sensing a great secret that has to be learned. It may not be discovered at the first reading or during the second; it may always be in doubt. But the reader knows that it is there, beneath the sand, and this makes the story's lasting power.

A successful story can be *both* Wet and Dry. A good example of this is J. D. Salinger's "Raise High the Roof Beam, Carpenters." It deals with a few hours in the life of Buddy Glass, in New York on leave from the army to attend the wedding of his brother, Seymour. Seymour fails to show up for the wedding, and Buddy finds himself thrown in among a handful of wedding guests who are, to say the least, incompatible with the specialized viewpoints and mores of the admirable Glass family. The prose is distinguished, accurate, comedic, and supremely entertaining—yet beneath it is a bone-dry and almost anguished *reaching* after the character of Seymour, who is the reason for the story's being told.

The same combination of Wet and Dry can be felt in an early Fitzgerald story, "The Offshore Pirate." It has a flimsy plot, tacked together like a Florida cabana, barely strong enough to last out one season. Yet beneath the barely believable manipulation of young and privileged and careless love is a fierce dry belief in its message—that first love is as precious and as evanescent as a color of sunlight dancing on blue water. True dryness, the aching core of revelation, doesn't always show up at once on a good story's surface—but when it is there, it can give infinite extra value.

Stories by John O'Hara have surfaces purposefully dry and "unpoetic." The emotion in them is usually revealed almost entirely through dialogue; action, with the random exception of a few stories which end in violence, is held to a minimum; but the adrenaline count is high because such suppression makes seemingly small events extremely important for the reader. For instance, a man who has received a shattering emotional shock simply puts his hat on the wrong way round as he leaves the room. And from this single uncharacteristic trivial mistake we know how much and how deeply his life has been changed.

If your story inclines toward the dry side, it's necessary that you feel Character beneath it so completely that, as its author, the character vibrates under your heels with each step. If you lean the other way and happen to be gifted with a fluid, lyric ability for evocative words, you need to rein yourself in—never using the words for their own sake, but simply to pin down Character.

For Action *is* Character. It is, first of all, the action yeasting in you, the writer; the urge to fix and corral Character in a story. This is transferred to the action of your story people—to what they say and what they do, and how they say and do it; to stories Wet and Dry.

Description and Character

While talking about Dumas's "Citizen Bonaparte," I emphasized the fairly common mistake of isolating character description from the real movement of the story. But this is such a constant temptation—an "easy out" offered in the heat of writing—that it needs a little more illustration.

In the story cited back in chapter 6, "Sweet Chariot," the first draft was twenty-four pages long. It was all there, complete, making its point without shouting at the reader; but it was also too leisurely in rhythm, and self-indulgent when it came to halting the forward motion and giving the reader a guided tour of scenic wonders and outside appearances of people. At one juncture its main character was described as if he weren't inhabiting a *short* story at all, but happened to be in a roomy Sir Walter Scott sort of novel:

> *Journey was a looming, rangy man with the high cheekbones of middle Appalachia, descended from hunters, ballad-singers, keepers of their own secret counsels. His eyes, the color of very good, sun-faded denim, sometimes held hints of wildness—of wanting to rush away, like a deer startled from dreaming.*

That is passable character drawing; but it stands by itself without any kinship to the quick, demanding music of Character in Action called for in a short story. It is neither Wet nor Dry writing. It's a trifle show-offy, like a set piece meant for recitation rather than reading in silence. In the process of cutting the first draft from twenty-four pages down to ten, it was thrown out without a qualm. All that remained in the final draft was:

> *His eyes held hints of wildness and rushing away.*

That line does the job, summarizing everything in the original windy passage and allowing the story to move on without hanging fire.

Let's assume for a moment that your story concerns a robot—and the plight of this robot when it (or she or he) is about to be melted down for scrap metal and cannibalized parts. What your reader will expect here, in swift and accurate presentation, is the inner emotion of this robot; a communicated feeling of terror and frustration; not a disquisition about rivet placement and circuit connections.

Or let's say that part of your story is about the reaction of a woman to a snake. (Excellent stories along this line have been done—in the King James Version of the Old Testament, for instance, and in more recent times by John Steinbeck.) Your task, to be performed in a minimum of words and space, is to make your reader know the essence of snakedom, the elixir of woman. You may have read half a hundred volumes about herpetology; you may have spent an instructive summer working in the snake house at your local zoo. But in your story what you're after is the valid center of the experience—the point, for instance, that dormant snakes smell like new-cut cucumbers; that they inspire atavistic fear, even though they're amazingly sentient, easy to handle, and overmaligned. And without doing an essay on it, you will need to quickly interpret the woman's reaction to the encounter; to tell how she takes it, what she does, which will give immediate insight into the middle of her character. This is a section from a short story of mine, which was later, with slight changes, incorporated into a novel, *Glory Day*; among other things, I wanted to show the impeccable calm of the woman, Phyllis, in a moment of natural crisis. The writing could be classified as a mingling of Wet and Dry, and it comes in on a slant, by indirection, embedded in the action so that inside and outside factors are working in harness. The reader sees what is going on and feels it at the same time:

> *She took hold of another weed; this one deep, calling for a side twist to bring the root webs out. When she had tossed it back and was reaching for another, she saw the intruder. It was uncoiled, a flake of sun touching the triangular, turned-away head. The serrate, arid scales looked as though, if touched, they would whisper like autumn leaves. The body of the copperhead was a thick single muscle, relaxing. She sat back, hand hanging in air, then withdrew it gradually, from shade to sun.*

Woman and snake are somehow together; the confrontation is mysterious and double. Here, the word *description* is misleading as a cover word for what is actually happening. The eye sees, the ear listens, the skin feels; the hand of the woman becomes the hand of the reader as it is drawn back from the shadow into the sunlight. The inwardnesses of snake and woman are respected and let alone to be themselves. There are just sufficient words to allow the reader to participate wholly in the experience.

And here, for full contrast, is a sample of Dry writing at its best, from Elizabeth Bowen's short story "Maria." (It was Elizabeth Bowen who said of the process of writing, "One must regard oneself impersonally as an instrument." This is the classic professional attitude; it is especially useful in moments of self-disgust and despair.) The story is one of the funniest ever written, and the intricately horrible character of young Maria comes through without one extraneous label offered by the author:

> *"I can't tell you what I think of this place you're sending me to,"* *said Maria. "I bounced on the bed in the attic they're giving me* *and it's like iron. I suppose you realize that rectories are always* *full of diseases? Of course, I shall make the best of it, Aunt Ena.* *I shouldn't like you to feel I'd complained. But of course you* *don't realize a bit, do you, what I may be exposed to? So often* *carelessness about a girl my age just ruins her life."*
>
> *Aunt Ena said nothing; she settled herself a little further down* *in the rugs and lowered her eyelids as though a strong wind were* *blowing.*

A thousand labored "signpost" sentences couldn't tell you more about Maria or more about Aunt Ena's stoic endurance. Their inwardness has been expertly and beautifully externalized.

What I am calling inwardness here—a certain center of withinness in all people, and in animals and birds, and in sunlight and rain—is nearly always seen and simultaneously felt in what we name, too lightly, "good story description."

This withinness, insideness, is there in so-called inanimate objects as well as in the obviously living and breathing. An awareness of it stands behind the wholly Dry story, in which the author feels it around him or her during the act of writing; it is this awareness that informs the story (even a fantasy) with reality, and it can make the *unsaid* more potent than what is put on paper, and richer than if it were stridently spelled out. When you admire understatement in a story, this is what you are admiring. You are praising considerably more than good taste, which like fastidiousness is not a particular virtue when it stands alone; you are impressed by the author's constant consciousness of the entire world of people and things, as well as that author's ability to suggest these in microcosm without turning up the volume.

So for a minute now, consider:

The In-Ness of Things

Going into a raw, newly constructed house which nobody has lived in, touching the fresh wood, sniffing the plaster, you feel neither alien nor at home. You are in the no-man's-land of the untenanted.

But after a few years, when the house has been occupied and rubbed by humanity, it gains a special aura, even when its occupants are not at home. A quality more important than furniture or familiar belongings or food and light is there. People have brought to things a felt impact of themselves.

The lived-in story is very like this. Each corner of it reflects, refracts, and responds to the tone of whoever lives there . . . whoever wrote it with innate understanding of its inmost character.

There are stories which have never been lived in. They may be built of the most durable material; their authors may have applied every rule laid down by generations of good, indifferent, and long-retired or defunct teachers, and still have produced handsome and hollow shells.

Stories such as this are sometimes published—but when they lack the heat that lies outside technique, readers forget them. They suffer in silence from a need for the character of people *and* things.

The things of a lived-in story don't have to be "described"—sometimes they don't even require mentioning. Yet during the writing they were known by the writer as familiarly as his or her hands and feet and heart and bloodstream; they were *felt all through.*

In the story I am going to write in the middle of this book, it would be wasteful and foolish to include the fountain in front of the Plaza, the haunted—and unfortunately dangerous—paths of Central Park after dark; the upright-tombstone feeling of Fifth Avenue when viewed in a certain glancing spring night restiveness. It would also be out of key with whatever style I have; I prefer frugality. But I cannot forget that all these things are there as I write; I cannot discount their interaction on Grady Calman, Amelia Sammons, and Hamilton Ferris; I cannot feel these people in a vacuum.

In a story of ten manuscript pages there are hundreds of sensory impressions about place, time, and immediate background that I shall leave out. But *they will still be there*—behind what is written, buoying it up, as implicitly indicative as a Rand McNally map.

In his giant gusto and superb recognition of the Things that Surround

People, Honoré Balzac flanked his story and novel characters with floods of description—whole ecstatic catalogues of personal property, methods of papermaking and banking, histories of the psychology of gambling, pointers on various styles of French architecture through the centuries. For this he was sharply chided, generations afterward, by Willa Cather, in a cool essay called "The Novel Démeublé," or the "Novel Without Clothes." If he were writing today, he might omit a lot of these furnishings—though I doubt that the Cather essay would influence him greatly. But the sense of them, their weight and presence, *would still be there for the reader.*

In the paragraph about the discovery of the snake by the woman while she was weeding an onion patch, I left out the intense fury of the late-afternoon, Fourth of July heat above the simmering Ohio River, the arcade of sun-stunned, leaf-drooping oaks in the near distance, the musky smell of the riverbank, the friable, powdery touch of the baking earth. But they are there. They're in the silence around the snake, around the woman.

And the in-ness of Things is present to a touchable degree in "Maria," whose voice needs no description because we know it is pinched, haughty, and insufferable, from hearing it on the page in her words, which characterize her completely—as do Aunt Ena's eyes, barely visible above the rugs as she lowers her eyelids "as though a strong wind were blowing."

Your perception of the in-ness of Things is not something to worry about; but you should know that it is there, and that it can be strengthened, and that it accounts for the extra value you receive from a good story. You should remember, too, that although it may not be visible to the reader, it informs the story in unseen and magical ways. When asked by a friend how he "thought up a story," Chekhov pointed to an ashtray. "That could be a story," he said.

And, if he had felt like writing it, it surely would have been. Perhaps it was—and simply never got around to describing the ashtray itself. *Things* lead mysteriously to many stories which remain untraceable to their true origins. Such stories are always fully inhabited.

Still Another Suggestion

Find a Dry story and a Wet one. Read them slowly, and feel how the character in them moves through the different surfaces.

Now, imagine a room suspended in a void, without anything in it, with the walls themselves indistinct, undecorated. Try to picture someone you know—or yourself—living in it; acting out a story in it. When you're done with that, do the same thing with a tenantless, treeless, grassless dullard of a landscape.

Then, in a few words, try to sum up the character you can see, feel, and put your finger on in an old wicker basket, a pair of well-seasoned shoes.

Chapter 13

A Sense of Place

*B*ackground is a poor and parochial word to describe what is so essential to most stories it really shouldn't have to be mentioned. *Ambience* is worse, one of those fashionable, vague words that show up repeatedly in articles about fashion. *A sense of place* is a better definition. Without this, characters in a story seem to gasp for breathable air.

As emphasized in the last chapter, all background doesn't have to be described. But when it is felt by the writer, it moves into the story like woodsmoke in autumn, pungently existing between the lines. When it isn't present during the writing, the story is likely to have a metallic ring—withering in some dark basement, like Rose of Washington Square in the old ballad.

Characters presented to the reader by an author who lacks sentient memory of place or the ability to evoke it seem to have been knitted, not born. Fiction is frequently distorted and condensed for special effect—but in it, when a butterfly is introduced it ought to be a real butterfly; a monarch or a swallowtail, impinging for a moment on the reader's eye, evoking lightness of wing and random flight. All of your built-in sensory gifts are present to help you suggest background. They are allies ready with richness of suggestion—found in the best of the Dry stories, as well as more frequently in the Wet. Of all short story writers who used the English language, D. H. Lawrence had the most instantly communicated sense of places and creatures. You may disagree, sharply, with his earnest theories about the dark gods in the blood and with his extremely ambivalent ideas about Woman—but his fiction happens in a true, touchable environment. When a fox flashes across a meadow, it is a real fox, feral and whole and unrelated to any cunning Disney representation.

Your story's foreground and the people in it should be lighted by your feeling for background—the shape and presence of Things.

Now this so-called background is no stage flat, put there to give an audience the easily destroyed illusion that it is looking at a drawing room or a doctor's office. Its windows are real. Its walls have substance. It is never merely imagined. It is made of your ability to bring out the whole solidity of place. It reminds the reader of *something she or he has known*; and it influences the depth of a story as well as its topsoil. And this is true even when the place you choose is an alien planet or the (highly idealized) jungle of Lord Greystoke in his role of Tarzan, the lodgings of Sherlock Holmes at 221-B Baker Street, or the San Francisco underside of Dashiell Hammett's Sam Spade. In many commercial stories of the kind published up through the twenties and into the thirties, such background was as bulky as a horsehair sofa, dominating the induction of a story while its characters and its readers waited for the action to start. Dress styles were lingered upon, furnishings were depicted at paragraph length, fabrics were named and sometimes priced. This opulent sandbag approach to a story is no longer necessary or at all desirable—but without *some* fragrance of background reaching the reader, the story will hang in the air, a depthless and curious mobile.

Place is the Latin *Locus*—creator of the atmosphere where drama happens.

Bringing it closer, it's your own hand gripping the rocks of a gulley down which your chief character is perilously moving; your observation that these rocks are stippled with tiny deposits of quartz, which glitter in late sun beside the shadow of the mountains; your nostrils expanding to smell time-worn stone; your eye catching the light on a circling hawk's wing; your ear listening to the shuffle of pebbles as they slide below you with the sound of snare-drum brushes; the taste of danger drying the roots of your tongue. Even a story delivered entirely in dialogue—an experiment not to be encouraged—should have this thereness, witness, the felt knowledge of background beating behind the words.

But background is double-edged. When it begins to take over, it can slowly swallow up and cover over what began as a story with a clean line of action and event. A story drenched in background is always on the verge of becoming an essay. Every writer has, inside, a pendulum that swings toward background and foreground—and if you allow this to linger in the direction of mood and scene, you'll discover that your main character has turned into an observer and *only* an observer; that his or her vitality has become muffled.

Keeping that character alive to the least hair in her or his eyebrows, neither dominating the background nor subservient to it, but *in* it, is one of your primary concerns. At this point, if I believed in illustrative charts—which I do not—I would draw one, splitting the page in half, and at the top of one half I would inscribe **BACKGROUND,** and at the top of the other I would write in the same boldface type, **CHARACTER.** I'd much rather you would imagine this; as a writer, it's considerably more healthy for you to think in words than in geometric designs. But consider the chart as limned in your head. The moment you feel yourself spending too much time, too many sentences, on one side or the other, go back to using your personal pendulum in steady balance; back to the rhythm of Background Place and Foreground Character.

But we are not clocks, we are people, and to point out this necessity for balance between human character and the character of place, a story of mine, "The Thief," is usefully handy. This one depends more than most of my work on a careful division of character and a full realization of background; for the background becomes a "character" in its own right, yet it cannot be allowed to obliterate or even slightly to dim the reader's understanding of the boy, Raoul. (When I was writing the story, I did not think, even remotely, in such reasonable and logical terms. I did not realize them in words. My words were bent toward the making of the story; I realized the problems involved without actually naming them or looking at them; I knew the country where the story would happen, and I could see it with the attitude and through the eyes of Raoul, who was about ten years old; this was all I had when I started, but it felt like a great deal.)

"The Thief" begins with Raoul awkwardly shoving open the screen door of the summer cabin he shares with his father on the Altamaha River in lower Georgia. He carries a rod, a reel, a creel. It is a blue hot morning. His father, a judgmatic sportsman-broker on vacation, nods over his first gin and tonic of the day and wishes him luck. The saturating heat and quiet mystery of the morning take over; Raoul is a noticer, a seer of the small and the large; he appreciates the minuscular flowers that go to make up a bed of moss; the enormity and silence of the river. As he comes to the river, the reader enters its aura of mysticism—and is reminded, in a few lines, that once, before General Oglethorpe's men drove them away, elk roared along its banks, and that until the naturalist and explorer William Bartram discovered it, it was known only to Indians and wild animals. (Carl Van Doren once suggested that reading the journals of Bartram, published in London, inspired Coleridge to write the interrupted *Kublai Khan*; this is not mentioned in the story; but there is a glassy, gliding touch to it, and somehow both Coleridge and Bartram are present in spirit.) The river is, in essence, a god.

As he casts and waits for a strike, Raoul breathes into himself its agelessness, its binding self against his puny humanity. Yet his humanity is important; he is more alert than ever before in his brief years to the presence of Things—to being watched, perhaps judged. Seeing an egret on the far bank of the sun-mirroring water, he recalls that egrets are called cowbirds by farmers—considered pests and casually shot as such. He has started on this morning to become someone else—someone who was waiting within him to appear... older, more alive and aware. And what he wants, tangibly and terribly, is to catch just one decent fish, to carry it back to his father and remark offhandedly that it isn't such a bad catch.

And then he has his strike—a respectable trout of about two pounds. It fights with fury, and for the first time in his life he remembers to apply the controlled skill his father has tried to teach him, to play it as an old hand would; almost miraculously, he lands it, swinging it over his shoulder and back in a shining arc to the firm sand beach. But before he can touch it, a red-tailed hawk is upon it and has snapped the line and sailed to the mesalike top of a sandstone and shell cliff. The cliff is sheer, thirty feet almost straight up, appearing to be unscalable. But in his stricken, ice-hard rage Raoul climbs without real consciousness of anything but raw injustice. He finds barely enough handholds to keep moving, but never pauses to look down. Attaining the tabletop ledge where the hawk's nest is built, he dives at the hawk, finds his hands around its thin throat, its life under his fingers. The hawk's wings, its crazed and courageous saffron eyes, with their own rage like a lion's, and its searching beak, are all demonic. And in one blinding second, impossible to sustain but only to recall later and to keep with him perhaps to his own death, Raoul understands that the hawk's need is infinitely greater than his own. He drops it. He looks at the already torn, diminished trout, its live river-self faded and gone, its colors paling semblances of what they were. With strong caution, going slowly and nursing his bloody scratches, he makes his way down the side of the cliff. He gathers his snarled gear and starts back; the revelation he has experienced stays with him, invisible, but as hoary and intense as the river and the heat; he knows an exaltation he will never be able to speak completely.

At the cabin he merely mentions to his father that the line got tangled in brush and that he was scratched getting it out. But he has changed completely, and we feel he will forever be.

Keeping Raoul in balance, never allowing him to be subsumed under descriptions of Nature, or the story—which was only seven pages long—to turn into a "nature study" piece of charm, were the only recognizable problems at the time of writing. The rest was swimming underwater—perhaps the water of the Altamaha. "The Thief" was the obvious title, though I played with "The Hawk Fight" for awhile. The story is terse, Dry, with a few sentences of Wet illumination threaded through it. So far as I know, "The Thief" has no easily explicable theme. It would be simple to say, "A ten-year-old child becomes a discerning man," but it wouldn't be true. The wrestling in Raoul is strong, and it is brought to an end by his recognition of the purer and more violent wrestling in the hawk, yet there are overtones there which I can only hear, not define.

All of which tells us that mystery is at the heart of many stories and that unraveling the mystery as far as words can is one of the challenges that keep writers of stories for bread young in their nimble minds.

Some writers' ability to see background immediately, so that it forms at the same time that the idea is tested and found solid, is almost automatic. If when a story comes along in fledgling form, you say to yourself, "*This* has to happen *there*," you are lucky. If background grows reluctantly, lagging behind character, shifting position and place as the forefront of the story outstrips it, you will need, for a while, to think more about place than about people.

And this is not nearly as odd as it sounds because background is also a kind of dormant action—place, waiting for event. Eudora Welty's *Golden Apples* is imbued with a splendid, tactile, and emotional sense of a certain part of the South at a certain time; it is a series of short stories, flowing together so seamlessly they make a long narrative, related like family members forming a single warm entity. Without an acutely developed, lifelong awareness of her native ground and the people in it, Miss Welty would not have brought to her book the inward continuity it contains. I am not talking about "regionalism"—I am talking about a quality of place that goes far beyond local mores and ways of speech. It dictates the actions of the people in a story, surrounds them, and becomes in its own right a sustaining character.

As Robert Louis Stevenson once observed, some houses wait for murder to be done in them—and this impact of place is more than mere atmosphere. In preparing her special writing ground for the novel *The Haunting of Hill House*, Shirley Jackson caught one glimpse of a blackened, surly house seen from a train; and this was enough for the genesis of Hill House—which, among other things, is a superb study of the evil that *place* itself can hold.

The short stories of Kipling, Henry James, Flaubert, John Cheever, Faulkner, Fitzgerald, Stevenson, Welty, Flannery O'Connor, Chekhov, Frank O'Connor, Maupassant, Walter De La Mare, D. H. Lawrence, Jessamyn West, and Katherine Mansfield are only a handful of those which, in the history of the story, evoke *place* so powerfully it is inseparable from foreground event.

A story can start with the plain emotion brought up by remembering background. It can stir like a fountain forcing its way into the sunlight from the depths of a half-recalled dream.

Hold high among your storymaking weapons the elements of withness, thereness, the texture through which mankind lives. Treat it as a gift that must be kept in balance with your people to be seen, touched, and heard at its finest—often changing the people, for good or for bad, but never for a second standing in front of them to shut them off from the reader.

The Nowhere Story

With that said, it must be added that sometimes a story will achieve excellence without being presented against any known environment or with any recognizable anchor point for the reader.

Such a story is likely to be written in a stream-of-consciousness narrative—like that delivered by a hospitalized patient coming out of anesthetic. A story of this kind demands intensity and the realization that the reader must be held by situation alone. It is told in a sort of gleaming void; the reader is filled in on what *may* be happening by bits and pieces of suggestion. The urgency of these stories is their whole reason for being; the trap in them is that they appear to be simply constructed and as easy to toss off as a three-finger exercise on the piano. They aren't. They call for a bonfire of plotting behind each allusive sentence. Dispensing with the whole tapestry of background, they exist as pristine shocks leading to the revelation at the center of mystery. "The Damned Thing," by Ambrose Bierce, is a case in point; so is his "An Occurrence at Owl Creek Bridge." In one way these are both trick stories—yet their emotion is so artfully centered, their readability so focused and realized, that the trick is forgotten like the conjurer's patter as he performs the impossible. On a more obvious level—and on any level, a sterling sample of the commercial story with an ace up its sleeve—there is Gertrude Atherton's "The Foghorn."

This is stream of consciousness at its most persuasive—the inward and, at first, seemingly idle and quick-running thoughts of a patently beautiful young woman in a luxurious situation. She is waking; we hear her speaking to herself. In a matter of two or three pages we are aware of something wrong—the intrusion of a foghorn into these blithe, still half-sleeping commentaries on current styles in a San Francisco society aura. Wedges of scenes from her past are inserted; the reader picks up the glancing knowledge that she may recently have sustained a serious illness, since her hair has been cut short. We learn by further swift allusion of her love affair with a "respectably" married man; of their night meeting in a rowboat and their going out through the Golden Gate—of the foghorn, the foghorn crying again—of a ship looming through; a catastrophe as the little boat is caught between two ships and crushed, her lover's head nearly severed; then, finally, as she stirs and in the dim light of her cell looks at her hands—those of an old woman—we realize, as she does, that she has returned to full awareness after half a lifetime of insanity. And this is dryly confirmed by the almost pedantic conversation of a doctor and a nurse beside her barred window. The voice of the foghorn outside the asylum continues in the reader's mind....

Attractive, even fascinating as it is to many beginning writers, the nowhere story which beomes a somewhere story with a vengeance isn't advocated by this writer as an ideal on which to rest a career. It *is* a trick, and it doesn't come off in beginners' hands. And even these specimens of the tour de force aren't quite minus a little earth for the reader to stand on; they are usually written by old hands who have a canny sense of what their readers will stand still for. They are hybrid offshoots of what O. Henry spent a lifetime doing; emulating them can too easily lead to the spillage of words which makes an editor's teeth hurt.

If you feel the need to write completely from the inside out, speaking from the chaotic brain of an unhappy heroine or hero—or better, just a human being—simply be sure you're nailing the whole story down with perceptible craftsmanship. While you're careening along, give the reader handles to hold on to.

The Eleventh Experiment

Write three short paragraphs of pure background. Don't let anybody, man or beast, inside them. Pick whatever subjects feel right for you—an old barn, a rolling estate shaded by elms which have happily escaped Dutch Elm Disease, a ghetto alley.

Now, in three more paragraphs, people them—put your people into them as if they belong there, were born there, and couldn't exist in any other air.

Does it feel as if you'd started a story? It should. If it doesn't, change your backgrounds and start over. Keep at it until you can recognize the relation of your story characters with their background—until one complements the other, without either standing out so far it takes charge.

Your backgrounds should have the general look of a watercolor wash before the picture has started to take on definition—they should be comfortable, not too heavy, and seem to be waiting for the sun to come up, a curtain to rise, someone to enter. The people when they appear shouldn't be trying to startle anybody—they're not pop-up pictures in a child's book, they're people engaged in living. If you're writing fantasy, remember that *Alice in Wonderland* has stunningly clear backgrounds; that's a real rabbit hole she falls into, a genuine White Rabbit nervous about being late for an engagement, even it it does speak understandably.

Now turn the experiment around—start with three paragraphs of people (or animals if you prefer them) in action, and in the next set of paragraphs, give them solid places to live in.

And then, when you've become exhausted or exhilarated by this experiment, go back and review all the previous experiments; there's no need to do them again, unless you sense that you need more limbering up on one or the other. But review them; and do the same, however light-ly, with the suggestions.

At the close of the following chapter, we're coming to the largest ex-periment of all. For this reason the chapter ahead is a piece of final prepa-ration for it, a hold-all of last instructions before we finally shoot the moon.

Getting Ready: The Matter of Flashbacks

*F*lashback is still another word which this writer wishes had never been invented, because it unsettles most starting storywriters' equilibrium and has a haughty, secret ring like the key to a closely guarded secret.

There is nothing in the least mysterious or hard to conquer about it. It's switching backward in time to sketch in necessary reader information about what has happened before the story began. In certain novels page after page is given to flashbacks, so that their readers sometimes know more about a past event and its effect on character than they do about what goes on in the immediate present.

In the short story there isn't room—never was; never will be—for long explanations of the past lives, adventures, and peccadilloes of the story characters. If the story, tentatively entitled "Three Writers," which I shall write in the next chapter, while you are writing the first draft of your own story, were a novel, I could expand a flashback to my hungry heart's content, as follows:

> As he followed the trim girl into the hotel Grady recalled his first meeting with Hamilton Ferris. Ferris had, astonishingly, phoned him on a sultry afternoon after the lukewarm public reception of his first novel, Midget on Horseback. The great poet's voice had been masked by a veil of liquor; he was known to drink a great deal, to the possible detriment of his liver but not the quality of his work. On the phone it was vibrant with an underlying sincerity; it lifted Grady's spirit like a hand from interstellar space. Grady still remembered the husky, slurred words: "Now, son, don't let a little thing like sales bother you. You wrote one hell of a book—and when you get another one ready, I want

to see it and say something about it on the jacket flap; I want to help you get it off the ground and make the public install it on every goddamned plastic bookshelf in this more or less literate nation." Grady had believed those words. He wanted to believe them so badly it was impossible to keep his usual healthy skepticism about the machinations of Manhattan's literary cliques. So he had met Ferris for lunch; the scarred and triumphant lion, the reputation-maker—and while he hadn't been totally disillusioned, he had disliked every moment of the encounter. It had taken place at Tonelli's, a restaurant distinguished for indifferent Italian food, haughtily served by what seemed to be uncaged gorillas wearing limp white ties—an extremely popular and astoundingly expensive place, that year. And Ferris had been surrounded by a retinue of trucklers; men and women who hung on the poet's increasingly blurred speeches as if these were cut in bronze. "How," Grady had asked himself, then and later, "can he live like that and write as he does?" The question still bothered him as he caught up with the girl and, for a breath, they stopped and looked at each other as if they had met on a treacherous island.

There is nothing much wrong with that; it yields up a quantity of information, and it is consistent with Grady's character as I want it for the story; it also tells a good deal about Hamilton Ferris. But it is told with the spacious feeling of a novel. For far too many sentences the girl, Amelia, is left out—presumably walking a bit ahead of Grady while he does all this serious thinking about the famous poet. In the story, as I write it, the first draft will condense all this feeling and reaction in as brief a time as I can squeeze them and ideally will bring out by inference in dialogue what has been narrated above. In fact, the above effusion is as out of place in "Three Writers," as I now visualize it, as a treatise on hummingbirds might be. In any commercial story's action the so-called flashback should consist of a few sidelong references, probably in dialogue, to events in the past which have helped shape the present drama.

And such swift references aren't "flashbacks" at all. They are simple, quick links between what is going on *now* and what happened before *now*. They are worked into the texture of the story like buttonholes in a garment whose stitching doesn't draw attention to itself but is adequate to do the job. They cannot become overimportant, suddenly taking off with a flourish of trumpets and drums; if you avoid classifying them as flashbacks, it will help you to see them in the right perspective.

Some stories—and yours may be one—have the general nature of a meditative idyll. In these the flashback will often become the whole story:

> *Jane never forgot the summer her Uncle Jacques took her to every home game the White Sox played in Comiskey Park. There he would be, as enthusiastic as a fire in a wastebasket—chewing his gallant brown bandit's moustache; urging on the players with cries of "March, my old!" and sipping a noxious mixture of cheap wine and Coca-Cola, while his warm eyes grew redder in the corners.*

But there again, it's not vital to call the enfolding flashback by a special name. I think you will be much happier as a writer of stories if you look at the flashback with the lofty attitude of a scientist dealing with a fly that has crossed his microscope lens—treating it merely as something to be dealt with in passing. To tell yourself, "Good Lord, I'm about to commit a *flashback*," is to give it an awesome importance it doesn't deserve. It is also likely to make you freeze up a trifle, so that you lose the forward impetus and eagerness you started with, and take a chance on losing the first draft in a mélange of half-remembered rules. Starting writers who memorize new rules every day, placing these above their desks and stopping to consult them as they grow increasingly complex and numerous—and sometimes inconsistent as they accumulate—have been known to turn into story experts. A story expert is someone who has read all the rules and who keeps on learning new ones, and who is glad to leap into your life with stern advice gleaned from hundreds of articles and volumes about the short story—and also someone who has never written a publishable story.

Getting Ready: A Few Words about Formula

I have already said that formula is the tactic of setting out in a story to please a reader's aesthetic or sentimental side, with the single-mindedness of a burglar about to make off with the family silver. Or at least I hope I have implied this. But the real formula story is the one in which these aims show through like bones in a transparent fish slice—the one in which, from the aesthetic standpoint, the reader is told by heavy implication that life is unfair and cruel and nothing is ever going to change it for anybody; and its sister-under-the-skin, the story in which rosy sentiment is substituted for transferred emotion or thought, and every character is pushed into living happily ever after like so many bisque Kewpie dolls. Real compassion, as well as honest joy, is absolutely impossible to pin down in any commercial story—so is complete irony, as long as it isn't thrust upon the reader like a dose of necessary medicine. The blatant use of formula bypasses the heart of all storytelling—it neglects the storyteller's ability to live inside his story until it becomes, by highly artificial but laudable means, alive and quick and kicking—it presents stereotypes.

In a phrase *formula is forcing*—treating the story as a piece of work without a life of its own; making it illustrate a generalized thesis. (By thesis I do not mean theme; I mean a preconceived notion of what the readers of a particular market will swallow and the ladling out of this with a generous spoon.) You can recognize a formula story of the first and most adulterated water by its peculiar thinness of vision—as if everyone in it sprang into being from tap water instead of blood. The overaesthetic formula story is the story that works very hard *not* to be *popular*—it comes out of art for art's sake superciliousness. Its practitioners speak highly of Chekhov, whose humanity they have never understood, and whisper the names of Harold Robbins and Mickey Spillane as though these were monsters; their stories are precious in the extreme, are printed, when they reach print, in magazines of sharply limited circulation, and never achieve the honesty of craftmanship found in either *The Paris Review* or *Redbook* or *Good Housekeeping.* Genuine sentiment is, in itself, no sin; as Faulkner once remarked, around the stem of his pipe, it is a very sentimental thing to be a human being. But when it is carried to pink-washed extremes, with people turned into biddable pieces shunted by the author around a mushy checkerboard, the resultant stories are as much anathema to the large and well-paying magazines as those which strive to be overliterary and end up stillborn.

I have also pointed out, and reemphasize here as you stand on the brink of creating the first draft of your story, that genre stories—the sci fi, the Western, the romance—are *not* by any definition formula—unless their authors lean sharply to the dead clover of the avowedly literary or the soggy sentimentalization of everything they touch. A bad story can fit in any category. So can a great one. A good or great story deserves the largest possible reading audience and the highest monetary reward; this plain fact is often sloughed over or misinterpreted by those who should know better. Rust Hills, in his often discerning treatise (from an editor's-eye view) called *Writing in General and the Short Story in Particular*, makes the, to me, snob's error of suggesting that Scott Fitzgerald was among the few "serious" writers able to earn a living in the big slicks—and he goes on to say that this was because Fitzgerald possessed a romantic outlook. But the Fitzgerald magazine stories are *not* formula by any stretch—unless you consider an impeccable style a hallmark of formula—and the names that filled *The Saturday Evening Post* in its fat years were, among lesser ones, Faulkner, James Gould Cozzens, Kay Boyle, John O'Hara, B. J. Chute, William Saroyan, Jessamyn West, Shelby Foote, Thomas Beer, and on occasion, Gertrude Stein and James Thurber. (There were plenty of formula tales as well; but guilt by association should be discounted as fairly petty.) Far from harming his sense of storymaking integrity, writing for a huge audience and aiming the product honed Fitzgerald's genius toward the making of *The Great Gatsby* and *Tender Is the Night*, while enabling him to live the life he wrote about, and it is time somebody said this.

Somewhere in the untapped reaches of your convoluted storymaking mind you might cherish the notion that your story ought to end happily for the sake of pleasing an editor. If this is the sole reason you have for making such a decision, it's a very bad one. The story itself will tell you where to go. There are stories which, to be true to themselves, must end on a note of resolution that may well be optimistic. Others resist the intrusion of cheerfulness for all they are worth—they may not be unrelentingly grim, but their subject matter is such that to twist them, however slightly, in order to bring about an ending which is out of key with the rest, will ruin them as believable experiences for both editor and reader. Cling to the story's own innards, which are a sacrosanct part of your own persona—if you envision any editor or eventual reader as an arbitrary Pollyanna, you are creating a false image that, like a will-o'-the-wisp, can lead you into swamps of fatuity. No outside force, teacher, guide, mentor, or imagined editorial reaction should be allowed to interfere with your essential writing self once the story is in progress.

More on Getting Ready:
Writing for Children

The greatest storywriting for children—the hardest in the world to accomplish—is comparable to etching in miniature on the head of a diamond all that goes into the good adult story. Oscar Wilde's "The Happy Prince" and "The Birthday of the Infanta" have this quality—read to, or by, a heterogeneous bunch of children, they still move listeners and readers deeply. In the durable children's story the earth's wonder, unfairness, terror, and laughter are faced head-on—and their scope goes far beyond the library habit of labels that say, "Ages 5 to 9" or "Suitable for 12 to 14."

Children, from the foulest to the fairest, the nearest to animate poems we have on this besieged earth, are not as a rule analysts—but they are unrelenting critics. They are closer to the cave-hunkering barbarian and his gimlet-eyed demand for *a good story* than most writers can remember. They love humor and will sit still and rapt for sublety in it—but the second humor becomes arch and adult, containing one meaning for the children and another for the grown-up, murmuring, in effect, "See how smart I am as I talk down to these moppets," they lose all interest and are keenly aware that they are being condescended to and may well, indeed, wish that they could throw a pie at the narrator. The use of "easy," "comprehensible," "understandable" primer words is never enough. A child will plow through polysyllabic words by the score if the center of the story is gripping enough—indeed, many vocabularies have been enhanced because, on the third or fourth reading of a favorite story, the child began to wonder what those mysterious words meant. Children's chanting games glory in odd words and chiming rhythms. Kipling's "Just So Stories," written for his own children before the stories were published and containing, in "How the Elephant Got His Trunk," such magical phrases as "The great, green, greasy Limpopo River," treat the child as a confidant who is already familiar with inside jokes; and Kenneth Grahame's "The Wind in the Willows" is written *from a child's viewpoint and with a child's elemental appreciation of nature, the roots of laughter, and lurking evil*—in spite of the point that it is also an adult hymn to the vanishing wonder of the English countryside.

Moral stories, those which strive to teach, for instance, that good manners never hurt anybody, or more important, that surface ethnic differences are nothing *but* surfaces, present preachy traps into which all but the most earnest respecters of children may too easily tumble. For all her occasional prunes-and-prisms moralizing, Louisa M. Alcott was a great respecter of children—which is why children still gobble her work, steering around the preachments as easily as fish glide around obvious hooks. Such modern classics as Madeleine L'Engle's *A Wrinkle in Time* and all her other novels and stories for young adults respect their audience fully—and though they are intensely "moral," they are never for a breath vapid. The Narnia stories of C. S. Lewis, the beautifully told stories of Lloyd Alexander, the direct and wholly contemporary books of Judy Blume—in which sex is a miracle to be contemplated in the same light as Blake's burning tiger—and, of course, the children's books of E. B. White are all, in their ways, direct successors of Hans Christian Andersen, the Brothers Grimm, George MacDonald (*At the Back of the North Wind, Curdie and the Goblins*), storytellers who wrote on the precise level—not an inch above, not a hair below—of the children they spoke and speak to.

Much too frequently, this writer has encountered the stories of beginning writers who, asked why they wished to concentrate on stories for children's markets, said, in effect, "Because they're easier than the other kind." Such confidence, along with a paucity of distinction in the stories themselves, evokes from me a stunned tribute of silence. In fact, it makes me pity the fiction editors of children's magazines, who must be more subject to nervous breakdowns than their equivalents in supposedly more complex fields. I am not demeaning the confidence itself; I only marvel that anyone approaching blank paper in the mood of tossing off a tiny exercise for the tots hasn't yet recognized the right attitude of spirit—the emotional equipment for the job. I think this attitude should be one of great joy and need, coupled with a high concern for craftsmanship and steady alliance with the child in every writer—somewhat like the attitude of John Keats, who "Adonized" by putting on his best clothes before starting a poem; or Emily Dickinson, who dressed in white and took up her pen with a calm white fury of hope and trust.

If you feel this, putting everything you possess behind, into, and after the wondrous words "Once upon a time," you have a nice start. Hosannas to you.

Still More: Occupational Hazards

About the time you are set to write your story, meeching uncertainties may walk out of the woods. Mere daily irritations—telephones, necessary chores—can take on the power of malevolence. You may feel you have been singled out for attention by gremlins determined to distract you from your real target. Actually, the act of writing is its own defense against these fancies; once into it, this writer has found that very little can lead him badly astray. Telephones can be answered, words can be spoken over them, while the story is held in immaculate suspension at the back of the mind and in the working corpuscles. But there is a dominant fear more potent—as a fear—than any of these more minuscular threats. It's the result of a multitude of varied and sometimes simultaneous possibilities—bad weather; star-crossed love; galloping hypochondria; a thousand elemental atavistic intimations of doom. And these lead inevitably to the assumption that, perhaps because you have this dull pain across your dexter eyebrow, and the cat has been at the typewriter ribbon again, you are developing Writer's Block.

It's not restricted to writing. Painters get Painter's Block, or Visual Wipeout—hours of staring at canvas, wondering why they didn't listen to their wealthier friends and learn an honest trade. So too with musicians, zookeepers, baseball players, and teachers, speculating on burnout as they gaze valiantly at another freshman class—each blankly considering his or her own field with a temporary lack of love and enthusiasm. It is, in some part, a realization of the gap between the dream and the product; a comeuppance of the soul brought about by hard critical standards. It is a splendid excuse for not working, too—and for drifting in a moody, masochistic void and learning to recoil from the waiting weapons of your chosen profession; or, to accurately revise the metaphor, from the waiting arms of your first and only love.

In this writer's lifetime Writer's Block has attained the status of a gloomy badge of distinction. In the right circles it can be spoken of with the instant expectation of sympathy. It rates well with gout, perpetual charleyhorse, and tachacardia as blights which are not openly deadly; it stands somewhere between hiccups and poison ivy as a conversational springboard.

Yet the chances that you have it are about one in four million. And the chances that you will find it overtaking you one morning after you have written and sold short stories are less. It is one of those afflictions which lour in the background and pounce when they are given enough leeway to be let in. It is a usurper, to be classed with pretenders to the throne of Alsatia and purveyors of snake oil and voodoo charms. Recognizing this early, and still understanding it late, is important to everything you do in the short story—and in all fiction.

I am glad to present here a passage from the work of a man who put his capable finger on the bogie of Writer's Block when he was young and who recalled it in a splendid book for all writers, *Margin Released*, done in his sixties. In one earnest and profoundly felt burst he sums up what happened to him on a dire day when he had every reason in the world *not* to write; when his first wife was in hospital, dying. The author is J. B. Priestley.

> *I got back to Chinnor Hill, late one afternoon, so deep in despair I did not know what to do with myself. I was nearly out of my mind with misery. Had I been close to town I might have visited friends, gone to a pub or a cinema, wandered about the streets, but Chinnor Hill was miles from anywhere. Finally, just to pass the time while I was at the bottom of this pit, I decided to write something—anything—a few pages to be torn up after I felt less wretched. On my desk was a rough list of chapters for the Meredith book. I chose one of the chapters, not the first, and slowly, painfully, set to work on it. In an hour I was writing freely and well. It is in fact one of the best chapters in the book. And I wrote myself out of my misery, followed a trail of thought and words into daylight.*

Notice—and now I address the aspirants in the audience—the subject was far removed from my own life; I didn't lighten my woes by describing them; both the release from anguish and the good work done came from the necessary concentration, the effort, the *act* of writing. Perhaps, as I have already suggested, it would be better not to be a writer, but if you must be one—then, I say *write*. You feel dull, you have a headache, nobody loves you—*write*. It all seems hopeless, that famous "inspiration" will not come—*write*. If you are a great genius, you will make your own rules; but if you are not—and the odds are heavily against it—go to your desk, no matter how high or low your mood, face the icy challenge of the paper—*write*. Sooner or later the goddess will recognize in this a devotional act, worthy of benison and grace. But if what I am saying seems nonsense, do not attempt to write for a living. Try elsewhere, making sure the position carries a pension.After reading that, if you can't break through the false skin of Writer's Block and plunge to the subterranean wrestling of your story people, you might conceivably try hypnosis. William Saroyan—who had no need for ways to avoid thinking about Writer's Block, since it was as alien to his gladness in being a writer as a convention of certified public accountants—was once asked if he'd like to try being hypnotized, during which process it was suggested that he be urged to write something. He said, "Fine, as long as it's fiction."

I suggest that if you think about Writer's Block at all, you visualize it as a piece of real estate where working writers live.

Getting Ready: The Great Experiment

In the pages ahead I shall write the story about the three writers. It will be printed on the left side of the page, in column style, with my running commentary as it takes shape appearing on the right. This will be a *first* draft—hot from the furnace, imperfect, but approximating the version I'll send out for editorial eyes. The comments won't be the result of hindsight, but jotted down in the fire and fun and challenge of composition.

Before you read this shaggy first draft, I want you to write the first version of your own story. Do it from start to finish, in one sitting or several, but *do* it. Never mind strikeovers or bollixed-up sentences—just get it out as clearly and completely as you can. Your first consideration here will be the point made in the second chapter; let the adrenaline of honest confidence get into every word. If you don't feel it pumping when you sit down to begin, keep on working until it's there. Think in terms of about ten double-spaced pages (if you write first drafts in pencil or with a pen, make an educated guess about the length), but don't fuss at yourself if you run over. The main thing is to bring it out—all the cosmetics, pruning, clarifying, and beautifying will come later.

Before you start, refresh yourself anywhere in the preceding chapters. But as you start, drop everything but the vitality and stubborn confidence you need for your story.

You are, of course, free to read straight ahead without doing your story at all. But if you do that, you won't get half the good out of what's to come as you will if you read it with a fresh story of your own under your belt.

Chapter 15

Three Writers: First Draft

*T*he actual writing of this first draft, including the raffish personal notes on the right, was accomplished in about five hours. At almost every completed paragraph, I switched to the commentary; it is inelegant, heated, and pretty accurately reflects what I was thinking and feeling as I produced the story. If spread out on the usual 8½x11" manuscript pages, this original draft would amount to fourteen of these or just a tad over 13. And here it's needful to clear up what might be interpreted as a discrepancy. At the opening of chapter 2 I said with accuracy that your story will stand a better chance in today's market if you tell it in 3,000 words. That's the ideal; a target that was somewhere in the rear of my skull as I began "Three Writers." It should have remained your rough target as well. This present draft is subject to paring, and as we get into the process of editing it may be cut; at this point I'm not sure it will be drastically cut, because I was lucky and it has the right feel as it stands. I'd rather go a bit over than present a pinched manuscript.

But without that amorphous yet restraining ideal of 3,000 words, "Three Writers" could have sprawled like an octopus in the first draft, waving its tentacles at will and turning into at least a young novel. As it is, even though it is very slightly overlength by my original standard, it is clear, rounded, and tight without being jerky: a draft I am happy with. If you kept the 3,000-word ideal generally in mind as you wrote your own story's first draft, not worrying about it in any rigid way, but knowing it was there, chances are fine that it has a shapeliness, a contained impact, it wouldn't have had if you'd merely let the whole affair hang out. And chances are equally fine that you now have something to work with which, in its final form, you'll be able to present to an editor with a tasty soupcon of pride.

This writer's glands, fingertips, skill and discernment were working together in the draft that follows. Remarks are on right-hand pages.

Most of the people in the hotel lobby had the startled look of sudden appreciation—as if the spring wind whirling around outside had blown them here, and as if they might have to join it again to enjoy it fully. It was fourteen minutes until nine by the ornate clock over the curving marble desk; glints of plans for the night shone from eye-corners, the smell of briskly stirred April furs and good perfume lifted from women ready to go somewhere exciting; only the girl and the man seated on the blue satin chaise longue were wrapped in a kind of tentative waiting.

The girl was about twenty-three; she sat with her whole body leaning forward, her black hair rumpled by wind, her green skirt and the matching green garden hat with its large rim like leafy articles from a summer garden. Her eyes were wide, she was smiling slightly and with hope; the sheets of paper under her arm had no restraining rubber band, but were clutched there as if they might be children she was having a little trouble controlling. Her shoes weren't quite right for the hat and dress—they looked eminently practical, low-heeled, scuffed a little from a lot of campus walking. The man, at least ten years older, sat a trifle more stiffly, guarding something—it might have been the girl, it might have been something he kept to himself out of old habit. A thin scar went from the corner of his mouth to his forehead, vanishing in certain lights, stronger and reddening now as he shifted his good hands on the briefcase—a tough old briefcase, rough with use—and said, "You ought to get a folder for them. You could have lost more than that one. Let's get something to put them in. There's a stationery shop around the corner, down the hall. They'll have some kind of envelope."

"I didn't even lose one," the girl said. "You were so fast. How did you know they were poems? I mean, it happened so quickly—and when you grabbed it you said, 'That's no way to treat any poem.' "

"I'd been looking at you going up the steps," the man said. His scar was very vivid for a second. "I could read a little of one of the pages. It just looked like a poem. Don't you want to get some sort of protection for them?"

"No, they're all right now. Out of the wind. I'm bringing them to be read, by—by a man who's staying here. They're safe all right from here on." She laughed. "I'm so scattered—when I left Maine this morning I was at sixes and sevens—I'd never expected this person to call and tell

◄ *Third Person; First too close-up for this, felt so all along. And why the hell start outside Plaza—why name Plaza? It will come through stronger without this. Paint atmosphere, hard and sweet; circle in fast, establishing time, look of clock, on Grady and Amelia. Stir and brilliance of night, place, around them. Then right on them, and this feels damned good—has the right taste, touch. Excited about it, controlling it. No joy like this, never could be. Forward!*

◄ *Let the describing be complete at the start, full as possible without stopping motion and quickness, aliveness, not telling too much, surfaces indicating depths—I'm looking at these people as if I were from Mars and yet very concerned; only one I'll get inside thoughts of is Grady, and that will come in second scene or third.*

◄ *Nobody knows yet that Amelia's sheets of paper are poems, but the children idea's right; leads to what they really are. Mystery moving here—if I were reading this I'd read on, to solve it; shoes a right touch, OK, they'll appear later (it was Chekhov who said that about the pistol on the wall in the first act and somebody using it in the third, no come-on without dramatic satisfaction—Grady held in like a time bomb. Scar there in my first thought—Vietnam—from the first. Only really surfaced now.*

◄ *Now to the poems, and let the reader—bless your guts, old good reader—find out about what happened just before they came in. By a little indirection, a little overhearing.*

◄ *I've already said there's wind in the April night outside, this is clear enough, don't lean on it, Boles; let it move through as they talk.*

◄ *The word protection is important here. Don't have time to expand on this or I'd lose the story. It overrides the whole story, though, or will. Protection of a certain innocence; extended from protection of weather and other factors for the poems.*

◄ *I can hear her, all right; all I have to do; let her show what she is, give smattering of background. The "man who's staying here" is enough, too; she thinks so much of Ferris's work she doesn't even want to say his name; yet she has to say something more,* me to meet him here tonight. He's very famous. He's a wonderful poet. He was writer in residence at school up there last year. I didn't think he cared a damn about anything I'd done, and then, this call—I had to borrow the fare from my sister. And I couldn't find anything on the bus to wrap them in—newspaper didn't seem right. They're my best things. I wouldn't want to insult them."

The man's gaze was level and intense. His eyebrows were black and heavy, and his knuckles tightened slightly around the briefcase. He said, "The man you're meeting. Is it Hamilton Ferris?"

"Oh my Lord," the girl said. "You know him? You mean you're actually acquainted?"

"I'm not his friend," the man said slowly and carefully. He was looking at the girl with his eyes narrowed and assessing. "We've met just once. Two years ago when my first novel came out he read it, and after it had been out awhile he called me about it. We had lunch. He said when I'd written another book he'd like to see it in galleys." His right hand tapped the briefcase. "I read in the Sunday literary section that he was in the city, staying here. I called, and he asked if I'd have dinner with him tonight. That's all it is. I don't really know him." He was quiet, as if he wanted to say a great deal more but decided to keep it down. He looked like a dark cat burglar studying diamonds to see if they had any paste in them.

The girl said suddenly, "What happened at the lunch?"

"Nothing. There were a good many other people there. It was a long, wet lunch. He did most of the talking."

She nodded. "He was like that at school too. Very liquid. The English Department followed him around and took care of him—when he was about to fall on his face. But you see—it doesn't make any difference. There are the poems. Like Dylan Thomas, you know. You can't blame him for being less or more than human outside the poems." She was leaning forward farther now, her eyes as bright as if she'd carried the spring night inside and still preserved it wholly inside her. "You're Grady Calman. You wrote *Midget on Horseback*. The Vietnam one. There was a picture on the flap. I hope it sold millions. It was one of the best books—novels—I ever read. You don't look like the picture—it was softer."

"I'm older," Grady Calman said. "Thirty-five. It's goddamn near decrepit. I was married then too. Maybe it made a difference."

point out his eminence. Not deigning to wrap her poems in any old newspaper is right for Amelia. I like this woman and I'll keep on doing it.

◀ *Quick report while I write: I'm giving some blood and love here, that's why it feels right. Don't always get it the first time, but thinking about this one did it—in spite of that outline, which really only hit the high spots. Inside a thing is always different. Feeling way, with absolute confidence I'll get there.*

◀ *All through this can feel Grady's control, deep anger; this man's a good novelist, and better, a hell of a man—keep bringing that through. Amelia's reactions are closer to the top—he—and I—sense the other depth, or hope it's there.*

◀ *Can sense Amelia's strong intuition. Let her say it, bring it out.*

◀ *Respect and joy in the Ferris poems must come through; part of her depth, her own mystery which Grady and I now know. I'm riding this story as if it guided me, but the path is clear even if sinuous.*
◀ *She probably started to recognize Grady a short while back. Right now she's sure. She's even a little sure of how he feels.*

◀ *All the background I surmised is floating deep now, showing in the story in sureness and kept close enough to the chest, but not*

"I don't see what difference it could have made," the girl said. "You look wiser now. Age doesn't mean much, does it? I'm twenty-four—anyway I will be in May. I don't feel that way. Not any younger or any older than any other poet alive." She put out a hand. After a moment he took it. The handshake was brief and just sufficient. "Amelia Sammons," she said. "Nobody's ever heard of me, but that doesn't matter either. It doesn't change anything."

They sat stilly, in a hiatus through which the murmur of the lobby was like scented surf. Then Grady said, "All right." He glanced around at the clock. "Going on nine. I'll say what I want to and get it over. You saw Ferris in action—you know how he is. Maybe you want it that way. I don't know. This isn't any moral lecture. I could use his help—a good review would get the new novel off the ground, if Ferris did it. *Midget* sold about a thousand copies. Big reviews in some literary quarters, but no splash. Not the kind that bring in the fancy offers—the kind that let you live where you want to and clear the way for more of what you have to do."

Amelia gave another nod. "I know. But you don't like him."

"I think he's a high-rolling bastard. Nothing to do with his poems. I think," said Grady, his scar bright, his head forward, "he'll take you and eat you for breakfast and throw you away. It's something I want to say. It's not advice. Take it as stupid, opinionated, parochial observation. I even think from the way you look, from what you say, that you may be a real poet yourself. So you're absolutely free to make up your own mind before you do—or don't—go in that famous dining room with me. And to Ferris's private table, and lay those poems at his feet."

He got up quickly, as decisive as a fullback in action. His tie was a little slipped at the knot, a little sober and worn. "This is a book better than *Midget*." Hoisting the briefcase with the galleys in it, he gave it a quick trusting stare. "However I feel about Ferris, that's the big idea right now. So come on or not, Amelia Sammons."

Amelia said from the chaise longue, "Lord, oh, Lord, you're mad." She stood, making a pass at her tumbled hair with the unoccupied hand. "He didn't ask me to dinner. Just to drop off the poems. Did you get that scar in Nam? It shows how mad you are. Somehow it reminds me of Donne— 'a circlet of bright hair about the bone'."

"That's interesting," Grady said. "That would have interested the hell out of the medics in the Mekong Delta. It would interest the shrinks *so close anything is going to have to be unscrambled; what code I'm using is clear. That's a wonderful mingled metaphor, also exactly how I feel. Can hear and see them both, these people—feel Ferris waiting too.*

◀ *From standpoint of back chapters, story is both Wet and Dry, but that kind of naming is only useful when thinking about a story, not when writing it. I'm happy and I could be interrupted by an earthquake and still finish this the right way.*

◀ *Letting this much out is important, vital. Grady doesn't have to be described in tone of voice. All in the words.*

◀ *He hates being here, hates even more the suckered life of having to ask Ferris in effect for a favor no matter how sincerely it's offered; as in any story when it's going right I know him as if for a thousand years. What he hates even more is what Ferris can do to Amelia. Putting him to the point of getting this out at least partway, though his control (and mine) is needed right here. All I have to do is stand aside and let him say it.*

◀ *Think Amelia should bring out how much he detests being here and will have her do this next. She's perceptive with the perception racing under the skin of the story. Feel a solidity of action and talk—sensory being of the people—which comes only during writing at these times.*

◀ *Didn't mean to have her bring up John Donne, it was her idea, but it seems right and I think should stand. Straightforward mention of the scar okay.*

◀ *Tone here is savage enough not to need any qualifiers, adjectives. This is as much as Grady will say about his past on top of what* too. They worked on me awhile after I got back. It would even have interested my ex-wife. She was very intellectual. She'd never have thought about anything like that to say."

When they reached the entrance to the dining room, a maître d' bowed beside them and lowered his head when Grady said, "The Hamilton Ferris table." Amelia put her free arm through his. She walked with her head lifted, her eyes shining and amused and, in their corners, observant of Grady. She didn't notice the people who looked after her approvingly, as if they liked this woman who for all her fairly sloppy shoes summed up the chancy spirit of the night outside the windows.

Flanking a well-polished potted palm, a violinist played Noel Coward and Gershwin in ribbons of nostalgia, but the Ferris table stood beyond that. It had a verdant green cloth on it and many candles. The people around it, ten or twelve of them, seemed to be riveted to attention—no one of them was speaking; only Hamilton Ferris held forth. At the head of the table his face was that of the Emperor Nero and an old boxer—deeply lined, flashing with malice, the eyes alone living; eyes like cold opals with skins of light over them. Grady said to Amelia, "The occasion for the dinner. He's delivering his new manuscript to his publisher tomorrow. Trumpets and drums. First book of poems for twelve years. He makes just the one original manuscript. No copy."

"I read the columnists too," Amelia said softly. "We get newspapers and magazine up in Maine."

Ferris was finishing his oration—or soliloquy. His voice was a piece of gravelly velvet. It was slurred at the edges—no dinner had yet been served; the table was heavy with drinks—but it was distinct and bell-like in the center. The voice seemed to soar out like a noose and lasso everyone within fifteen feet of the table. "... and if the Nobel committee in its infinite wisdom should see fit to choose me for honors before I reach my seventies, I'll tell them in my best and suavest manner, up yours, you Swedish idiots. I never did write for prizes—just for people with the perception to read." He leaned back, addressing a glass. There was visible nervous relaxation around the table. His eyes flickered past the candleshine and caught sight of Amelia and Grady. He half-stood, a shade unsteady but foursquare, and this time the voice purred. "Mr Calman. Young Calman. And the lady—she attended all of my seminars during an excruciatingly boring stay at her fine little rustic place of learning. Messieurs, Mesdames—Mr. Calman is an excellent novelist.

he's already said. In scene coming along he'll be its center and the need then will be to stay in his reactions all the way.

◀ Quick picture of Amelia from outside as she nears the Ferris table—feels right and makes the right lead-in to next scene.

◀ Point is always, for me, not to stop and look back at last scene but to move straight into next. Here a two-em drop space between scenes. Need overall picture of table without wasting space on nonessentials, sort of bystander's overview. With Ferris as its focus.

◀ At the end of this table approach, need—thinking five beats ahead of the writing but not hurrying, just letting it all form on paper—a mention of the Ferris fetish about no copies of manuscripts, which may or may not be true but is a fostered part of his legend...have Grady mention this, with cold straight scorn.

◀ All this will be Ferris's; show him by hearing what he says first, something demeaning about prizes for writing, then going fast to his seeing Amelia and Grady, and keeping him objectively in sight as if reader stood just behind or at elbow of Amelia and Grady. Voice and eyes most vital sections of him to see in story. Waspish tone taken for granted. Words frame it, phrase it.

◀ Keep in mind, for God's sake, you don't need anybody else but these three people, they're the whole path to the whole story. Don't get into how hangers-on look, let this be implicit—stay now with Ferris and have him go quickly to his arrant "plans" for Amelia, real reason (apparently) he asked her here tonight.

Welcome him. Miss—Sammons, that's the name, a round old New England moniker—please come over and stand beside me. She"—he bowed low, sweeping upward in a sketch of an introductory gesture—"God help her, is a poet." He sank back, grinning. Amelia detached her arm from Grady's. She made her way past the glimmering backs of the women in their evening gowns, the men in their tails and white ties, past a projecting floral piece which wept leaves over the table rim, and stood there, the garden hat's wheel brim catching points of light and her face as calm as a far-off morning.

Ferris's right hand, a sinewy liver-spotted talon, extended to grip her left wrist. "Ah," he said. "Ah and ah." The cold shining eyes traveled upward, downward, upward again. "Words," he said. "Fully inadequate. Amelia Sammons, I'm afraid I haven't made provison for your dinner in this celebrated seraglio and infamous hostelry. Because I have other plans for us. You have brought your effusions—those damned things under your arm. We'll study them line by line, word by word, no matter how long it takes. We'll perform this in privacy. Far from these succubi who surround us. In my suite—and why in God's name shouldn't a great poet live greatly—there is food, drink, comfort. Run on up now and wait for me there—"

He was digging in a coat pocket. The suite key came up heavily, in brass that winked under the flames, and it thudded on the table with a soft clank. "There; pick it up, and run on off upstairs—and some time during the very small hours we'll observe your poems, I do promise that."

His face was bland under its network of creases. "Yes, my dear Miss Sammons, this is an advance—a pass performed in public. Yes, you know my obvious reputation for libidinous rites; surely you observed it at that little school. I have no shame; why should you?" In a lower voice which still penetrated he brought out "Pick up the key, love. Pick it up, or run on back to Maine and cultivate whatever cherished virginity you have. Hurry, now, hurry along."

Grady Calman stood beside a chair someone had pulled out for him. His scar pulsed, but no one was looking at it, or at him. He thought, this is how it was, how it always was, with the children in the villages— when the firepower was turned loose, when the napalm started running and roaring. They stood without moving and they didn't lift a finger or an eyelid because what had happened to others and was about to wipe

◀ *Staying outside and yet tightly inside this scene is the imperative. No elaboration. Do it fully, roundly, but keep Ferris's action, what he says, to the point; no going back to Grady yet for any reactions. If this were First Person it would be impossible to balance; even in retrospect Grady would bring overemotion to it—as it stands the implied impact on him and Amelia's handling of it are enough. This walking a tightrope is as necessary as though I were the late Karl Wallenda going across a gorge. Say plenty, but let the plenty be uneditorial, staying with the whole view and not the fascinating parts.*

◀ *His making her pick up the key was a fulcrum on which the story first turned. It's still a high moment, but the story is going deeper than it was when I planned it and has its own autonomy; this is just a part of it necessary to get over without pressing it too hard—to make everybody see and to burn into Grady—and now a deep solid breath and into:*

◀ *From here for a while this has to be Grady thinking; no italics, just get into him and let it run, not exactly a stream but the real way he does feel and see this—the undertow of baffled rage pulling him while he watches Amelia fed to the whims of this excellent poet and—for now—inferior man. Keep it down inside him, as it is, enough to taste it all the way.*

153

them out had its roots in something so old it couldn't be defeated by crying out or protesting even with the body. They were without help in the center of raw power. The ceremony of innocence wasn't just drowned, it was obliterated in dirty fire. This is the same war and I'll never be out of it. And however she handles it, it isn't even her choice—it's between her and those poems.

It wasn't a long wait. Once during it he told himself, now she'll pick up that key and throw it in his face—and when she does I'll walk out with her. And this man whose own poems are part of everybody who loves decent writing will grin again and shrug his shoulders and write her off. But then as her free hand came out, wrist gentle, and closed around the key and he saw her start to smile, uncommittedly, a social smile, and saw her turn and walk away, something in him seemed to burst—what had been a furious center of heat turned cold as an iceberg's belly. Good-bye, he said, Good-bye Ms. Sammons—as he sat down, propping the briefcase with its load of galleys against his leg, a woman next to him on the right, a woman in long pearls and with green tired famished eyes whispered, "After all, I wouldn't feel too terribly about it, Mr. Calman. She's one of an infinite number. Here, have a drink—you seem to need it."

But he didn't drink; a sip of the good Scotch was enough, the rest didn't feel as if it would go down well. The table was full of general conversation now, nothing that remotely mentioned Amelia Sammons; through the buzz which touched on the new, singular, and unduplicated manuscript of the fabulous poet, and speculated on his fetish—well publicized—of making no copies, and dealt in old literary scandals whose center he'd been, and his first four wives—through this Grady Calman watched, via the shapes of spring leaves and the light of candles, the heavy yet witty and masklike face of Hamilton Ferris—he thought: When I get up, it will be any minute now, I'll pick up the briefcase and walk down to the end of the table, and from there on its a matter of logistics—I could swing it from the side, those are pretty bulky galleys, I don't write small books; the briefcase should catch him on the side of the cheekbone and get him out of the chair without any extra trouble. There'll be a certain amount of fuss; my own publishers won't like it any too well. This hotel won't call the police, it'll just ostracize me, which is all right because I couldn't afford to stay here anyhow. The able violinist in the background had changed melodies; he was concentrat-

◄ *Keep holding my breath, trying to keep Grady in full focus, but the feeling is still all here, the emotion working with the words—same time, I'm in the room, Palm Court of Plaza probably, seeing from edge of my consciousness all the Things in it and not mentioning them because they're not on balance important to the whole of the story.*

◄ *Betrayal but not so much of Grady as of Amelia herself—then the cold following it, the anger not gone but turning baffled. And settling into steady wash-my-hands-of-it unsimple observation and I think plans to lay one on Ferris's jaw before leaving. (Doing these notes is like hanging out of an aircraft by the heels while flying.)*

◄ *No feeling like the power and command of knowing the illusion is complete, and riding through to the end; this has to be done here wholly inside Grady, could use italics but don't like them.*

◄ *Grady's studying out of the plans he has for Ferris done in almost an angular way, presupposing his cold steady rage without saying it.*

ing on Rudolf Friml now, and his ribbons of music soared as if they drifted through the windows into the alive, traffic-sliding, many-lighted night with its beating of excitement and charmed the shadowy trees in the park beyond.

No, he thought; no, I'll simply keep the briefcase in my left hand and use the right, not to damage him—he probably has a good many years of wonderful writing left—but to make him remember and know why it was done. That's the ticket now; just get up slowly, slowly and quickly both, like moving through long wet grass on a night patrol, and go to the head of the table and get it over with. Come on now, do it. Do it now, unobtrusively at first, and do it cleanly.

He had his left hand around the handle of the briefcase and was stooping a little below the table when he saw the old, comfortable, campus-easy shoes pass the varied footwear of all these hangers-on; they seemed to drift like small safe boats along the dark carpeting, and he felt a surge of joy as he sat up with the case in his left fist and his other hand clenching and then relaxing. At this precise moment Hamilton Ferris was busy in low-toned talk with a white-faced neighbor at his elbow—somebody'd said he was Ferris's long-suffering but patient editor, who of course would be here on the eve of the great manuscript delivery; how many poets made money for their publishers? As Amelia drifted along, Grady Calman noticed the faces turn in half-profile to see her, and heard the whispers, but he was looking at her, not anything else. In tiny spears of light the hair around her forehead under the capacious hat brim was moist and dewy, a child's after the bath. She was smiling again, not a social smile this time, something with repressed delight in it. A waiter who'd appeared at Ferris's other side stood with order pad poised for the moment when Ferris might choose to order. He took a step backward as Amelia appeared; for another three seconds she merely stood there, the loose poems under an arm as they had been before. And then Hamilton Ferris felt the waiting, and he turned to look up and around.

There was near silence except for the soaring of the rapt violin. "Thank you," Amelia Sammons said into it. "Thank you so much for the opportunity to freshen up. It's a beautiful suite, Mr. Ferris—I had a marvelous shower. And then—."

She dropped the key, not heavily, but with a distinct little sound beside one of the candlesticks. Its brass flashed through the crystal base. "—and then I read your manuscript. I didn't think you'd mind—it was so

◄ *A glance here, and an ear bent, to the night itself; it feels necessary, part of the rounding out of the felt scene.*

◄ *I know I am preparing the way for the return of Amelia, but I have to keep her coming back a surprise to me as well as to the reader; this willingness to amaze myself is something so needful to the rightness of the story it's inherent in the act of writing. That's as far as I can dissect it without straying from the central drive of the story and its whole being around me.*

◄ *I'm going in and out of action and thought like a needle through silk here, but keeping it forward-moving as Amelia is seen again, and if anybody wonders where those shoes would come in once more, this is the place.*

◄ *Skimping on one word would be fatal here, this is the kind of ample but still tight story which has its own built-in cadence from the first line, and while I'll consider cutting later, to even think about it seriously now would be to cut my storywriting throat. Two moods always to the making of a story—this one like steering safely in the eye of a hurricane, the one afterward meticulous and withdrawn and editorially minded but not too much so.*

available. I'm naive, I'm too raw to offer a critique; I was terribly moved. Thank you for that, too." And when she said it she was wholly serious, her lower lip showing it, the same emotion in her eyes; the next second, the light simple half-bantering tone was back. "I'm afraid I did an awful thing then. It was so stuffy in your suite, on such an airy night—I opened a window. And part of your manuscript blew out before I realized there wasn't any screen. Twenty or so pages. It looked for a few seconds like a ticker-tape parade—snowing over the city, whirling up and then settling lower, spreading out—maybe a flock of gulls when they scare themselves and go off in different directions. That's a sort of Maine image—provincial, I know. But I thought you'd like to realize how strangely moving it was...." She was turning away at last, not quickly at all; no hint of haste. "I'm sure all this publicity about your having only the one manuscript is nonsense. You're much too self-preserving a person for that—" Her voice had lowered. "Aren't you?"

Grady Calman found himself, stirring, rising, swinging the case at his thigh, following her as the green skirt swung and the wide hat floated away. The violin loudened as they passed the violinist in his palm grotto. Then it was fainter, and from the Ferris table behind them voices broke loose at last—indignant, maybe horrified, who could tell from here? Amelia put her arm through his again, gave him a quick upward glance; she whispered hastily, "No, of course not. It was a little lie. I had to say it. You can see I had to say it."

"I can see," Grady Calman said. "Here, though." He stopped, and took the loose poems from her, and opened his old briefcase, and put them in carefully on top of the folded thick novel-galleys. He snapped the case lock shut. "Against the wind outside," he said. There were plenty of mirrors in this lobby, but he wasn't a man who looked into them much when he didn't have to, he knew what was there, and he knew the scar wasn't bright now, just faded back to where it ought to be when he was feeling all right.

He was still feeling that way when Hamilton Ferris said from just in back of him, "Damn it, wait up a second will you? I'm not agile, I'm not one of your joggers." When they wheeled around, there he was, a slight red-wine stain on his cheekbones, from hurrying, and his breath coming in short puffs. But he was grinning, too. Behind him the man who was probably his editor, and a couple of others, were standing with their eyes like horses in a pasture when lightning had struck an old favorite tree.

◀ *Again, Amelia's tone doesn't need elaboration; what she says will carry its own adrenaline. I'll give no side glance to Ferris, but let his reaction be imagined. He isn't a comic character piece, a slimy villain, he's a self-tortured man, also a genius, needing his own implied respect in spite of what's gone before. All this stays underneath, where it should be, in the wrestling muscle of the story.*

◀ *I have to let her describe this, just as an earnest child would; and let her unchildlike self come through with a barbed edge as well.*

◀ *I'll imply Grady's curious look at her—did you really let part of that manuscript blow away?—by letting it stand in her volunteered answer to it. This is a place where leaving out is also important.*

◀ *There's an inevitability here I had to have, a sort of union between Grady and Amelia sketched and perhaps symbolized, and it's all I need except for the point about Grady not looking in any mirror but knowing the state of his own soul and self.*

◀ *From here on in, the story is coming to its end like a sled coasting to a true halt after a long brisk run; can sense the underlying truth of Ferris coming to the top, the thing that makes him a great poet in spite of all the rest. This lack was what bothered me in the original outline, and I knew later he would have to be what he really is.*

◀ *Just enough of the real Ferris has to rise to the surface now and*

Ferris waved them back. "Go away," he said gently. "Go eat somewhere else. I don't want you tonight. Tell the rest; I'll be engaged the rest of the evening. Go on, old boy—aroint, get out."

After that he said, reflectively, even thoughtfully, looking first at Amelia, then at Grady Calman, "My sweet God, that was funny. A couple of very funny people. Naturally I have copies. And you probably couldn't even open one of those windows with a derrick. Now let Ed clear out those blighted breath-holders and let's sit down and eat and talk. And leave your novel with me, Calman, and your poems with me, Miss Sammons—when you go. I think I'll even stay relatively sober in honor of both of you. Come on, we don't have forever—nobody does, writers least of all."

"That's a very pertinent observation, Mr. Ferris," Amelia said.

His shrewd elderly child's eyes blinked. "No more of your lip, Miss Sammons. We have serious things to discuss. Calman's future and yours. Things no literary parasites would dream about. Come on, please."

Grady said, "It wasn't my idea. It was all hers. If you're giving credit."

"I saw you," Ferris said. "You would have knocked me off that chair if she hadn't come back." His hand on Grady's shoulder was momentarily gripping, almost beseeching. "Don't you know all this foolishness is unimportant? There's pride, and then there's false pride. Do you think I'd help anybody I didn't think was worth it? I care about very few things anymore, but what they call integrity's one. Listen." His head went up. The eyes shone in the battered monument of the head. "you can hear the wind, just a bit of it; the spring wind. Even in this cosseted place. We have too many things to talk about to waste time. Join me now, will you, the both of you?"

After another moment Grady nodded. The three of them walked back toward the dining room. Now and then through the serene rhapsody of the violinist in his corner, the murmuration of talk from the tables and the clink of china and glass, there came from beyond the richly draped high windows a high free note of moving air in the dark.

A Quick Postmortem

You will notice at once, if you enjoy comparing the rough dream represented by outlines with the plain fact of the finished product on paper, *make itself permanently felt. This doesn't amaze me but it's right and I want it to be a revelation to the reader; the last piece of sleight of hand (and truth) before rounding out the end with a line that's already forming in my head, something about the spring feeling we started with.*

◀ *Let Amelia get in this quiet fresh sardonic thing; it's needed.*

◀ *And Grady's flash of anger should be here too—judgmatic, yet holding back some judgment, waiting to put Ferris's action in perspective with what Ferris actually is and has to be.*

◀ *All right, and building him as he is in fact and all truth.*

◀ *Now for the last paragraph and in this one it has come by itself and won't need changing; a rarity but one I'm grateful for, and a summing up I am not backward about saying is absolutely right. I have been on a lofty knowing plane of existence, with people I respected and knew much more about than I expected to, and I shall hold this to the end.*

that the substance of "Three Writers" is far different from that first idea of an outline. For one thing it's somehow become a story of the celebrated poet as much as it has the story of Amelia and Grady. He permeates it. This *is* about three writers, not two writers and a convenient straw figure. Whether or not Ferris planned his public abasement of Amelia, using it as a kind of test to see if she possessed the fortitude necessary to respond well (a fortitude needed by any poet, just as a working knight always needed tough armor), is left in doubt. It's one of those questions that deepen a story and make it resound; as far as I am concerned, it shouldn't be answered. There is a unity among the three at the end that represents a welding of purpose—the purpose of three people which has emerged from misdirection, misapprehension, and mistrust.

It would have been easy to "annotate" the story in those remarks on the right—to give an after-the-fact, fully hindsighted rundown of why I did this and that at such and such a point. The remarks as they stand are honest, and they have the inchoate quality of truths as I felt them and as they were scribbled down during the hot fire of writing. (I am not used to talking to myself while writing, and this approximated doing exactly that. It's not a process I recommend as conducive to calm. I thought, and think, that it is more useful as an inside exposition of a story than many pages of laborious analytic guesswork and analysis.)

After such a story is done, in the fading glow of the coals as the forge cools down, the euphoria—the magician's power, the emotion of command—cools too, and special questions and memories come up. The first question that may be of use to you as you sit looking over your own completed story in first draft, is this: Is this a commercial story? Will it appeal to as broad an audience as possible? The answer as it applies to "Three Writers" is yes. The people do happen to be writers, but they are intensely *people* and not sticks on which the label of *writers* has been stuck. There is a plausibility about the setting and their action in it that happens to be universal. The problems of integrity they face are those of everyone in any field, unrestricted to writing. And the second question is: Could the time frame of the story have been more restricted, more narrowed and focused than it is?

I doubt that it could. As it is, it starts *inside* the hotel, in the lobby—not with the sheet of paper with a poem on it whirling out of Amelia's keeping and being rescued by Grady, as in the original outline. The clock time of the story is about half an hour, all told; events and pressures of the past—both the immediate event preceding the story, Grady's capture of the windblown poem, and patches of Grady's *and* Amelia's specific backgrounds—are suggested in dialogue (and directly in Grady's internal, self-to-self remembering while he is at the Ferris table). There are no "flashbacks" as such. There are three main scenes, the first almost the same length as the third, the second sandwiched between them like a muscular bridge from one to the other and ending with Amelia's only apparent submission to Ferris's raw use of his poetic eminence. Each scene opens a wide door to the next. Seriously truncating any one scene would pull the story into another shape and hurt its balance.

My third question, meant to be applied to your story as well as this one, is: Are there any self-indulgent side trips which linger too long on some aspect of a scene—lyrical side trips or flashes of the brush which pull away from the mood and drive of the story? Take the violinist—could he be cut out? My answer here has to be yes—but not with profit. He is briefly shown, or *heard*—what he plays, the Coward, the Gershwin, the Friml, is in ironic and silky contrast to the real mood of Amelia, Grady, and Hamilton Ferris. He takes up very minor story room. If a magazine editor (perhaps one who hated parent-imposed violin lessons in his or her youth) suggested that the violin sound ought to come out, I would obliterate it as neatly as possible. But if the story were being reprinted in some anthology, or a collection of my own, I would quietly reinstate it and feel it was back where it belonged.

And my fourth question, which applies to your story as firmly as it does to mine: Is the title right? Farther along, we'll go into the fairly large matter of titles—those that are inevitable and those that are dragged in from left field and have the ring of sweaty fakery about them. Some titles don't emerge with any conviction until the second draft is done, and still others stay shy and elusive even then. This one seems to have embedded itself early and taken up residence for good. It is the kind I trust. Its umbrella nature is cut from the same bolt of goods the story is made of. There is no infallible test for "a good title," but a useful rule of thumb is that if you can imagine no other, and feel a fillip of satisfaction when you think of it in relation to your story, you and the title are both right.

I said a minute ago that memories as well as questions rise as the afflatus of having again surmounted the agony and joy of writing a story dies out. At this second I remember stories that, like "Three Writers," came out right the first time—the results of years of stories that *didn't*; stubborn stories that had to be cut, bullied, shaped, and reshaped to lean, comely, and commercial worth. But whichever way first drafts went, they all felt as this one feels now. The great surge of making was over, to be replaced by a self-critical ear, a tough but not chilly editorial eye.

So at this point let's try to slip into the shoes of a deluged editor in the process of picking up a manuscipt and an anonymous reader roving through a magazine—with respect for both, and equal respect for the selfhood and strength of our labor.

Chapter 16

Easing into the Second Draft

*A*fter finishing your first draft, don't spend much more time than it took you to read the postmortem in the preceding chapter in mulling over it. Set it aside with firmness. If roseate clouds of accomplishment still hang around your ears and buoy you up, take a long, brisk walk until you are good and tired and the last shreds of exultation are dissipated. Your story isn't going to be as good as you think it is now when you go back to it tomorrow. (Neither is mine; for all my talk about it having "the right feel as it stands" and my solid defense of its general tone, it can use cutting and cosmetic surgery here and there.)

Wait about twenty-four hours before you pick up your story once more. And at this point be extremely careful to hold on to a completely professional attitude. That is, don't gape in despair and groan because strange gremlins seem to have been at work on the story, and, conversely, don't start beaming fatuously and call up all your friends to read them choice passages.

Just read it through once more, quickly but thoroughly. A splendid attitude at this point is that of treating the manuscript as though it were someone else's—as though you were trying out somebody else's bicycle for overall balance and road-worthiness. Stifle any impulse you may have to start marking up the manuscript as yet. If you must make notes, make them on the side, separately. What you're reading for is to get yourself on top of the story again, to surround it and to see it with the attitude of a craftsman—no more than that and not one whit less.

Depending on your personal fund of sensitivity, pride, and a number of other unfathomable factors, this may, at first, be tougher than writing the first draft. A rigid, *fair* critical and self-critical capability is built into some writers at birth; others have to develop it, and sometimes they can reach it only through a lot of inward battle. It is never exactly easy to apply to your own product. Humility and doggedness are qualities that will help you here—a remembrance of Chaucer's "the life so short, the craft so long to learn" will help too. As you move toward the making of your second draft you're walking a hard but wholly necessary line between despair and ebullience. Pretending that you are dealing with the work of another can, indeed, be a useful attitude—but it can all too easily give way to angry, ruinous ruthlessness. (The word *ruth* means tender; if you are without some degree of tenderness toward your own work, you may slash away until you have nothing left but cattle tracks on cryptic pages.)

What you are doing now is going through a rather mystic but wholly comprehensible process of change. You are becoming your own editor. In doing this, you need to keep your self-respect and the belief in your story you had during the time of writing it. At the same time, you need to exercise this same self-respect sufficiently to be intolerant of anything you recognize as bad. *Nothing about this is really difficult in the least.* All you are doing is moving from one plane of understanding to another—a new plane on which, as you revise, reject, and improve, you will gain constantly greater knowledge of all forms of writing and, specifically, deeper insight into your own.

Few processes are more wonderful—more steadily *educational* in the highest sense—than that of making your manuscript shine where it was rusty, tighten where it was flabby, speak clearly where it mumbled. The process can be like breathing life into a baby struggling for air; or like discovering, against the damp straggling background of a public park in the dead of winter, a unicorn.

There are, of course, beginning writers—and they will always be beginning writers—who cannot be driven to admit any defect in their first drafts. They will argue, with Dionysian heat, that what is done in the consuming fire of inspiration is necessarily sacrosanct and shouldn't be meddled with in cold blood. They feel that tinkering with, or talking about, a story, once it is done, is a debasement of what has been written out of pure feeling—their arguments are loud, fervent, and intensely self-serving. (They serve *themselves*, not readers.) Occasionally, such writers achieve limited publication in the teeth of their completely anti-intellectual, creative-versus-analytical bias. In pointing out to these fortunately rare specimens of art for art's sake the need for the use of a little mind along with an ocean of matter, this writer sometimes mentions that John Keats certainly improved his second draft of "On First Looking Into Chapman's Homer" in the rewrite and that another superlative poet, Edwin Arlington Robinson, summed up the whole school of I-can't-touch-my-holy-work advocates with his sonnet "New England," which begins:

> Here where the wind is always north northeast
> And children learn to walk on frozen toes,
> Wonder begets an envy of all those
> Who burn elsewhere with such a lyric yeast
> That you can hear them crying at the feast
> And crying loudest who have drunk the least.

The possession of at least slightly chilled toes is a healthy attribute for any writer when he or she sits down to address the hard-won first draft of a story.

A Few Possible Pitfalls

This writer feels that it's better not to show the first draft of a story to anyone—except perhaps a passing cat which happens to look over your shoulder. But I didn't feel that way when I started out, and I did receive decent and logical criticism from a few friends, not all of them writers. This is a matter of personal preference—combined with your assessment of the taste and honesty of the reader or readers you choose. Many good readers are good critics as well. And if they're also good friends, they'll pull no punches and also be careful not to go overboard by criticizing for criticism's sake. Groups of writers, meeting to go over one another's first and second drafts, can be warmly and sincerely helpful—this is especially true when the group is a relatively small one, guided by a spirit of strong professionalism. Groups of this kind can, to an extent, take the curse of loneliness off a lone-wolf profession; at their best they are useful blessings. At their worst they are suspicious cliques, engaged in dull internecine warfare which has nothing to do with the development of talent. If you feel settled and at ease and earnestly bettered in a writing group, that's your criterion of its value to you. If you feel it is full of show-offs exercising their egos at your expense, leave quietly.

Apply the same standards to the individual nonwriter to whom you might feel drawn to show your work. You probably wouldn't have thought about him or her in the first place unless you had already recognized an appreciation for good writing somewhat like your own, and the rest is a matter of plain trust. Closely allied relatives—husbands, wives, sisters, brothers, aunts, and uncles—usually have about as much objectivity in these affairs as can be fitted into the eye of a small needle, but even among these there are rare and happy exceptions. Rudyard Kipling's father and mother were hard, fair critics around whom the least sign of a swelled head was the signal for instant deflation. Growing up in a reading, well-booked family to whom stories and novels are as important as bread is a lucky start, but if it can't be arranged there are often stout substitutes—the dedicated teacher of literature, the friend who haunts libraries looking for the lost golden books of the Incas. Caustic criticism can be immensely healthy for you, as long as it remains concerned with the work and not with its maker. The difference is something you have to decide for yourself.

And there are high risks involved in handing your work to others. Even when it's done with discrimination and plenty of character-weighing beforehand, your trust *can* be badly betrayed, setting up a host of needless tensions between you and the first draft of your story. Informed readers are the people you're writing for, and most writers are not so self-centered and cutthroat by nature they won't say what they do mean, but it's possible for you to pick the wrong reader, the wrong writer—and if you do, and everything backfires, go back, no matter how much you may be shaken, to your desk and try, patiently, to separate the dross of the critique from the useful, taking into account the many crochets of humanity, and again regaining the forthright confidence you had at first—along with a resolve to edit well.

What Makes You a Capable Editor?

Why are you able to edit at all? And why should you be able to edit your own prose, to which you have been closer than anyone else will ever be during the hours of writing it? Doesn't this latter fact blind you to lapses and bad habits, peculiar quirks and reader blocks which only a completely different pair of eyes can see?

The answer to that first query is that not only are you able to edit but your editorial skill has grown, even though you may never have recognized it or used it up to this time, from the moment you first learned to read, and it will be developed in exact ratio to the amount and range of your reading. The more catholic your reading taste—tomato-can labels through Spillane through Plato—the better equipped you are as a sound, all-round editor. All great editors, including the late Maxwell Perkins, have been to a great degree autodidacts—self-taught, even though they may also have received splendid formal educations. They were—and are—helpless when faced by a line of words printed on a page. For good or bad, they have to read them.

This same helplessness is your editing, and finally your writing strength.

To the second question and the third, the answer is that only you know how close you came to articulating the vision behind your first draft. What the professional magazine editor will see is the result of your attempt to move closer to your ideal. It is *not the ideal*, which remains your personal property—and who is better equipped than you to recognize, and to try to narrow, the gap between vision and execution? Who can better recognize lapses, quirks, reader blocks, carelessness—the need to preserve cadence, the need to take out a paragraph?

Step cleanly around the overhumble mistake of telling yourself you've never been "trained" as an editor. Neither have some of the best editors. They are in the business, first of all, because they love what words can do and deplore what many words don't do, and have learned, by trial, error, and with the occupational risks of ulcers and corporate takeovers, to tell the difference almost immediately. They started flying by the seats of their Brooks Brothers or Balenciaga pants by sure instinct and an affection for the craft. As they went along, this grew into second-nature sureness. You, on your side of the fence, are practicing the same art—with the inestimable advantage of working with your own manuscript. At this point you know better than anyone else how close you came to what you wanted—and how far you fell short.

Like the professional editor, your job at this stage is to fit yourself into the mood of that golden generalization, "the general reader." And, by dint of your native intelligence, your eye for error and ear for truth, bring your story nearer to a challenging heart's desire.

You've read straight through it now, surrounding it, assimilating it, all in acute silence. Now is the time to clear your throat, assume that mechanical whisper already recommended in chapter 11, and read it aloud.

Hearing the Sound of Effort

As you took in your first draft through the eye, skimming it with quick comprehension some hours after the heat and hope of writing, chances are that you saw a dozen or so places where it could be improved. Now, in your reading of it—in this unresonant, unfaked voice—you're listening for awkwardness, clumsiness, out-of-key sentences, the sound of strain and indecision—anything that bothers the ear of this editor-reader you're turning yourself into. *You are not reading out loud merely to find flaws.* You are reading with a little pride as well, gladly discovering good spots, points at which a happy union of words and desire took place.

As you go on doing this, with the present first draft and others to follow, you'll find yourself able to hear the story without using your voice at all—hearing its words sound in your head as though they'd been transferred to a tape or cassette. This will happen almost automatically, like the musician's ability to read a score without touching a piano. It is one of those gifts that come along when you try for them, such as whistling and learning to wiggle your ears. But for the time being you will need to speak the story softly, and as you speak it, use a pencil as dark and soft as your vocal delivery to make circles aorund everything that strikes your ear as wrong.

What you're working to perfect here is the inside rhythm of your story, a certain *chiming* that isn't yet complete, but that, when you have brought it out clearly, will take the place of the sound of effort and uncertainty in your original draft. You haven't yet started to cut or to look for the right words to replace those which seem to limp or drag. You're listing for clinkers, putting rings around them as they sound. Depending on myriad, devious factors—the fullness of your talent, the range of your taste, your ideal of what you really want the reader to understand—these clinkers will be clichés; or phrases which, while they might fit another story, are out of place in this one. Or they may be flights of poetic fancy occupying an alien background—Phoenix wings tacked to the body of a sparrow. Or again, they may be just the plain, garbled foolishness that gets into most first drafts no matter how pure the writer's aim was during the writing.

The Dawn of What Can Be

Writers concerned with metaphysical science often refer to the "leap in the dark" which has come out of the blue to inform great searchers after truth—Copernicus, Galileo, and Einstein among many others. Such writers consistently underline the point that, after years of laborious research, these men were strangely visited by certainty—certainty that did not rest on previous experiments or positive proof. They jumped, in a bound, overnight, from speculation to understanding. Without perceptible guides or visible pointers, *they knew what had to be.*

On a far more modest scale, but deeply important to you and your whole writing life, this is what can happen while you, in your new editor-reader skin, are murmuring to yourself the now familiar words of your first draft. A distinct change can take place in you. You can see and hear differently, more acutely, with sharper eyes, keener ears. Your points of reference can widen amazingly. You can see a bright shimmering of new light on what your story can be.

The excitement of this discovery is, to the real writer, superior to winning the Irish Sweepstakes—a breakthrough full of lasting delight. For when you sit down to go over the fresh draft of your next story, it will still be there—a feeling of mastery, beyond the arduous ache and joy you experienced while you were dueling with yourself to find your story and get it all down.

I wish I knew precisely how, why, and where this is made to happen. If I did, I would divulge the full formula in this exact spot. But I think it defies formula and analysis. I have a notion that it is the result of trying, of giving all you have—and some elements you didn't know you had—to every story; the upshot of wanting to make your story match the urgency of its conception. But the editing breakthrough, the dawn of what can be, happens to every writer of good commercial stories—and I urge you to work toward it with the first draft of your first complete story. When it comes about, it appears with a rush, as if Merlin had appeared on the scene with a hatful of magic; enabling you to tap a discerning area, a well of clear water in yourself which you hadn't known was there, brimming and ready. Egoistic, anxious, self-protective scales fall from your eyes; plugs of self-sealing wax pop out of your ears. And you're able to see, and hear, just under the surface of your first draft, the ghost of a finer story rising.

The Coming Forth of What Can Be: Part One

This finer story is not always one that has been drastically cut. The editing breakthrough—the near epiphany to which I just referred—brings with it discernment about what to save, as well as firmness about what to throw away. As your soft pencil circled boggy places, this was an indication that they might be cast out; but it wasn't a hard-and-fast signal for rejection.

Often, what you ringed in dark pencil only required tightening—the use of fewer, better, simpler, or more aptly used words to bridge a piece of slackness. Keep this in mind as you put aside your manuscript again—and now walk away from it once more. You have been very close to it for an intense hour or more, and no matter how eager the *writing you* may be to go on—this is true whether you are sixteen or eighty-five, built like a fullback or a leprechaun—the physical you will be in rebellion. Both your optical and your aural equipment have begun to fade. So has your judgment.

Force yourself to take a long break. It's ridiculously easy (and on occasion, fatally easy) to become fed up, sick to death in the spirit, stricken with what in the Middle Ages was known as *accidae*, over any story—especially one you wrote yourself. And revision calls for all the fresh insight you can muster—the hawk's stare, the composer's ear. Also, fatigue is a self-deluding as well as a physical enemy. Balzac's phenomenal stints of creation, Thomas Clayton Wolfe's midnight-to-dawn churning to the contrary, short story wisdom is better gained in short, bright sessions.

When you have returned, rested, clear-eyed, calm, pencil like a little lance, decide once and for all what has to come out and what can be retained but has to be rewritten. Go straight through the mushy, pencil-encircled spots from A to Z, drawing X's through those the story doesn't need at all and making some other mark—an *R* or any cabalistic reference point you can read later—on those that are going to be redone.

Now study the rejected, X-marked passages. Does their elimination create a real reader gap—a gulch in sense and meaning between the passage that went before and the passage that comes after? If it does, you're going to need a transition—one that is as seamless as invisible mending and in close approximation of the rhythm of the sentences which precede and follow it and in the identical spirit and tone of the rest of the story. Start working it out, on the typewriter if you work that way, with pencil if you don't; and in the interest of preserving your original manuscript as completely as you can and ending up with something legible enough to transcribe to your second draft, I suggest that you do this on a separate piece of paper. (I have worked my way from first to second drafts with manuscripts which, finally, resembled code-breaker's nightmares, but I assume that you are neater.) When you have worked out and assembled the last of these transitions, you have finished this session. Stop and go away, resisting the powerful temptation to sneak back and take one last look at what you've accomplished so far.

Please note: I have spoken here of cutting out *passages*, not words. Cutting *words* is a dangerous, delicate process. It can lead to wholesale, well-meaning manuscript slaughter. Of course it must be done here and there, when the word is egregiously wrong, misused, or for some other reason totally out of place. But to begin revision by crossing out a word and then another and then another ad infinitum through the manuscript removes all rhythm and power, leaving a sort of baby-talk telegraphese. Under the delusion that the shortest route to becoming Hemingway is the junking of every other word, many beginning writers have decimated first drafts beyond redemption.

The Coming Forth of What Can Be: Part Two

Before you go back to your manuscript, we need to settle another point about self-editing. There are, miraculously, stories that ask for very little of it. They have been felt so firmly, known so thoroughly in their first drafts, that any final touches are merely the patting in place of a necktie, the final tug at a hem. William Saroyan—as a rule—wrote a short story in one sitting, revising very slightly as he worked, saving paper and amusing editors by single-spacing, and sometimes sending it off an hour after it came out of the typewriter. There are other storywriters (not generally of Saroyan's caliber) who insist on similar procedures, but I do not believe their record of sales is astonishing. Jessamyn West once remarked in an essay that the only trouble with Saroyan was that he made writing look easy. It *wasn't* easy for him, but the travail came before production. With the majority of storywriters it comes before, during, and after.

When you have been making short stories for a while—four or five years, at a roundhouse guess—you will sometimes find a story emerging strong and whole, needing only a few pats on the back and tugs at the necktie before it goes out into the world. "Three Writers" is, I mildly regret saying, such a story. I regret it only because I meant to use it as an example of where and how to edit, pointing to excised areas galore, clicking my tongue over my own errors of judgment, and doing a graceful little tap dance as I proved how editing skill had refurbished it as a fully salable item. In future I shall produce stories subject to the knife in quantity, but, as intimated in the postmortem, this isn't one. It does need a few touches: the half-soliloquy of Grady Calman at the drink-laden Ferris table asks for shorter sentences—not blunt or terse, only shorter—and the ending, for all my first blatant approval of it, may be a shade too lyrical. But I will not insult it or my trade by using it as an example of a story that could be improved by strenuous line-by-line labor. I could, of course, substitute another manuscript for it; but at this point I think that would be cheating, like turning back the odometer on a used car; and at any rate I like its subject and what it says to writers and about them to readers. I also hope that you know me well enough by now to realize that nothing of mine is immune to editing and that I take solid, fussy pride in stressing its importance to my stories and yours.

On the hazard that your first market-aimed story is not yet an untouchable gem, use your next editing session to do the rewrite portions. What you're after here is both complete clarity and tightness—like stretching sails that have gone slack, without disturbing the way the craft rides in the water. You are not tinkering, you are *editing*; which means that you're keeping everything you thought was valuable when you read the story aloud. In your rewritten passages never cut back so far that you feel yourself slicing through the blood and bone of the story. The hoary adage about not throwing out the baby with the bathwater is a good motto to follow here. And once again, remember while rewriting that a sentence from which key words have been plucked has a tendency to lose momentum—like a bird flying into a wall. Here is a sentence that, found in a first draft, might reasonably be marked for rewriting:

In the grim, gray, grainy November twilight he got down from the mud-caked tractor as if his back was broken, straight across the pelvis, and he now had to hold it together with fumbling hands.

The logical way of shortening this sentence is to remove that dubious alliteration without disturbing the rest. Doing this, the sentence would read:

In the November twilight he got down from the mud-caked tractor as if his back was broken, straight across the pelvis, and he now had to hold it together with fumbling hands.

Yet a self-editor full of an overzealous desire to shorten without regard for mood, rhythm, and impact might spoil the whole picture with this:

He got off the tractor. His back felt broken.

The original sentence, for all its bad start, had a singing, convincing, overall strength behind it. The words "grim, gray, grainy" were extraneous, editorial as well as overfancy. They were not key words, but flourishes. With them gone, the sentence was strengthened and could still complement the sentences around it. But with the last example the sentence became two flat statements, each as characterless as a cheese rind. Unless the rest of the story had been written in the same bony, sightless style as those statements—which, from the evidence of the original sentence, it couldn't have been—the statements would be ludicrously out of place, throwing off the whole balance of the story. It would have been better to throw out the whole sentence than to reduce it to its minimal value.

Decisions similar to this one will have to be made again and again as you go through your rewrite. Some will entail the use of meticulous trial-and-error experiment until you arrive at something that truly fits. Some will be much easier than that—so that you say to yourself, as you come across them, "Why didn't I do this the first time around?" But as you go on, your perception of what is right for your story, and wrong for it, will increase, and your comprehension of the story as a whole will be wonderfully sharpened. For self-editing is not simply working with cold iron. It is, strangely, the reheating and strengthening and honing of that metal, an *inward seeing* which can tell you more about your writing than a thousand friendly savants, experienced teachers, and earnest guides.

Chapter 17

The Inside Secrets of Coming Forth

*A*nd now that you have cut out the bad sections of your story manuscript, inserted brief and clear-cut transitions where that was necessary, and done all the patches of rewriting that were necessary in other spots, take another salutary deep-breathing spell. And then start the fresh session by cutting *words*—as if you were a combination of concerned surgeon and prayerful patient. This must be done with care and slow, thorough judgment. You have already been cautioned as to what it can do to power and rhythm. Test every sentence out of which you contemplate removing a word. If the sentence reads haltingly or cryptically with the word removed, either put it back or find another that says more capably what you wanted to say the first time. No matter if you treasure words and have a naturally abundant vocabulary, *keep a good dictionary at your side at all times during every step of revision.* You will also need a good, comprehensive style manual which will give the *rules* of punctuation, paragraphing, and other niceties—there are plenty of these on the market, and they are as indispensable to the serious writer of marketable stories as eyes and ears.

I am taking for granted the point that you will learn these rules thoroughly to produce literate prose. In the sections to follow I am dealing with aesthetic choices, not grammatical ones. I want to communicate the *feeling*, rather than the established strictures, of paragraphing, of the use of certain connectives, of word repetition, and of punctuation. I want to suggest how the rhythms of prose are affected, even on the page, by how they are punctuated. This is a matter of professional finesse—not mere literacy. It is, in my immodest and considerably seasoned judgment, a matter of as much importance to your potential storytelling career as anything else so far brought up in this book. So in the pages to come, don't look for English rules; look for "English" as you think of it in the spin of a well-struck pool ball.

The First Inside Secret: Paragraphing

In the well-tuned, finished story, paragraphs are notable mainly for their quality of being present without being noticed, like line soldiers who have learned to look as if they aren't present when asked to volunteer. The reader just doesn't pause for most of them—unless they run on too long, in unwieldy unindented rows like massive building blocks, in which case the reader is likely to develop an itch. But now and then, a single sentence or truncated sentence will stand there by itself, at full salute, stopping the eye of the commander.

Exactly like this.

When this happens, it should be the result of no mere whimsical urge on the part of the writer; the writer should have in mind arresting the reader's attention for a good and crafty reason. The writer wants to illuminate what is ahead and at the same time cast a backlight on what has already happened. The gentle shock effect of a one-line paragraph is, as a loose rule, used more in novels than it is in short stories. It is particularly useful in passages of cumulative action, such as this one from a hypothetical adventure story which will not be written this year:

> When Bill had finished skinning out the tiger he stooped above it for a moment, reflecting that the brassy taste of fear he still felt at the back of his tongue was an illusion created by the nearness of the jungle, the darkness of the foliage twenty feet from his tent. He studied the long, splendid pelt rolled up at his feet, wrinkled his nose at the viscera littering the grasses, and was about to turn to the basin of water to wash the knife, when he heard it.
>
> The cough of another tiger.
>
> Directly behind him.

Such paragraphing, presented above in double force, was almost a special hallmark of Victor Hugo, who in his gigantic novels, such as *Toilers of the Sea*, liked to give a comprehensive picture of whatever the principal subject was—in *Toilers*, the awesome history and ominous habits of a giant squid, followed by a single, simple, and gripping statement calculated to make the reader jump and swallow sharply as Gilliat, the hero of that book, wheels around to see what has disturbed him in an undersea cave, and finds that:

It was the octopus.

The lonely action sentence, or flat statement, can be powerfully effective in some short stories when it is isolated in its own paragraph—as effective as if the reader had been collared in a dark alley by a mugger. But like any other effect, it is easy to overuse. In hundreds of stories by beginners this writer has found it repeated, each repetition less forceful than the last, finally creating a visible hangnail in prose. Any trick that keeps on advertising itself, flaunting itself before the reader, turns phony when it is used as a substitute for communicated emotion.

In fact, the story paragraph is a weapon that asks to be used as quietly as possible. It signals a very small scene change, a shift of attention within a larger scene, and its artful indentation should seem as logical to the reader as the systole and diastole of the act of breathing. Now, as you go over your first draft again, especially if it was produced at white heat, you are more likely to find that you've come down heavily on the side of long paragraphs than on the side of brief one-sentence signposts. There is no rule whatsoever about precisely where to paragraph—but it is a process you begin to feel safe about as soon as you have turned yourself into an editor-reader; if you think of the paragraph as a kind of story digestive, used to make prose tastier and easier to swallow and relish, that too can be helpful. Good, careful paragraphing always falls into place with a series of silent clicks, interior noises heard only by the writer.

Dialogue should, nearly always, be emphasized and set off by paragraphs. Without this space distinction, the job of separating dialogue from narrative background is shifted to the reader. The exceptions happen when you want to refer in narrative to significant dialogue that was spoken before the story started and is now needed to highlight what is going on in the present. This is from my novel *Parton's Island*, but it could just as well have been taken from a short story:

When you went west on the bank a while you came to where the river widened out. There were great big clumps of brush looking like hills on each side there. They had leaves like feathers stick-

ing up, always green, and the oaks on top of the lower leaves were bright red and yellow in the fall. But even when the oak leaves got old and died there was still the other mess of leaves, staying green. I mean, Alabama, you know? My father said when we moved here, "This is the ever-green land." "Yes," my mother said, "but not like money." "Well," my father said, "maybe you should have married a banker. After sixteen triumphant years of marriage you ought to know better than mention money." "All right," my mother said. "I like leaves too."

By paragraphing at *My father said when we moved here*, then paragraphing the rest of the father-mother talk as recalled by the fourteen-year-old narrator, a certain closeness of texture would have been lost. The passage simply needed to stay inside a medium-sized block of words where it was comfortable.

In your present vital position as reader, editor, and arbiter of the final look of your story, your acute sense of what is comfortable is the equivalent of an old shirt or blouse which simply *feels right*. Everything that fits your cautious, watchful, instinctive good judgment about unobtrusive, effective paragraphing is going to bring you closer to satisfying the reader.

Another Inside Observation: The Ubiquitous *And*

As the most useful connective in the language, *and* is a verbal rubber band linking segments of thought into complete sentences. It's also a great deal more; it radiates Old Testament strength, somehow evoking the flash of spears and the clash of shields, an atavistic music that drums through the subconscious mind. It can be a singing word in its own right, as in:

I will sing a new song unto thee, O God; and sing praises unto thee upon a ten-stringed lute. Thou hast given victory unto kings, and hast delivered David thy servant from the peril of the sword. Save me, and deliver me from the hand of strangers, whose mouth talketh of vanity, and their right hand is the right hand of iniquity....

A psalmist caught without *and* would be a muzzled poet. Most of our effective prose has its taproots in biblical word-music, in which *and* bears a muscular dominant place. It is, in its own manner, more distinctive and fitting than *then* when used as a pointer to what happens next; in Flaubert's ending to his retelling of the Story of Herodias, *then* would be acceptable but not quite as firm as:

> And *all three, having taken the head of Iaokanann, went off in the direction of Galilee.*

And is a forward-leaning word, tough and universally useful. In some places it has a majesterial ring for which there is no substitute. But when it's used as a crutch, it turns weak under the hand, losing life and juice and drawing attention to itself rather than what surrounds it. Its most unattractive usage occurs in the nonstop, breathy sentence which should by rights have been three or four sentences to start with:

> *We came into the room and it was dark and Julia shivered and said she couldn't stand the clamminess and Pete shrugged and said old houses felt like this what the hell did she expect and the baby was crying and I thought it would be swell to be back in Cleveland and I wished I'd never seen Pete and Julia and the little kid and everything was all gone out of the world and I just stood there.*

Somewhere beneath that sentence something important, even moving, is going on; if the narrator hadn't covered it with *ands* draped around the action like strands of kelp, it might have reached a reader. The sentence is purposely exaggerated. But the monochromatic application of a sensible bridge-word is typical of many stories which are hustled onto the page and offered to editors in their weedy first condition. Their authors mistake speed of statement for strength, the bathtub bubbles of random emotion for the Niagara of felt-through writing. As a suggestion only to be acted upon if you are in the mood (I would much rather have you concentrating on your second draft), you might rephrase the example, breaking it down while keeping its emotional level clear.

As you revise, it's sometimes healthy to think of *and* as a durable, flexible servant of your prose—a word to be kept in its place and not encouraged to shoulder its way to a central position. It's a servant you inherited from generations of wise and foolish storytellers. It's there to help you run your writing establishment, not for a second to take over. You can't get rid of it; you can't let it get too uppity, either. Here once more the criterion of comfort is valuable.

Still Another: Pet Words

In chapter 4 I spoke of word cherishers. The collection of special, favorite words is practiced by thousands of storywriters, and not storywriters alone; happily, it's a habit of many readers, for whom collecting never stops. Tidy aphorisms for beginning writers—cautionary reminders to use "plain" words at all times, to depend on words with Anglo-Saxon roots, to avoid Romance words—fall on stony ears when these enthusiasts write or read; they look for the better, more apt word throughout their lives. They learn by a process of acceptance and rejection—as the human body takes in some foods and refuses others—which words fit their needs and which ones their instinct denies. But they are forever adding to their personal word stock. (This process of the appropriation of words for their own is a strong contributor to what we very loosely call "style" in a writer. Style is a *way of saying*. It is, to some extent, born into its owner; for the rest it is a result of individuality as firmly expressed as a fingerprint. It is the reason why situation, plot, and general story line—as in Shakespeare's *Romeo and Juliet,* which he "borrowed" from a rather namby-pamby Italian source—are subordinate to the method of presentation; for style is also a *way of seeing.* When *Gone With the Wind* appeared in the thirties, hundreds of southerners said, "Why, I could have written that." But only Margaret Mitchell could and did write that; she alone possessed the way of saying and seeing that made it possible.)

In the novels of Iris Murdoch—to take one example from a multitude—the word "rebarbative," meaning "crabbed and unpleasant," shows up with somewhat charming regularity. It is not distracting. Instead, it is accurate and enhancing. Plainly, it means a little more to its author than the dictionary definition—as the word "fine" meant more to Hemingway than its usual connotation of something better than good. The author's spirit has, to a degree, taken over the word and made it her own. And a variant of this same method of taking over may easily have happened to you with certain personally appealing words—words which you consider pattable, strokable, more utilitarian and worthwhile than the ordinary. Such words simply suit the one-of-a-kind temperament you write from. (It is also worth saying here that very few writers *talk* the way they write; they adapt their workaday speech to the speaking pattern of those around them and save highly regarded words to use as integral parts of the public mask, or persona, which they put on while they are writing.) In *The Physiology of Taste* Brillat-Savarin observes that "the discovery of a new dish does more for human happiness than the discovery of a star." And the discovery and adoption of a new, versatile word may be a comparable gourmet experience for you.

Now, in a novel, where you have ample elbowroom and enough space in which to repeat a pet word without any but the most observant and analytic reader noticing it, you are as a rule able to indulge this pardonable, and even useful, fetish within reason—keeping a sense of decent proportion and making sure you don't flourish the word inside the span of two or three pages or closely connecting chapters. This isn't a severe limitation, and few writers are really conscious of it; it is taken in stride, like the act of running the half-mile on a summer morning; your "good" words come up smiling on the page, and you welcome them as they appear, using them with confidence and automatically remembering not to repeat them too soon. But in a short story the danger of reusing particular pet words is multiplied in ratio to the restrictions of the form; the reader, concentrating on the story which you have asked him or her to read while shutting out countless outer distractions, is jarred and perturbed by obvious pet-word repetition in so short a time, and what was a well-meant and rightly used flourish the first time turns into a second-act flop. (An editor of my acquaintance has said of this phenomenon, "It's like following a trained seal with another trained seal.") The mistake is more common than you might think. In a recent, otherwise excellent published story encountered by this writer, the word *rictus* showed up three times in nine pages. Its use was perfect the first time and equally perfect but deeply irritating the second and third. It wasn't especially important to the story, which wasn't primarily concerned with gaping or the corners of the mouth; the character trait it exhibited could have been emphasized in a thousand other ways. And yes, an alert magazine editor could have eliminated the repeat performances—but still better, they could have been caught by the writer at the source before the story was dropped into a mailbox.

So when you are self-editing, check for pet-word proliferation. Once in any story is enough for the most faithful of any of them. Twice takes the shine off and underlines sluggishness or stubbornness on the part of the writer. Using the same special, prized word three times or more in the same story is—in a word—rebarbative.

And Another: Tone Change

In the rewriting, reshaping, refeeling mood I hope you're in at this point, you may feel that something alarming has happened. Your first draft, starting out on one level of emotion, may have shifted during the writing to another. What began, for instance, as a story whose dominant theme was revenge may have ended with its people discovering that revenge was foolish and that understanding each other's motives was far more important than "getting even." In brief, you may well have discovered in yourself depths you didn't know were there and transferred them to the page as you went along. If something equivalent to this happened, it's no cause for agitation. The reverse is true: every short story is a voyage into the self as well as a dramatic adventure in public entertainment and legerdemain; if a story could be written *without* plumbing the self, the mystery of what we are and who we are would no longer be essential to its making, and short stories could be produced by the plastics industry in great volume.

But they can't be, and so in many first drafts the emotional tone of a story undergoes a sea change on the way from its opening to its ending. When this comes about, the best way to react is with thankfulness for having been surprised on the way to market, and to set about repairing those first passages which, like tricky broken-field runners, feinted in one direction but finally scored by finding an unexpected opening in another. If in "Three Writers" I had stayed with the original outline, and during the writing had still considered Ferris a complete villain of the most polluted water, with no potential final redeeming feature except for his published poems, only discovering on the last few pages that any man who can write great poetry has also seeds of greatness and forgiveness and inward alliance with all other worthwhile writers, the first of that story, and its center, would have been subtly out of key with the last. I was hard on him, and, in the character of Grady Calman, sardonic about him as well as strongly troubled about Amelia's future; but before

I plunged into the story I had thought enough about him to know I had to be fair to him—and to myself.

If your story has undergone a change of tone, this doesn't mean that your second draft will be far away from your first. What happened in the first draft will usually be redeemable; the repair work consists of accommodating yourself to the chemical alteration your characters have experienced and altering the reader's attitude accordingly. In many stories there are one or more subsidiary characters who (especially in first stories) are likely to be treated as punching bags, lifeless parcels of canvas on which your more thoroughly realized characters exert their power. Often they come alive in a second draft—to the betterment of the story—and in these situations rewriting simply means a little clarification for the reader, a sentence or two showing that your central characters don't live in a world of stereotypes. As you read over your first draft for possible change of tone (although when it is there, you'll have *felt* it during the writing), remember that, Adolf Hitler and his ilk to the contrary, pure evil is never embodied in one person—it is an essence, and those who practice it are pitiable, but they are still, to a degree, human, not possessed of tangible horns and forked tails. And the same is true of saints—they are fallible, not amorphous enhaloed heroes and heroines, but people with warts and occasional hemorrhoids.

The power of rewriting lies in its ability to make the writer see both where change of tone has happened and where it *should* have happened. It increases your comprehension of where the real writing is going on. It is your second chance at the admittedly impossible but wonderfully worthy target of perfection. In some cases your opening itself will have to be rewritten to accommodate the change of tone. When you realize this, it won't be difficult—only inevitable. Recognizing the presence of, or the need for, change of tone is like being jolted into another time and place by a gust of perfume on a sharp night. It shapes and sharpens your understanding of character—whetting your most formidable storywriting weapon.

Chapter 18

The Diplomacy of Punctuation: Commas

*W*ith the reminder that this is not a handbook of remedial high-school English and that what we're concerned with is the impact of your short story on the greatest possible number of readers, let's move behind the general rules of punctuation to look at it as series of diplomatic messengers serving your storytelling need. Actually, punctuation is as much a part of your personal imprint on a story as is your choice of words. The decision whether to insert or leave out a comma may never appear as important to you as it did to Oscar Wilde when he said that he was exhausted because he'd spent all morning putting in a comma and all afternoon taking it out. But the comma can be important enough to merit a little sweat in its behalf. It is more than a slight pause for breath. It is a *mental* pause as well, and when it is left out, its absence can create a gap through which all sorts of misconceptions leap to assault the reader.

The following sentence is not nearly as rare in its ridiculousness as it may at first appear:

As she was singing to her ears came a faint wail.

The prospect of a lady serenading her ears has a peculiar attraction, but it is highly doubtful that this was the impression the author had in mind. The phrase *Punch, the Fabulous Puppet* undergoes a lightning change and becomes a plea for direct action when the comma is omitted:

Punch the Fabulous Puppet.

And in less glaring examples of the commaless sentence, the reader is left with an impression of breathless haste, of a quality of slapdash improvisation rather than the steady gait of hard, clean prose. For straight-forward narrative has a good habit of moving along in rhythm, with each sentence setting up the next, doing its appointed job without distracting the reader or giving him reasonless pause. This is not "distinctive" prose, but it is as clear as daylight through a north window on a cloud-less day:

> *It didn't seem so long till Jean got back with Dr. Simson. He had his bag with him. He took Max into the dining room where he turned on the chandelier and also used a flashlight to examine Max's throat. By this time Max was squirming around a little, normally. I felt a little better about the whole deal when Dr. Simson said, "He'll be all right. Here—" From his bag he took a bottle. "Have him gargle with this, two teaspoons in a glass of warm water every hour. What happened?"*
> *I said, "He was fooling around with a little turtle. He swallow-ed it by mistake."*
> *"Could have choked him to death," Dr. Simson said. "Though a turtle would probably go down easier than most objects, at that. Had a child try to swallow a fire engine last night. Good night, no charge. Merry Christmas."*
> *When Jean went to let Dr. Simson out, Max said in a furry, far-away, hoarse voice, "Thanks."*

There are eleven commas in that brief passage. Each performs a special function in the creation of plausible, quiet storytelling. None is obvious or at all outstanding. The penultimate comma, placed between *faraway* and *hoarse* in the last sentence, could have been left out. But without it the sentence would have had a slightly different rhythm—the absent comma would still have been supplied in the reader's mind.

Again, omitting the comma in Dr. Simson's remark, "Though a turtle would probably go down easier than most objects, at that," would have hurried his observation, changing him, however subtly, from a calm, meditative, and amused doctor to one who talked more swiftly and was a shade more impatient.

Commas, like all other punctuation marks, are pocket handkerchiefs, arranged in the breast pocket of a story's suit coat with neither excessive fussiness nor too much modesty. And they are more than this; they are there because they enrich your story without drawing attention to themselves or detracting from the effect of the complete ensemble. Whether or not Oscar Wilde was talking for the sake of good talk, the rightly placed comma is an excellent diplomat—unobtrusively smoothing the path for real communication.

A Pointing Finger: The Dash

The dash has a different nature from that of the comma—it is not quite the same sort of pause. Because it has more airspace on both sides, it becomes a little flag, a pointing finger sometimes aiming at what is to come, and sometimes replacing parentheses when it is used in double form to set off a sidelong thought inside a sentence. In both uses it is invaluable. If it is used too much, it gives the impression of a speech impediment on the part of the narrator, with the effect of a series of nervous gasps:

> She came in—Lily Dache hat on the back of her head—left eyebrow curiously arched—as if—I thought—she'd just discovered an angleworm in her martini—placed there by a surly member of the working class—

Those dashes are bad substitutes for commas, and, as such, destroy the impact of the sentence by breaking it into brittle segments. They make the eyeballs jump like fleas and the stomach react as if rocked by choppy water. But here are dashes used with a friendly, easy, conversational quality—the tonal quality of a man seriously discussing his puzzling past, in Stephen Vincent Benét's "Everybody Was Very Nice"—a story that says more about divorce than a courtroom full of expensive lawyers:

> Now, of course, we've been married eight years, and that's always different. The twins will be seven in May—two years older than Sally's Jerry. I had an idea for a while that Sally might marry Jim Blake—he always admired her. But I'm glad she didn't—it would have made things a little too complicated.
> And I like McConaghey—I like him fine.

Such dashes are small bridges between thoughts, casual areas between confidences. The dash can also be lifted to complement enormously effective prose, as it is in Fitzgerald's often and deservedly quoted final lines in *The Great Gatsby*:

> *Gatsby believed in the green light, the orgiastic future that year by year recedes before us. It eluded us then, but that's no matter—tomorrow we will run faster, stretch out our arms farther...And one fine morning—*
> *So we beat on, boats against the current, borne back ceaselessly into the past.*

Then too, the dash can appear to handsome effect in front of separate sentences indented for a purpose, creating miniature moments of remembrance more poignant than "flashbacks":

> *Maggie sat in blue darkness, her hands sculpturing a beat of music, most of it concentrated in the fingertips, all of it grasping after what had been gone for seven years—*
> *—Isn't that our favorite tune? Wasn't it always? Won't it be, f'r ever 'n ever?*

The dash is remarkably intimate—a low, precise, controlled alto note of your storytelling voice. If you hate dashes, shake your head when you find them in other people's work, don't find the need for them in your stories, just forget them—anything you can write and live without doesn't need your attention. But if you feel that they're diplomats par excellence, use them whenever they can exalt and point up your story, as the indicative fingers of artifice from which natural style is made.

As alternatives for parentheses, dashes have a quick, lively, and still low-voiced impact on the reader, which is much more comfortable than, for instance, these well-meant parentheses:

> *"God, Charlie," she said (rushing up to me, always rushing) "The thing about Milton is he's so tough to get into! I mean" (forever saying I mean as if explaining the Ten Commandments) "he's so iron and monumental!"*

That thumbnail picture of a flighty coed stunned by the works of John

Milton would read more easily with dashes in place of the parenthetical observations. And this brings us headlong into the bosky mysteries of parentheses—but before we get there, a brisk word: you are now requested to turn yourself into a copy editor as well as a magazine editor. Each magazine has its own style and sometimes stylebook. So what you may regard as paragraphing and punctuation essential to your story may appear to a copy editor as wrong by the magazine's arbitrary standards. If this happens, and the story is published and you sit up with a shock when you detect the changes, don't fret, and don't write any sharp letters to the editor. Remember that you have given the story what you thought was best for it and that this was a contributing factor to its purchase. It may even have been improved by the assiduous copy editor. (If you don't think this, just hold your tongue anyway; and tell yourself that if the story is ever reprinted in an anthology, personal collection, or textbook, you will insist on going back to your original paragraphing and punctuation.) A copy editor's goal is, largely, consistency. And professional copy editors exist in thankless vacuums; they become dour at early ages and are reputed to have a high suicide rate. Rest secure in the knowledge that you've done your utmost as both bleak-eyed editor *and* copy editor—and that being a blend of both is as necessary to your life as a productive, selling writer as your original talent was. It's an extension of that talent, as well as a guard for it. Its lack has reduced uncountable thousands of potentially good storywriters to dilettantes fribbling on the fringes of the arts, consoling themselves by eating crumbs when they could have bitten deep into the hot bread of the gods.

Parentheses: Walk with Care

In this nontextbook and overall guide I have frequently resorted to parentheses in which to enclose sidelights which I think important to your deeper understanding. In a novel, and particularly in a short story, I wouldn't dream of scattering them as liberally as I have here. In *Tristram Shandy*, one of the most whimsically punctuated novels in the history of literature, Laurence Sterne—his punctuation is part of his odd and permanent allure—makes parenthetical notations multiply like guinea pigs; but what we are concerned with here is the commercial short story in our own century, an art form directed to those who read as they run. If you simply like parentheses for their own sake and enjoy their turtle-shell appearance on the page, try to restrict this enthusiasm to essays and letters to your friends. Keep your stories as free of them as you can, depending on the dash for internal thoughts inside the body of a sentence.

For parentheses, unlike dashes and commas, *do* draw attention to themselves—they are born boasters, born breakers of rhythm and reader attention, and if allowed to get the upper hand, are as prolific and unpleasant as wire coat hangers. They are especially obtrusive in fiction. Their appearance in longer fiction is more easily forgiven by the reader's eye and ear because the sweep of large scenes swallows them up—and they may even be regarded as necessary to contain whole pages of action and information, as in Faulkner, whose *Absalom, Absalom* might not exist if the parenthesis had never been invented. But in the best short stories—Faulkner's briefer ones included—they are used sparingly, and then only at moments when an equivalent of the actor's aside to the audience is really called for. Here is one of those moments, from Henry James's "The Beast in the Jungle," which I submit that, given the Jamesian prolix style and tendency to squeeze the most from any delicate emotion, is inescapable and inevitable in its context:

The escape would have been to love her; then, then he would have lived. She had lived—who could say now with what passion?—since she had loved him for himself; whereas he had never thought of her (ah, how it hugely glared at him!) but in the chill of his egotism and the light of her use.

But in the contemporary commercial story there are few chances for anybody to have an abstract motive hugely glare at him, in parentheses or outside them.

Unless parentheses feel, sound, and look inevitable, don't use them in a short story. The only exception to this rough rule of thumb might occur in a story written in letters, where the fictional letter writer's character was underlined by his or her parenthetical interjections. But the story-in-letters is a rare form, challenging to the writer and slightly forbidding to the reader; chances are rare that you'll tackle it in your first two dozen stories. Before leaving this spotlight on parentheses, let's take one more example from a short story, James Gould Cozzens's "My Love to Marcia," where, as in the Henry James sentence, their use seems fully justified; this is in part because the passage is closely related to the work of Henry James and presents an unusual narrative problem in which dashes would be out of place:

> *Since she had nothing to reproach herself with, Marcia would long ago have forgotten; but Curtis might reflect, so uselessly late, how much better it would have been if, instead of insulting her with all those disgraceful lies, he had said: "I want to marry you, but not enough. As it is, I have no money, but I can stay at the club. If I made any change, I would have to give up (because I would not be able to live suitably to entertain them, nor dress my wife properly to present them to her) acquaintances who will be important to me in my plan for becoming, sooner than Mr. Fitzmorris or any of them expect, a vice president of the Premier Union Bank and Trust Company. I cannot tell you how dearly I love you, yet, after all, I seem to love myself a little better."*

There, for once—as in the James excerpt—the parentheses don't show off or draw extra reader attention. You will notice that both passages are extremely close-knit, illustrating states of mind in which characters are talking to themselves and presenting modes of conduct impossible to clarify without vital second and third thoughts. And it is arguable that even here the parentheses could have been skipped with some profit to the reader, creating a more forcible, clean-cut look on the page.

Parentheses are treacherous diplomats which have to be watched closely at all times to keep them from spoiling the precious détente between writer and reader. Let them into your stories only when they promise to enhance rather than to intrude. I would guess that this will happen once or twice in every hundred stories.

Dots: The Dying Fall

Dots are lapses in time…indications of unseen action, which is nevertheless *felt* by the writer and the reader; and when they are used at the ends of sentences, such as this one, they represent a statement left hanging…a music sensed but not wholly heard…a dying fall….

They are, in general, more agreeable to the reader than parentheses—perhaps because they're open-ended and unclaustrophobic. But it's easy to overindulge them, simply because they seem to trail without effort across the page and because they can be substituted for what slow, intense, careful thought on the part of the writer could have brought about in words. Too many dots seem to fill a story with the smell of cheap incense. Also, they make a story sag—as though its spine had fallen out and been replaced with bits of knotted string. English (or more important, American, the language in which we are doomed, fated, and privileged to write) is enormously flexible, packed with silk, steel, and gold; it never forgives a languid lover. No matter what a story may say about the virtues of being alive in every muscle, if it is hung together with dots it turns into a faded valentine.

Yet dots, in the right places, can serve as ideal punctuation for indicating a change of scene, an alteration of mood. This is from a Fitzgerald story, "The Intimate Strangers":

> "Abby's down at the beach with the others," she said. "Oh, is she? Look, do you know this...?"
> ...Twenty minutes later, she jumped up suddenly.
> "Heavens! I'm supposed to be feeding my son—the poor little— see you on a wave!"
> She tore for the nursery. Margot greeted her tranquilly at the door.
> "You needn't have hurried, Madame. I gave him his bottle and he took it like a glutton. The doctor said it did not matter, today or tomorrow."
> "Oh."
> But it did matter. Sara knelt beside the crib.
> "Goodbye a little bit," she whispered. "Goodbye a little bit, small son. We shall meet."
> Her breast felt heavy with more than milk.
> ...I can feed him tonight, she thought.

Without those particular dots the stretch of time between Sara's volatile and impulsive trip to the beach, followed by her uneasy self-assurance about feeding her son later, would not hit so hard, be so immediately poignant. The conflicting moods—ebullience and regret—are telescoped by the dots; they have allowed much communication in modest space. In a rather wonderful way they are not mere surrogate emotion, but the emotion itself. And this is where the dot becomes a diplomat with a deft touch in the short story, a brief but important link between you and your reader. Applied with caution, *felt* as it is utilized, the dot represents your implicit trust in the good reader's imagination—a quick little poem sketched in the air to bring you closer together.

Exclamation Marks: The Bristlers

Where the dot...or three dots...can be gently and sometimes miraculously effective, the exclamation mark is a braggart and a bristler. Used *as* precisely what it is, a mark denoting a louder and surprised tone of voice in dialogue, a contrast to preceding and following talk, it is safe enough. Used with a free and careless hand, it is as ridiculous as a grizzled Shakespearean actor ranting at the top of his lungs: Hamlet conceived as Falstaff. It can become overbearing—and pretty unbearable—very quickly. Many otherwise worthy and possibly reclaimable first stories are sprinkled with exclamation points to the exclusion of common courtesy, as though their writers were dealing with the deaf. Victorian side-whiskers are suggested by this tone:

> *Andrew Montmorency and the Masked Wolf are one and the same man!*

The exclamation mark, when splashed around overabundantly, can be catsup poured on good food, drowning out all flavor and subtlety in a plebeian flood. It can also be neatly, forcibly, and rightly used, sometimes as an urgent call to attention, as in the opening line of Eudora Welty's "Powerhouse," which sets the stage for a great, powerful, and tragic jazz musician with:

> *Powerhouse is playing!*

And it can become loudly tumescent, much funnier than it means to be, in purple passages such as this:

> *The first time I met Juan, a torrid afternoon in Cannes, he—literally!—swept me off my feet, scooping me up from the sizzling sand, his long eyelashes coming closer! closer! till I went blind under his kisses!*

Certain readers, who don't like being sandbagged, will have gone blind themselves at that point. For the exclamation point, although it may indicate a surplus of vitality in the storyteller, is not by itself vital at all. It is the most contumacious of your ambassadors of punctuation, the most inclined to take over and detract from the real balance and message of the story it is allowed to dominate. It is a diplomat designed for a flash of emphasis alone. In a good story most of this emphasis vibrates in the well-aimed sentences themselves. When the people you are writing about raise their voices in gladness, grief, alarm, warning, and exultation, or you need to lift your own writing voice to express the same qualities in narrative, you will sometimes need the simple strength of this unruly mark. But not often—and its use is, finally, a matter of your taste, your understanding.

Chapter 19

Answers to Potential Revision-Rebellion

*A*t this point I'm going to answer some questions which have very likely surged up in you during the previous discussions of aesthetic matters in your second draft. First: Do you have to go through this line-by-line rereading every time? The answer is that you do, or should—but also that it will become second nature as you go on writing other stories. If the cosmetic issues involved here seem to you tiny, insignificant, not worth your closely focused attention, and indeed, chores that pull you away from the noble wild spirit out of which you write, I strongly sympathize; yet I know that if you intend to be a professional storyteller, your noble wild prose is likely to wilt under an editor's stare unless you have cared enough for it to become a decent editor yourself.

And, strangely, the more attention you pay to your second draft, the better the first draft of your next story will be—you will find yourself moving into the job of revision with increasing skill and assurance. You will be sustained during the desk hours by an eagerness to reach the finished product—and you'll find that those carefully rationed hours (not too many of them at a time) somehow, mysteriously, pay off when you've finished and mailed off the story and have sat down to write the next. It's as if a residue of confidence has built up in you and that what you've learned by revision moves into pure creation. Why this should be I do not know. It may well be that Robert Graves's wondrous figure of the White Goddess, the muse of all creators, smiles only on those who care enough to become alert craftsmen—and that never in the history of the short story has she considered *craftsmanship* a dirty word.

Another logical question: Is all this strict attention to surface story-detail done only for the purpose of making your story sell? The answer is that this is the primary surface purpose—that the good laborer is worth whatever he or she can command in the market and that the blood, fire, and afterthoughts that go into a sound commercial story deserve the highest pay that market can yield. But there's another purpose behind this: While you work at revision, you are becoming more and more firmly acquainted with your genuine writing self—peeling off layers of self-delusion, getting down to the bright core of who you are, what you have to say that no other writer could.

The Fine Italian Hand of Italics

Italics are the more suave, smoothly mannered relatives of exclamation marks. They don't shout aloud, but they attract the eye immediately; their ambassadorial duty is to heighten the reader's attention and, ideally, to raise the pulse a few beats. When used to emphasize a single word, they tilt that word a shade to the right, and their typeface serves as a swift accent similar to the human voice when it stresses a word in conversation. The reader hears it sounding:

> *He knew her methods of teaching the short story were unusual. How unusual he didn't find out until the afternoon when she made a tent of his Hemingway imitations and set them on fire.*

Sometimes, usually in a story of the action-mystery or horror variety, one whose author doesn't feel is capable of putting across its large moments without typographical assistance, italics serve to strengthen a line of special importance to writer and reader, as a symphony conductor calls for *fortissimo:*

> *As Hilary stared at the sarcophagus, the full meaning of what the tiny man with strange feet had told her back in Athens came home at last:* Ah, Madam, you will never know the genius of your husband until too late.

In dialogue italics are often stand-ins for vocal emphasis, as in duplicating the gushiness of a nonstop talker relaying nuggets of gossip:

> "*You know how* Sylvia *walks, especially in a new girdle. Well, this* man came out of the Bull-Horn Bar—little bitty man, looked like he'd been in there since before the Alamo—and says, 'Ma'am, we're hiring nude dancers.' "

There is a common typographical convention of presenting a character's thoughts, as opposed to spoken words, in italics. Frankly, this convention seems to work more efficiently and with less reader distraction in novels; in the story, where a character's thoughts are rendered on fewer pages, the italicized portions are likely to jump at the reader with so much frequency they bother the eye. This writer prefers straight type for giving the reader the inside working of a mind; it preserves the flow of narrative without breaking it up, and the reader can make the lightning transition from action, or description, to thought, with ease. There are exceptions here—your story may move with a steady, if not leisurely, pace which accommodates a few italicized thoughts more easily than a story full of high nervous tension and quick movement. This, from my "Sweet Chariot," is a passage that deals with the mountain man, Journey, as he stands surveying the prospect below him:

Staring down, he saw the scene as it had forever been, this time of morning, this season of the year. There was the house. Linda had gone in now. There was the whacking log with chips surrounding it. There was the barn behind. Have to paint it someday, *Journey mused;* else it'll fall down of its own accord and ruin them cows some night.

That thought could have been spoken inside Journey's speculative brain without being underlined. But marking it for italics, giving it gentle emphasis, seemed to make it fit his mood more aptly. On the other hand, there are countless stories of mine with a different rhythm than that of "Sweet Chariot," in which I would avoid the use of italics for thought-transference vehicles, as I would avoid chicken pox. Once more, the standard of comfort applies—what feels absolutely right to you as you look at it, and as it sounds inside you, is going to be right for your story—and your judgment about these matters becomes steadily more accurate as you work.

Genuinely onomatopoetic words call for italics when such words might otherwise seem out of place in a sentence. This is an example from a barbershop scene in my story "The Kindred Heart":

Al's father was tucking the dollar bill under the roller in the dollar-compartment of the register, and Al was remembering—with

*a quick flick of wonder at how little things meant so much to a
small boy—when he had admired the working of the cash register, the bell-sound of it and the quick juicy* chuck *of the drawer
closing....*

Left barren of italics, the word *chuck* would have lacked the solid noise I
wanted to make the reader hear, and would instead possibly, have been
confused with a woodchuck, or a chuck under the chin.

As for the long italicized block of words found in many novels and
used to convey feverish inward speculation or the headlong rush of narrative action, this should, nearly always, remain a property of the novel,
a patent that is not covered by the storywriter's license to operate. For
one thing it takes up a lot of precious wordspace—and for another the
necessary transition back to upright type gives the reader a jolt. By its
nature a single italicized word is like a tympanist's mallet striking his
great drum's stretched skin or the isolated accent of a jazz snare-drum-
mer executing a rimshot. Heaped upon one another, italics can deterio-
rate into formless noise.

Sometimes, as a result of improvising at top speed in the middle of
first drafts, along with the availability of the underline key on their
typewriters, rapidly hyperventilating writers indulge in italics for no
other reason than that they feel they are "expressing" themselves. (They
sometimes do the same thing with dots, producing a lamentable sight
like this: ....)
Such wistful and fervent exercises have nothing to do with prose or the
making of short stories; when encountered, they should be excised like
the tumors they are.

The same goes for boldface type when it is used merely as a lazy onomatopoetic substitute or in place of narrative and dialogue words which
could imply strength without shouting. **BANG—CRACK—"SHUT
UP"** and innumberable variants are the equivalent of standing on, or
putting a lampshade on, one's head to get attention at a party. The use of
caps is justified when your story needs a tangible reference point which
is brought closer to the reader's eye by spelling it out—a signboard, a let-
terhead, a headline, a billboard, the identifying window-lettering of a
place of business, as in this paragraph from this writer's "Aunt Myra":

It was a pleasure to see him hold up a piece of meat by the small end, glistening red and smacking full of red juice, and to see the life ripple over his own face in the hot sun shaking through the window and painting the letters BUTCHER SHOP in a backward arc on the counter.

That is about the extent of the efficacy of boldface type in the short story, and if you look at it a moment longer you will see that italics *could* have been used in place of caps, with no real loss to the reader. I chose caps for their stronger graphic effect, but italics would have been a little more civilized.

The Conversational Semicolon

Look at the way semicolons are used in this excerpt from Joseph Conrad's stirring and bewitchingly evocative short story, "Youth":

I remember my youth and the feeling that will never come back any more—the feeling that I could last forever, outlast the sea, the earth, and all men; the deceitful feeling that lures us on to joys, to perils, to love, to vain effort—to death; the triumphant conviction of strength, the heat in the life of a handful of dust, the glow in the heart that with every year growssg"Youth":

I remember my youth and the feeling that will never come back any more—the feeling that I could last forever, outlast the sea, the earth, and all men; the deceitful feeling that lures us on to joys, to perils, to love, to vain effort—to death; the triumphant conviction of strength, the heat in the life of a handful of dust, the glow in the heart that with every year grows dim, grows cold, grows small, and expires—and expires too soon, too soon—before life itself.

In the first semicolon there is a meditative pause implied; the voice of the narrator rests for half a second before continuing his list of youth's merits and betrayals, and in the second semicolon the whole sentence comes to a grave if temporary stop. The first semicolon prepares the listening ground for the second, and the second is deeper, a beat longer, serving as the center of the sentence after that dark word *death*. Both are used with the sort of knowing artifice that is not natural, but creates what we call naturalism. Both are essential to the complete tone of the sentence.

To this writer the semicolon is an essential part of any short story's voice; it is a conversational beat in the air, hardly calling for a breath, but so firm that nothing else will do. If you consult a grammar or a style book, you'll see it defined as "a mark of punctuation, indicating a greater degree of separation than the comma." That is a little like calling a horse a graminivorous quadruped. Semicolons work as hard as horses and are as dependably faithful; without them many a story would lose its built-in rhythm and stature. If you don't like to use them (as in the case of the dash), then avoid them and find some other method for communicating to a reader the exact shading you want. (Some stylebooks warn against splitting infinitives, too; but a well-split infinitive, produced for a purpose like honest cordwood, is much more effective than any number of sapless "correct" sentences.)

The semicolon is a short story diplomat which can be kind to the eye as well as to the ear. It relieves the simple declarative sentence from its aspect of baldness and primerlike statement, strengthening words without bending them out of shape. In various books of instruction on how to write fiction, you have read—probably more than once—injunctions to vary the length of your sentences. This is exactly what the semicolon does; but it performs its work *inside* the longer sentence, bringing variety and grace and eloquence to what might otherwise be only a series of blurted gestures. It is possible to write gracefully and forcibly without it. It is just as possible to learn, while self-editing, where this eminently useful mark can do more than merely precede *and* or *but* when introducing a fresh subject and how it can illuminate your story.

The Cool, Efficient Colon

When I was a child, I had trouble with elementary arithmetic. This came about, not because God did not want me to be a mathematician, which was apparent from the first, but because despairing teachers could not break me of the habit of visualizing numbers as people. 2, for instance, was a pale small fellow with a retiring nature, and 9 was blustery, jolly, and given to wearing a bulbous hat at a cavalier angle. There was a world's difference between 3 and 7. 4 was feminine, a tricky girl, and 5 was masculine and given to snapping his bubble gum. This unrecommended method of free association caused havoc when it came to seeing numerals as mere useful methods of discovering how many bales of hay Farmer Brown had left if he started with twenty and sold fourteen and a half and gave his son a fourth of the remainder.

The need to personify persists. I see the punctuational colon as a brusque story ambassador, more commanding than his confederates, buttoned to the chin in a bellhop uniform as he briskly points to what is ahead: "Straight down the hall, governor, first door on your right." His use is limited; when prefacing dialogue, in place of the usual comma, the effect of a colon is abrupt and even sharp:

> *With a shake of his fox-red head, Balrondin boomed: "We can't follow such a path! Who knows where it leads?"*

And when colons pepper a page, they distract the eye from the sense of what is being said. But when used in quick, clipped dialogue—the kind that runs along on platform shoes—they serve to underline haste and urgency:

> *Mack said: "Look. In the tree."*
> *Suemae's voice sounded muffled by his mackinaw shoulder: "Bear?"*
> *"God I wish it was." He was whispering now: "Ever see a bear with a face like Richard Nixon?"*

When used inside a sentence, colons break it into hurrying pieces, as if time were stuttering by on stubby wings:

> *There were fourteen of us in the hold of the Coronado: fourteen: I wished we'd been fifty: there in the salt-smelling grimy North Atlantic dusk we could have used half the wartime Navy.*

As a loose but useful rule of thumb, whenever the colon begins to intrude, to look tricky and extraneous, to be leaned on, go to some other form of punctuation—or rewrite to get rid of it. And of course this same powerful intuitive recognition of what is right for your story is your underlying guide for all self-editing; when you're really inside the job of story revision, the best style manual ever compiled can't tell you much about your own work. Always ask yourself *why*—why this dash, these three dots, this comma, will or will not improve what you first envisioned.

You're the only first reader-editor your story will ever have. And it becomes more thoroughly your *own* story with every step you take to make it more attractive to the final reader.

On Bird Tracks and Mouse Marks

As you revise, it doesn't matter a great deal what mechanical means you're using. The main thing is to be sure that you can decipher the result when it comes time to transfer your second draft to fresh paper. If you write in longhand, depending on the facility—and sometimes the code-breaking ability—of a professional typist to transcribe your handwriting, just be sure the rapport between you and the typist is strong. If you compose on a typewriter, be equally certain that whatever interlining you've done and whatever mouse marks you've made in the margins are legible to you when the revision is finished.

There's a short story, by Sherwood Anderson, which has always struck terror to this writer's vitals. In it a somewhat fumbling man, afflicted with that spiritual fog which impedes Anderson's people, writes what he is sure is the finest story he'll ever produce. But when he goes to read it over, the pages are blank. Anderson doesn't explain that the unhappy author's pen had run out of ink while he worked in a dim light or that his typewriter ribbon had been eaten by silverfish. Anderson, with characteristic bafflement and despair, gives no explanation at all. It is probably the frustrating story to end frustrating stories. It illustrates Anderson's profound recognition of the chasm between a short story's vision and its execution—but it's an even better reminder to the storymaker to make sure that his or her editing scribbles are clear enough to be understood later by their author.

The mastery of a word processor and exaltation over its operation can produce, in the author, a sort of false euphoria which, while it swells word processor and software sales, is a long remove from story quality. Such technological advancements improve speed and ease of production; they don't influence the core of talent, responsibility, and integrity in the writer. Neatness counts. But this writer has never met an editor who said, "The *story* wasn't awfully good; we bought it because it was written and edited on a word processor." Faulkner wrote first drafts in tiny, spidery longhand which he transferred to a hoary nonelectric machine, revising as he went. Whatever method works for you is *yours*, even if it involves burning symbols on birch bark. If you feel at home with yellow second sheets, with blue, beige, or Nile-green stationery, with pulpy gray school tablets, with 25 percent rag-content watermarked white, or with legal pads, keep them handy and within reaching distance at all times. Totems and lucky pieces which seem to speak to your psyche—such as Fitzgerald's little stop-sign-shaped announcement saying *Business is Good*—can be more important to your writing life than a roomful of computers. (In the cluttered, book-heavy room where I write there is a dried-out coconut bearing Ernest Hemingway's autograph. He is not nearly as important to me as Fitzgerald and half a dozen other storymaking people, but if I looked up and found somebody had made off with the sere coconut, I would feel diminished.)

As to the look of the final manuscript, there is a plethora of patiently devised, rule-setting volumes on this subject. All of them talk about title-positioning, correct margin widths, double-spacing, uniformity, etc., with the rectitude of a conclave of penguins. Follow the advice of one or the other.

But don't mistake this ultimate needful step for *writing*. It has to be done. But it's in the category of making sure a child's socks are pulled up before you send him off to greet his teacher. It has no relation to his internal magic.

Keep solidly aware of what your bird tracks and mouse-foot notations on your first-draft manuscript will mean to the last draft—what they signal to you as you move toward light and clarity. And if you believe word processors are the harbingers of a Brave New World of communication in the arts, rejoice in your conviction—but not to the extent that you confuse methodology with story value.

Quo Vadis?

In 1490 the printer Aldus set up a press in Venice. He printed in Greek some of the works of Aristophanes, Demosthenes, Plutarch, Aristotle, Thucydides, Herodotus, and the then nearly contemporary writing of Dante and Erasmus. Because he used Greek punctuation forms, he's responsible for most of the marks you're thinking about now.

Among the symbols he transposed from Latin to Greek was one that finally became today's question mark—a big comma over a dot. Its application to today's short stories would appear to be self-explanatory, but fairly often it's not. It calls for special decisions in particular stretches of narrative where questions may be implied without using the mark. Here is a stretch:

> *Yes, Tom thought, but what about the time she came out of the Blood, Sweat, and Shears Beauty Shop with her hair in patterns like blighted corn. And the time she showed up for a P.T.A. meeting in a silvery space suit, face shrouded by a Plexiglas helmet.*

The absence of question marks in Tom's thought gives the paragraph a more hushed, intimate quality than it would have if the marks were there. It's as if the reader supplies them in ghostly echoes. So both sentences hover between a note of query and a declarative statement. Omitting the question marks is a subtle compliment to the reader, who, the author assumes, understands that Tom is asking himself questions about a fascinatingly eccentric woman.

If this distinction about whether or not to use the printer Aldus's comma-and-dot mark doesn't bother you, forget it. But if you hear the difference between an outright question mark and its implied presence, stop and consider that the questions posed in your story may be stronger if you leave out whatever question marks you put in the first time. While you're mulling over this decision as it applies to your story (it isn't a minor decision; no short story decision is small), remember that any question asked by your story people—or asked directly by you in the course of the narrative—is an intrusion. In effect, it asks the reader for an answer. In the short story a heavy spate of questions is often an indication that the writer is fiddling in the dark, desperately suggesting possibilities and hoping that this is contributing to the plot. This is such an interrogative flood:

> *But what am I to do? thought Amanda; will Lord Massingale think it forward of me to ask him to the Hunt Ball, when we have scarcely been introduced? Will he, Heaven forfend, turn upon me his peculiar grimace, that elevation of the lip which ex-*

poses so charmingly, yet so chillingly, his flashing teeth? Will he nibble the knob of his ebony cane, hunch his stalwart shoulders with ennui and rejection? Will he cut me dead, leaving me with blushes mounting my cheek to match my scarlet shawl from India?

Such extended internal irresolution has its decorative side. But in a short story it can wear reader sympathy to the bare bone—so that the reader can hardly wait for Massingale to break his ebony cane over little Amanda's whirling head. Along with throwing out a good deal of the lacy period-piece frills, the writer could have resolved Amanda's plight in a handful of words:

Amanda thought, Shall I ask him to the Hunt Ball, or will he think me an upstart. On a wave of impulse she decided to risk it.

An abundance of questions labeled as questions can push a story out of shape. The question mark, as a diplomat increasing understanding, is at its best when it seems inevitable; when it is used to ask a genuine emotionally charged question of fate or circumstance. Here, in the elevated, questing voice of a story by Shelby Foote, "Pillar of Fire," it is used with art that makes it seem as natural as an eddy of deep water at the foot of a cataract:

Remembering the Indian days, the exodus, he applied what he remembered to the present, to himself. Was it all for nothing, the distances, the ambition, and the labor? He and his kind, the pioneers, the land-grabbing hungry rough-shod men who had had, like the flatboat river bullies before them, that curious combination of bravado and deadly earnestness, loving a fight for the sake of the fight itself and not the outcome—were they to disappear, having served their purpose, and leave no more trace than the Choctaws? If so, where was the dignity of man, to be thrown aside like this, a worn-out tool?

Those question marks *needed* to be there. They are not idly used; the depth of the questions demands them. The little mark bequeathed to us by the printer Aldus cannot be bypassed in such cases; it takes on true muscle and moving utility. Asking yourself what function this mark has in your story is your own self-to-self question; asking yourself if you can safely, perhaps to the betterment of the story, leave it out—or if it is breaking down the door to be included.

The High Comma

Aldus, a forward-looking man, brought us the apostrophe as well. The word is Greek, and in its aspect of a high comma placed before the last letter of a word, it merely signifies that an interim letter has been left out, for the purpose of taking up less room to say more, or to indicate an ellipse in human speech.

In creating dialogue the use of contractions, with apostrophes to mark the missing letters, would seem to be as automatic as blinking one's eyes. A mother cautioning her child not to dip the gerbil in the cold cream seldom says, "Do not do that again." As previously mentioned, we speak in shorthand—as much of it as we can get away with and still be comprehended. Yet beginning storytellers, or those who have been writing awhile but haven't exercised their ears sufficiently, often have their characters speak in full-blown formal sentences for pages at a time. This is acceptable, to a degree, when the characters are placed in antiquity or rooted in a Mandarin environment. (And even there, its air of straining after quaintness can, unless the author has a great ear for duplicating what will pass for cadences of a far-gone time, rub the reader's fur the wrong way.) This same formality of speech is frequently used to suggest the language of alien races, where, depending on how skillfully you handle it, they speak with the voice of authenticity or sound like strays from a cartoon strip. And the same deliberate archaisms often issue from the mouths of people (or creatures) who are the protagonists of fantasies.

(Actually, the closer a half-lizard, half-human from Betelgeuse sounds like a resident of earth, the more convincing this hybrid will be. It doesn't have to speak like a native of Brooklyn. All it has to do is to express itself in a decent approximation of English-American, a language which, presumably, the reader will realize it is using as a convenience.)

But when contemporary story characters are steered around the warm gift of contractions and made to talk as if they had worn boiled shirts from birth, they simply fade away and vanish in midcareer. A few apostrophes here and there might have redeemed them. Their authors are infected with the disease of "nice" English—a rhetorical hangover from the last century, when Chautaqua tents reverberated to the rolling periods of silver-tongued speakers and the speeches of William Jennings Bryan made corn grow taller. (Louisa May Alcott, fine narrator that she was, fell into this public trap when she condemned *Huckleberry Finn* as "unfit for the youth of America"—so did Mark Twain's daughter when she said *The Prince and the Pauper* was a "nicer" book.)

If dialogue of stiff-collar caliber is causing your story people to strangle and leaching them of their humanity, try, once more, reading what they say aloud—then use apostrophes to help bring them back to reality. And use the same apostrophized contractions in narrative whenever it feels, sounds, smells, and looks right. Aldus's hardworking diplomat can heat up your narrative voice with wonderful effect on the well-cocked ear. Notice, in this Third Person passage, how the contractions caress and animate the scene and how giving the deleted letters would, in each case, cast a skin of slight remoteness over what is said:

> *She didn't want to take the chance of waking him. So she slipped the note under his pillow, thinking, He'll see it first thing in the morning when he throws the pillow on the floor. Then she walked to the door, wondering why her feet felt nailed to the doorsill, her hand felt frozen to the knob. She wasn't thinking at all by the time she'd reached the hall.*

Contractions applied in the narrative voice are useful for all stories, no matter what environment, year, and mood the stories evoke. In dialogue, in the genuinely felt story of long ago, contractions can be false notes. Here, from my novella, *Night Watch* the speaking tone of the narrator, Voldi, sums up a pre-Christian weight of the slow-speaking past. So there are no apostrophes in his speech, for *how* he talks is as important as what it means.

> *I said, "It has come to me, old man. The knowledge that I would rather die in the attempt than live as I have for a year gone on living. Breath without freedom is dead in the lungs. It stinks in the throat."*

In the usual story, contractions will serve you well and easily, as essential to your story arsenal of diplomats as your own ears, eyes, and your judgment.

Chapter 20

Hyphens—Yes or No?

*S*tyle manuals are reasonably consistent about hyphens. But how a word looks in relation to the others in your story shouldn't always be settled by referring to style-manual rules. An unhyphenated word has a different color, a different shape from a word separated from another by this stumpy little mark. "He dog paddled to the end of the pond" isn't quite the same as "He dog-paddled to the end of the pond," and saying "He dogpaddled to the end of the pond" puts the whole sentence in a different light. In this last instance, two words have been wedded to form a single portmanteau word, one which, in this case, gives an easy effect to the action and creates a strong verb. There's nothing in the least wrong with it *so long as the rest of the story accepts it.*

But to use a portmanteau word in one part of a story, then split the same word in two in another, with a hyphen or without it, is to go out of key—and although not all readers will notice this happening, there are enough fastidious, picky ones to make the slight mistake a hazard. And to hyphenate words on one page and leave normal single space between the same words on another can create the same feeling of reader uneasiness. Also, the elimination of space between too many words can lead to a razzle dazzle (or razzle-dazzle or razzledazzle) effect that makes some readers blink like owls under a searchlight. It is like a coat of glossy lacquer covering a painting, bringing out details in hard glare which detracts from the overall impact and meaning. Here is a sentence which might be valid in an impressionistic essay, but which turns out to be an intruder in a short story:

> *Like birdsong and prayercandles he flashed to the oakgleaming lectern, throatclearing as silence gripped the sweatbeaded congregation.*

This is not writing. It is juggling. It pulls the reader from the story to the author. It asks readers to applaud skill, not to listen to a good story. The habit of confusing pyrotechnics with storytelling, of avoiding the need to make decisions about hyphenating or not hyphenating by inventing portmanteau words galore, is one that sometimes grips beginning writers like a case of poison ivy. The remedy is to remember that, as a maker of stories, you're not creating vignettes of New Journalism—not competing with television, on its own grounds, by turning somersaults. You're writing prose. The profession is older than most, and it has never really been subservient to fashion. In it you have these decisions to make; in this instance, decisions over hyphenating. Each time you have decided, for or against, makes the next decision more accurate and more sure as it applies to your story.

Finally, "solving" the problem by hyphenating at every possible point is just another evasion. You are working with a story which is like no other in the world. To treat it as a piece of standardized merchandise is to sap its unique commercial value as well as demeaning it. Throughout these concentrated bouts of revision (with plenty of rest between them) you have learned to ask *what the story wants*. Or, even more accurately, to *let it tell you what it wants*. Nobody has yet published an individual style manual with your name on it which will answer these questions.

A Sidelight on Spelling

Many professional writers, expert and gifted visualizers, storytellers with a flair for getting and holding the attention of readers, spell so badly that a section of their brains seems to have been left out at birth. But their second drafts, the ones seen by editors, are correctly spelled—and their writing-room dictionaries are usually well thumbed, not merely for accurate definitions, but for the right spelling of any word they're a little unsure about.

Why, then—this is what is known as a rhetorical question, which, I feel, is needed at this point—do hundreds of stories which their writers believed in enough to pour blood into land on editorial desks with the spelling of even the simplest words altered to something so rich and strange they stick in the eye like cinders? Why does miserable second-draft spelling so often cause otherwise decent stories to be rejected like angels in the clothing of cockroaches?

Part of the reason is, I know, sheer haste—the impatient urge to get the story out *now*, blindly trusting that whatever misspellings the author feels may be there will be overlooked by a discerning editor. But this faith in editorial ability to see the substance of a story and overlook the surface is pretty much balderdash—certain editors *are* tremendously gifted at spotting fresh talent fast, but they are also human, and what they see, first of all, is that the writer of a badly spelled story doesn't have sufficient respect for his or her trade to spend a few minutes with *Webster's International* or a similar authority; and second, that they are dealing with an *amateur attitude* which doesn't care enough about the putative mass reader to clean up a product before shipping it out.

One of the best writers of stories I know writes her first drafts with a positive genius for spelling error. A letter from her is an adventure in deciphering scrambled words. She could not enter a spelling bee of fourth-graders without making her mother blush. And her second drafts are models of accurate spelling—so that if diamonds were awarded for this quiet virtue, she would by now have at least the equivalent of the Koh-i-noor. But there aren't any prizes given for good spelling in the adult world of the storymaker. There are only sorry little form-letter rejection slips meted out for its absence.

Nor do you have to be a collector, a polisher and cherisher of words, to honor yourself and your story enough to spell them straightly in your second draft. You do have to be possessed by a fierce and personal craftsman's pride—one of the indispensable qualities that made you want to make marketable short stories in the first place.

Sidelights on the Sidelight

Sometimes the secondary spelling of a word—the alternate following the preferred usage which will be listed first in whatever dictionary you consult—will feel better and look better in your story than the first word does. The way a word is spelled contributes subtly to its strength—in both preferred spelling and alternate but acceptable spelling, the meaning will be the same; but the shape will change

For instance, the Anglicized word *armour* is not quite identical to the Americanized *armor. Armour* has, somehow, a more mail-clad ring and depth—*armor* is a little lighter, less positive. In the same way, the word *glamour* doesn't possess quite the same overtone and essence when it is spelled *glamor*. It's quite possible that these distinctions make no difference at all to you—but if they do, and in going over your story to see that its spelling is right, you notice that the alternate spelling fits more comfortably, by all means use the spelling that you and the story prefer. Chances are that if the story is bought and published, your choice of spelling will be retained. No man wrote more hauntingly of the American past and present than Stephen Vincent Benét, but the title of one of his finest stories is "Glamour,"—and I am sure he chose that spelling for its evocative glimmer and richness.

To pursue the same thought for a second, if I refer in a story to a pair of *gray* eyes, I am suggesting that such eyes are softer and milder than *grey* eyes would be. The *a* in *gray* gives the word a luminous effect, like candleshine against fog, while the *e* in *grey* sharpens the word to give a hint of steel. Again, if you think these distinctions are trivial, ignore them—but if you believe they can make a difference to your story, consider them as choices to be made for the story's betterment.

As I have pointed out, many books on "How to Write Short Stories" underline, almost in the nature of a command, the need to reject Romance words in favor of the Anglo-Saxon. Like the favorite injunction to "Write What You Know," this is all very sound as far as it goes—but it leaves out a whole field of possiblilites and effects which the judicious use of Romance words, and often their European spelling, can bring to your story. In the public speeches, as well as in the letters and the (sometimes astonishingly moving) private poems of Abraham Lincoln, there are Romance words mixed with the blunt forward-going Saxon, words which vary the rhythm and enter the eye and ear to take hold forever. Uneducated (by simplistic standards), Lincoln understood at an early age what the good commercial storywriter discovers—that to reach as many people as possible, in the quickest possible way, *everything* must be used and condensed to put across a single emotional effect. This takes in spelling, the look of the word in print as well as its resonance in the ear. The Gettysburg Address is still around. Part of the impact of Lincoln's famous speech is produced by the cadence of solid Latinate words rolling and repeating like the sound of great bells: *continent, conceive, dedicate, devotion, consecrate, detract, people.* They and the speech endure. But, not strangely, no one remembers the name of the *Chicago Times* journalist who wrote this about it:

*We did not conceive it possible that even Mr. Lincoln would
produce a paper so slipshod, so loose-joined, so puerile, not alone
in literary construction, but in its ideas, its sentiments, its grasp.
He has outdone himself. He has literally come out of the little
end of his own horn. By the side of it, mediocrity is superb.*

Perhaps the unknown journalist didn't like Romance words, intuitive
truth, or great utterance in short form.

She Sells Seashells

Most beginning writers indulge, to an extent, in alliteration for its own
sake. The sound of words tripping along like a family of closely related
elves linked by their first letters charms your ear in nursery and kinder-
garten. You wouldn't remember Simple Simon half so well as you do if
his first name had been Albert. Peter Piper and those pickled peppers
would be forgotten if he'd been Joey, and the peppers marinated. Story
purists who cast a cold eye on alliteration are usually those whose ears
have atrophied—in the Gettysburg Address just referred to they would
change "brought forth upon this continent a new nation" to "brought
forth upon this continent a new republic." Clanking, oversibilant, or obviously and glaring alliteration is the result of the storywriter's inability
to separate method from content; to draw the line between the way of
saying and what is said. Like an abundance of portmanteau words, it
turns into juggling. When it is done unconsciously or "for it's own
sake," in the method of a pianist who vamps because he has forgotten
the melody, it is bound to be bad. When it is used with full consciousness of its effect and its place in your story, subordinate to and serving
the story, it is an admirable friend.

G.K. Chesterton's short stories—especially those in his *Father Brown*
collections and the collection called *The Poet and the Lunatics*—are alliterative amazements. Yet his dazzling use of alliteration contributes to
the full effect of every story and never merely shines for its own solo value. It becomes considerably more than a mannerism, carrying the eye,
the ear, and the spirit on an adventurous breeze.

These are three successful alliterative flights from one of Chesterton's most celebrated Father Brown stories, "The Blue Cross":

*Between the silver ribbon of morning and the green glittering rib-
bon of sea, the boat touched Harwich and let loose a swarm of
folk like flies.*

*He had a face as round and dull as a Norfolk dumpling; he had
eyes as empty as the North Sea; he had several brown paper parcels, which he was quite incapable of collecting.*

*Among the black and breaking groups in that distance was one
especially black which did not break—a group of two figures
clerically clad.*

If alliteration comes to you simply and well, use it with awareness of
what you're doing. Don't depend on it to expand an image to the point
that it is blown out of proportion. Don't put it where it stands out from
the rest of your storytelling words just because it tickles your sense of
wordplay. As you rewrite, look on it with fondness where it emphasizes
the mood of a sentence. But strike it out if it seems to take your editor-
reader mind off the movement of the story. Alliteration which features a
string of sibilants in a row (like snakes conversing at a tea party) is the
most distracting kind. In a lyric poem like James Joyce's "On the Beach
at Fontana" it is effective because it duplicates, to a marvelous degree,
the sound of water sliding on sand and returning:

Wind whines and whines the shingle;
The crazy pier-stakes groan;
A senile sea numbers each single
Slime-covered stone.

But even if your story is describing a hurricane, that many sibilants
should make the reader-editor in you reflect that story prose is not verse,
or a gallery of sideshows. (And, perhaps, that the ocean is very old, but
not necessarily senile.)

Gertrude Stein's *rose is a rose is a rose* sticks in the mind because of its
(somewhat nauseating) circular motion, with all those *r*'s snoring away
in concert. The same effect in a short story would be likely to make
readers wonder if the printer had been drinking more than usual. Alliteration cannot be casually inserted to dress up a story; it is there to make it

flow more freely, and knowing why you're using it, and how good you are at it, is as important to the process of revision as knowing why you choose a comma instead of a semicolon, a modest period instead of an exclamation mark.

If you find while rewriting that you have *unconsciously* filled your story with alliteration, mistrust all of it. Examine each example with a frosty eye before you let it stand. But if you remember saying to yourself while you were forging out that first draft, "This is alliterative, and it feels right," then it has a decent chance of being right.

By all means don't hurl it out of your story because you've read somebody's crusty and opinionated essay on why it has no place in the art of writing prose. It has—and if it brings your story closer to the reader, it is always justified.

Quirks and Crochets

The marketable short story has never been a model of standardization. Story prose that reads as if it has been stamped out by government directives (written by machines for machines) is as yet—like some variant of Smell-O-Vision—waiting to be perfected. I want to emphasize this now, because as you keep on, in carefully spaced bouts of work, aiming at your second draft, you'll find that a few quirks and crochets of your own character have slid into the first draft from time to time.

Of course the whole story represents a special facet of your view of the world and the people in it. But the quirks, crochets, and mannerisms I'm talking about will have entered the prose. Not as tricks—simply as methods of saying something, methods which appeal to you more than others. Like Chesterton's penchant for alliteration, these can turn out to be very valuable. They can be represented by what isn't there, as much as they can by what is actually on the page. For instance, for some deep-seated abstruse reason of my own, I don't like the word *thus* in one of my own stories or novels. (I don't mind encountering it in the work of other writers.) So instead of *thus* I use *so*. And every writer has these preferences—both for omission and commission. They help build his or her style; to worry about them, and particularly to try to get rid of them and substitute something more "like" other people's prose, is often a sad mistake—robbing the story of an essence of individuality. It is like exchanging the hand-carved for the manufactured—and all good merchandisable stories *are* hand-carved; they enter the world with the mark of the craftsman's knife on them.

Rewriting is as much—sometimes more—a process of self-discovery as the original first-time-around writing was. So keep telling yourself as you work along that what may seem a little odd or different in your first draft may also be part of your hallmark—and think awhile before you discard it for a phrase or a sentence that lacks distinction and quiddity.

Quirks and crochets aren't by any means always out of place. They're the sparks thrown off by seeing life as nobody else does.

A Word About Nooses

In my job as a guide behind the scene of the short story, I have already said that this is no grammar—and I've mentioned that for the able story-writer the split infinitive is no sin. (Sometimes infinitives beg to be torn apart for the music that can some out of their bodies.) But I do want to underline one grammatical *faux pas* which appears to me easy to dodge, and which I seem to find growing like graveyard lichen in a surprising number of stories—both published and unpublished.

It's the dangling participle—a glib and silky little rope which can strangle a sentence to death in record time. It's wiliness lies in the fact that, at first glance, it seems to make sense; to be almost plausible. Here is a good one:

Getting up in the cool soft dawn, the alarm clock said eight.

If you are lucky, the editor-reader's eye may skim over that without question. (But if you are even luckier, the same eye will catch it before it is allowed to stand.) If common sense and a critical spirit take over, you will find yourself wondering why the apparent subject of the sentence, the alarm clock, got up—was it bored with simply lying around, ticking its head off? Speculation of this nature can be fascinating, furnishing more amusement than the author intended. But it does stop the story as effectively as a curtain dropped between the reader and the page.

Here is another little exercise in skillful strangulation:

Curling around my neck, I felt her fingers brush the nape with a light electric shock.

At first look this seems to be part of the confessions of a contortionist—one who could certainly earn a good living by curling around his own neck in public. Without much travail, and with the addition of a few words identifying the subject in the first sentence, and a simple rearrangment of the placement of the subject in the second, the clock could be made to stop rising, and the contortionist would turn back into a story narrator.

The participial clause is a fine invention, as old as all storytelling, giving life and lilt and verbal movement to sentences and relief from flat declarative recital. But when its subject is bypassed or choked off, it leaves a hole in the air—a hole into which the reader pokes a questing finger to find just what *is* going on.

So if you find any of these unsightly nooses dangling through your story, cut them away. Your story needs all the breath it can get. Plain intuition will usually keep you from committing such rope tricks. But it's a sound idea to watch for them in everything you read—so that when they show up (which they will do, I am sorry to say, with some frequency), you will recognize them, nod quietly, and resolve to write better than the cowboy or cowgirl who unwittingly hung them there.

The Needful Artificiality of Style

During your hungry and extensive reading, you may have noticed that in published interviews many writers seem to communicate whatever floats into their heads—especially if it has a mystic, fuzzy ring. After years of casual analysis, I have decided that this is done to raise a protective wall against intrusion; also, it makes a nice smoke screen between the writer and the sort of interviewer who says, "I haven't really read your work, but we want to make this an *intimate* chat, don't we?" The way to know a writer you admire is to read everything he or she has published and then to read it again.

Among the "intimacies" disclosed in a great many of the chatty interviews is this one: "Style? I never think about style. I couldn't work if I did. All my stories come to me naturally—as easily as walking."

I find this guileless, baby blue stare of an answer vastly deficient in both honesty and iron content. For no writer worth half an ounce of coarse salt fails to think about style during all working and most nonworking minutes.

As I have said before, a short story *is* an unnatural act. You can be the best oral storyteller in your county, keeping spellbound children from their video games and other computerized toys, and old men from political argument. But until you make the leap out of your own skin and into whatever persona your writing self calls for—and until you teach yourself to become unnaturally natural on paper, editing while you're writing and afterward—you won't be able to take your talent to its limit or to try to move past it. You won't be able to spend years growing better at your chosen trade.

In Faulkner's short story "Knight's Gambit" Charles Mallison asks his uncle, Gavin Stevens, how it is that just years have brought him wisdom. Stevens says simply, "They made me older. I have improved."

The skill and seeming ease that come with mastering the artifice necessary to look and sound "natural" in the short story are products of work. Writing a good marketable story is as against the grain of "naturalism" as is the ability to pitch a shutout in baseball.

Style is one of the dominant reasons you're rewriting now; to instruct yourself to tighten and polish, to learn to appreciate the look of the page as a reader will, to develop the editor-reader inside you. Sometimes this can be accomplished in one illuminating surge of understanding. Sometimes it takes longer. In either case it leads to that moment when you can look at a second draft before it goes off in the mail and say firmly, "I have improved."

The Overrated, Much-Too-Simple Declarative Sentence

*A*t one time, in my misspent salad days, I served as copy chief for a flourishing advertising agency. Each afternoon at four, one of its founders, who had nothing much else to do but trim cigars in his office, would march down the hall of the Copy Department, chanting, "Nobody here can write a simple declarative sentence!" My answer to this canard was to write a very simple declarative sentence, in the form of an obscene command, and hand it to him as he strolled by.

I think he had read a brief hymn to the declarative sentence, in one of Hemingway's many and often cryptic comments on prose, or elsewhere, and had taken it to heart. While I do not believe such sentences are without their blunt usefulness in all story prose, there is no form of drumbeat which falls with a duller thud on the human ear or brings the water of boredom more swiftly to the human eye than a parade of them aligned together and masquerading as prose.

> *He climbed the stairs. He was hot. He opened the attic door. He went in. He looked out the window. He saw his grandfather's briar pipe. He picked it up. He smelled its dry crust. He put it in his mouth. He thought about his grandfather. He stood there awhile. He put the pipe down. He went down the stairs. He was still hot.*

Each corner-of-the-mouth utterance in that little group deadens the next one, until by the end of the paragraph any possible mood or effect has been chopped into dog food. We are back in the domain of the primer, with Dick and Jane exhorting their pet to "Jump, Gyp, jump." Thoreau, who urged mankind to simplify, did not, I think, mean writing man and woman to become lobotomized and deadened to the sound and color of storytelling. The mildly overdrawn example I have used here could be augmented by a hundred others culled from the work of those who mistake a brusque and cleanly sentence for a godly sentence and who follow it with another and another. This is not aiming; it is solemn and portentous repetition.

The short, straightforward statement can be magically effective—but only when it is used to vary a series of longer ones. It is sometimes contended by beginning writers that Hemingway wrote only in these tiny bulletins—but he didn't; he used them in conjunction with a rhythm which, within its boundaries, was very personal, artificially "natural," and an effective simulacrum of human speech.

There will be ample room for these much-touted donkeys of all work in your stories. But don't let them line up and bray in unison. Aside from again pointing out that style is a way of saying and a way of seeing, it's safe to add that it is never going to consist of battalions of declarative sentences frozen into humorless, rigid obedience.

Quotation Marks: Where and Why

Quotation marks around dialogue are, in most large-circulation magazines, as obligatory as the necktie, jacket—and shoes—worn when visiting a formal restaurant. They help the clientele separate the dialogue from the body of the story—and besides that, you don't stand a very good chance of getting in without them. This applies, as well, to the quote within a quote; if you're unsure of where and how to apply Aldus's high comma in these cases, consult your favorite style manual for the correct form. "Yes," said Phillip, "my great-aunt dropped the pruning knife and injured her toe, just as she was saying, 'Always whittle away from you and you'll never cut yourself.' "

The use of quotes around some word or phrase that you want to highlight because it has the nature of a cliché and, in your estimation, needs setting apart for this reason is a matter no style manual can really settle. It's a question of your own taste, sense of story balance, and your feeling for the appearance of the page. (Quotation marks used in this way are, no matter how slightly, snobbish—they imply that you and the reader know that the quotation-mark-framed phrase or word is hackneyed, and they are meant to take the curse off the fact that you have gone ahead and used the thing anyway. In this book I have used quotation marks in this context with some liberality; in a short story I would try not to do it more than once, and if possible not at all.) Here is a sample of a story sentence that may, or may not, require its quotation marks:

> They said he was "one of the boys" but as soon as he left them he became as aloof as a moulting eagle.

Does "one of the boys" really need those protective—and somewhat coy—quotes? The phrase is warmed by them, but without them the sentence would speak with a faster and cleaner impact. In these cases the problem of to quote or not to quote can only be settled by debate between your aesthetic sensibility and the demands of the particular story. On balance I would leave out the quotation marks and trust the reader to give the shopworn four words their off-the-cuff intonation. I would omit them because the murmurous irony of the quotation marks might well be repeated at another similar point in the story—and a story with more than one set of quotation marks outside its dialogue begins to look as if the author is soliciting sympathy for a superior viewpoint.

Occasionally quotation marks used in First Person narrative around phrases of humdrum shallowness can deliberately underscore the character of the narrator. This is the voice of Nora, a Civil War camp follower, speaking in Fitzgerald's "The Night of Chancellorsville":

> Well, I started to tell you how I went down to the army in "Ole Virginia." Never again! Wait'll you hear.

There the quotes give a droll and happy familiarity to Ole Virginia, and we can hear the exact scornful inflection of Nora as she says it, a woman outraged because the war won't stop long enough for her to make a few dollars.

In novels, because familiarity grows in proportion to length, you can, if you feel impelled to, dispense with all quotation marks. This has always seemed a sweeping and arbitrary decision, to this writer; it lends a certain mystery to the page, but at the same time the dialogue gains nothing by being presented without quotes. The exact sound of dialogue can be muted and a little fuzzy without boundary marks, as though something more than the quote marks had been left out. In your story, meant for as large an audience as it can command, I'm taking for granted that you'll frame all dialogue in quotes. And the decision to use them, or not to, in places where they may either highlight or give a different cast to a common word or phrase, has to be yours alone. Like all these matters of paragraphing, punctuation, and the general aesthetic understanding of your particular story, there can be no steel rules to guide you—only a steadily growing familiarity with the inner truth of what you want to say, of how close you can come to saying it with every story.

Rhyme, Assonance, Consonance

Assonance is actually the correspondence of accented vowels—it can best be studied (or at least, more obviously seen, heard, and understood) in the work of such passionate and successful probers into the sound of word-music as Gerard Manley Hopkins. Its use in prose is limited but rewarding; a line such as "skies of couple-color as a brindled cow" might precisely say what you wanted to, but if such lines were continually stressed, they would pull away from the central impact of the story and try to stand on their own; in general, great verse or poetry does this—stands for a multitude of impressions compressed in one—while short story prose is an able, agile, nimble, ever-changing servant dedicated toward the single overall recounting of the story, subordinate to it but keeping it fully controlled. The finest flight of assonantal poetry ever written can be out of place in a short story—a snake charmer visiting the local PTA.

Rhyme in prose—particularly the story—is much more obvious when encountered, and unless it is there very purposefully, to achieve a special effect by the use of repetition and chiming words, it is likely to come out like a virulent form of baby talk. I would advise anybody to avoid it and to take out poetic frustrations in some other manner than attempting to incorporate them in prose. Two or three deeply felt, rightly used phrases, blunt and unrhymed, are genuine poetry enough for a good or great commercial story—the great, simple, reverberant lines of the best prose become a people's poetry that sticks in the mind forever.

Consonance is concord—the induced vibration of one sonorous body acting in sympathy with another. When an A Major chord is echoed by another on a piano, many things happen inside the human ear—all of them mellifluent, pleasing, and somehow more right than the plain melody might have been. Less metaphorically, consonance is the repetition of consonant sounds in the middles or the ends of words—like the *k* sounds clicking away in alternation with the softer, more liquid *l*'s in "The sandpiper stalked along the water's edge, looking for snails to crack."

Unlike assonance and rhyme, consonance is often felt before it is chosen, and may frequently, in a seasoned storyteller, mean the deliberate selection of one phrase over another for its effect on a phrase already used—its doubling of the strength of the original. There is a certain kind of summer thunder that is full of consonance—the rolling of one peal of sound, answered by another, strengthening the impact of both. Consonance is not rhetoric; it is pure strong sound reduced to its most artful essentials. The relation between a good poem and a good short story has never quite been fully explored—but if you look back through the work of certain poets (Kipling, of course; Benét, quite naturally), you will find strong evidences of the same ear working on a storymaking level. And you can also discover short-story-making potential in the work of John Keats, Robert Browning; they were people who above all needed to entertain as they dazzled, amazed themselves, and served as practicing magicians of the word. These lines:

> The hare limped trembling through the frozen grass;
> The owl, for all his feathers, was a-cold

speak volumes of summary on a short story level; the Eve of Saint Agnes shines with terrible frost, and the reader is engaged in a vast physical as well as a fascinatingly religious-metaphysical adventure. And the consonance is achieved not by accident, but by the vast and successful artifice of beautiful storymaking.

With Browning's "The Flight of the Duchess" we are on the same intense level of narrative:

> Ours is a great wild country:
> If you climb to our castle's top,
> I don't see where your eye can stop;
> For when you've passed the corn-field country,
> Where vineyards leave off, flocks are packed,

And sheep-range leads to cattle-tract,
And cattle-tract to open-chase,
And open-chase to the very base
Of the mountain, where, at a funeral pace,
Round about, solemn and slow,
One by one, row after row,
Up and up the pine-trees go,
So, like black priests up, and so
Down the other side again
To another greater, wilder country.

That is narrative skill with a vengeance, and the working short story writer can learn more from it and its kind than from many weighty treatises on the status of the story through history.

The Transitional Space

In this entire section, ever since the writing of and commentary on "Three Writers," we have been looking at stories with a two-way vision—working our way through a forest, distinguishing oak from maple, birch from tamarack, poison ivy from moss; but never, I trust, have we lost sight or feeling of where we are in the forest itself—this story around us which is our purpose for being here. We have stayed outside it, and at the same time we've been moving through it, clearing away brush and bringing it sun and air. But a few points of forest cultivation remain to be touched on while we're in here.

The first is the use of the double space to separate one story scene from another.

A printer would merely refer to this space as a place to "drop two ems"—creating a visible break in the story where virginal white paper could talk to itself. And it is that simple in effect. But it can't be an arbitrary break, indulged in as a whim; it's there for a purpose, either because the passage preceding it rounds off a scene or because a slight break in time is strongly indicated. It signals more than the pause of a comma or a semicolon—more than the efficient pointing finger of a dash, the fading music of dots, or the sharp stab of a colon. In a stage play its equivalent is the dimming of the lights between scenes—to signify a change of mood, of time, of a fresh scene about to unfold.

Inside this white pause for taking breath before going on, the reader is subtly prepared for change.

In a story of mine, "Wet Night in Westmont," told in Third Person, and although done in straightforward narrative, keeping in reserve a certain occult overtone, a young soldier is home on leave in an Illinois suburban village. Yet the reader is not quite sure it is *leave* in the usual sense because the soldier, Nick, seems to be inspecting his past life with eyes more farseeing than usual, as if he were prepared for an overwhelming inner revelation which would explain his journey and put an end to all wrestling. Through the dark rainfall of evening he travels the familiar streets, moves across a glinting-grassed schoolyard with swings and ladders shining in the wet, and in his head, with his whole leaping imagination, begins to visualize his childhood home waiting, alive and alight in the sibilant darkness:

> *He was walking faster now. You took this angling shortcut and then you were, when you went down the short hill and reached the sidewalk again, almost at the front door. Already he could see the house; it was smaller than he remembered it, though it had a lot of depth, went back in room on room, like a child's imagined castle made solid in the night.*

This is a natural pausing place. The story ground has been prepared for another and ongoing growth; it would be possible to move onward without the transitional mute space, but it is a compliment to the story to offer this break in time and narrative. E.E. Cummings once requested an anthology editor to "surround my contribution with a little silence," and this sort of silence is precisely what the two-em drop indicates.

Of course the most carefully indicated use of white space may simply be ignored by the large magazine in which the story is published. This can happen for reasons of layout space, advertising, illustration, or even because a makeup editor feels a cartoon might look nice in the center of the page. If it happens to you, make a deep-sworn vow to smile valiantly and reflect that the magazine has paid you top prices for the dubious privilege of somewhat spoiling your best work; otherwise, be very quiet about it, and when the story is reprinted in a textbook, anthology, or one of your own story collections, put the white space back where it was in the beginning.

The (Happily) Rare Asterisk

Asterisks are encountered in today's commercial short stories less frequently than giraffes are seen grazing on suburban lawns. There was a time in the suggestive and often wonderfully coy rule books of editors when they peppered the page whenever "tough" language or lapses of sexual conduct might offend the readers of family magazines. It hasn't really been so long since poor old Colonel Cantwell, of "Across the River and into the Trees," found himself sold to Ray Long, then editor of *Cosmopolitan*—and his colorful language so bowdlerized by dash, asterisk, and other enigmatic mark that the result was like trying to read a telegram in a hailstorm.

Aside from the fact that they always did make reading difficult and seemed to do more leering than communicating, there hasn't ever been much use for asterisks in a good story. Michael Arlen used them deftly in his stories of the charming people of Mayfair, to poke fun at; but they have now gone the way of the passenger pigeon and the greater bustard, and the word and deed they once hinted at are mentionable.

But these same words and deeds don't require dragging into any story in the holy name of "reality." Beginning writers, feeling their oats, often rejoice in using words that substitute expletives for emotion. When the real word is necessary, it's simply inevitable—no word can shock when it's natural and proceeds from the real texture of the story. (When Grady Calman tells Amelia Sammons he thinks Hamilton Ferris is a highrolling bastard, he is saying just what he means; to have him modify this would be unfair to everybody.) A decent criterion for testing the power and efficacy of blunt speech is whether or not the words jump off the page and grate a little on the ear; if they do, they'll be overdone, and the writer will have exceeded and slightly betrayed the characterization. There is a balance of truth to be taken into account in these matters; in a so-called permissive society we expect the bare bones of statement to be taken at face value, but not indulged in to the detriment of the story and the danger of boredom.

(When faced by a problem of this sort, I often think of the splendid story about Sir Beerbohm Tree, the celebrated Edwardian actor-producer, a silky, sophisticated, and witty man who, after listening awhile to a group of chattering ingénues one afternoon, strolled to the stage and raised a finger and counseled, "Dear Ladies—just a *little* more virginity, if you please." I think many magazine editors faced by a surplus of virginity's opposite would sympathize with that heartfelt and suave request.)

The asterisk, if not as a symbol of something hidden and too esoteric for plain outright utterance, is still used in stories—to indicate that you've come to one of those two-em drops, but that you don't have room left on the page to separate the paragraphs. When this slight awkwardness comes about, place three asterisks—***—in the available white space and go on in the confidence that the editor will know you mean a two-line pause to be there. (If you have a word processor which justifies lines, plays Beethoven's *Eroica* in all keys, and is programmed to translate the Golden Books of the Incas, it may be taught to produce a final draft that is pure and wholly asteriskless.)

Story Endings

It is tempting, but not quite true, to say that there are only two kinds of story endings—those that came out right the first time and those that slid a little off the mark in the first draft and had to be carefully bullied back into place. Actually, there are infinite varieties of story endings; there are compromises which don't look at all like compromises by the time they have been made; there are simplicities which began as complexities and were reduced to their fine essentials through the refinement of rewriting. And, as I have emphasized, there are stories which have changed tone during the first draft so that the planned, too carefully preordained original ending needs to be recast and freshly shaped. In the ending of "Three Writers" I was lucky, and I am not going to falsely apologize for that; I have been a professional writer of stories for money for three good decades, and I am, after all, supposed to know my trade and to accept a little good fortune as occasionally earned.

It is in story endings that the true storytelling mind, art, and heart are cultivated most intensely; it is these that mark the "born" storyteller from the person who merely wants to tell a story. For many novels—especially long ones—can afford the leisure of vanishing piece by piece as loose ends are gathered up and the book becomes a sustained good-bye—but a story is over with one swift impression; and the impression speaks for everything behind it. It is like an invisible spokesperson with his or her head between the curtains, delivering the crisp implicit meaning of the drama, then vanishing forever. If you do not have this sense of swift, complete farewell in narrative, you may write fine stories but it will always be more difficult for you than other forms—I have called storytelling an unnatural act because I think it defies the inclination of mankind to explain—great stories do *not* explain, they merely speak and then go away.

Story endings can be Wet or Dry, juicy and resonant, laconic or sharply delivered. They can't be loose; they can't drift. They call for a special set of writing muscles, a mind geared to a single effect. Many endings are passionately suggested in the intonation of the storytelling voice, yet delivered as if they were mere offhand afterthoughts. Here is one of those—the ending of a story (I cited its opening much earlier in this book) called "The Big Beast." "The Big Beast" treats of many verities—of simply being young; of the mystique of the automobile; of dying; of war. But it also underlines the luck of being born in the first place. The words, delivered by the younger brother of the man who has gone away, say considerably more than they appear to, although they aren't abstruse words:

That's all for then. After that comes school and its problems and the beautiful complexity which never becomes simple, or straightens out in a clear line, till much later. And before the Christmas vacation there is a letter from R.C., laconic but to the point, telling us that he is enlisting because Pearl Harbor has happened. Then there are many more letters from R.C., none of them long, most of them humorous. Some of the last letters, coming years later, mention in a roundabout way, which the censor doesn't quite get, that he and his outfit will be moving out before long. I remember that I thought then, He could get as far as Stuttgart, and see the Mercedes-Benz works if there's anything left by then.

He didn't get to Stuttgart. Or Berlin, either. He was killed in the Bulge. I do not think he forgot the summer we had, and I doubt that he hated the enemy who killed him; I think he probably kept to the end the male pride and satisfaction that we'd been privileged to follow, to its finish, a youthful dream. He loved greatness, and women; and since they are both worth it, that can be a true love. He had the idea of mankind going all out

*for beauty. Sometime there'll be another like him, and he will
live.*

And here is an entirely different story ending, the completion of a piece
of puff pastry which I wrote for the plain, worthy need to entertain myself and as many readers as I could snare in my widely cast net. It is,
roughly, based on an old auto racing legend concerning hard times in Italy and the attempt to fix a famous racing event; there were those who
took knightly umbrage when it appeared in *Playboy,* and other professional, seasoned drivers, who said they had been there and remembered
the whole great debacle. The mood is one of joy streaming through the
racers, even in their defeat. The story is called, not altogether ironically,
"The Most Beautiful Race in the World," and it ends where it began, at a
favorite café table around which the racers sum up their betrayal:

> *Then the Stanguinettis had gone, the official gave us his blessing
> and let us go, and we five slunk off to our table in a corner of the
> plaza. We sat looking at Truffi for a long time, then fat Arito
> laughed.*
>
> *"I hope she was good," he said. "By God, I hope she was worth
> our money, all of it. Was she?"*
>
> *Truffi reflected. "Yes, pretty good. You know, I've had worse."
> Then we all laughed, there being little else to do, and ordered
> drinks; we put them on Truffi's tab.*

I can tell you if your story ending is right, but I cannot tell you how to
make it that way. These are intensely personal factors which have to do
with your developed or developing style, your taste, your feeling for the
right note in your own intimate music, and your sense of what a good
alert reader expects to carry away from the story. The old superstition
that iron, once chilled, can never be reheated to its first white-hot malle-
ability—that a story ending cannot be changed after it has left the forge
of the first draft—is false. Good endings can be achieved—made to fit
their stories, through sheer joyful, painstaking craftmanship and deter-
mination.

And with that said, it has to be added that there is no substitute for the
instinct of the great storymaker. A strong parallel exists in the life of
Louis Armstrong, a shameless, gross, often clownlike man who loved

the spotlight—but who in the twenties and thirties did things with a trumpet that changed the path of American music forever—majestic, joyful, superlative, *commercial* things. Overanalysis surprises and irritates most craftsmen, who operate on a deeper level than statistics can reach. Asked by a theory-ridden music major why he had held the great sorrowing opening note of "I Gotta Right to Sing the Blues," he said, "Oh, man, can't you hear there wasn't any other place to go?"

Chapter 22

Last Words: Titles

A good title for me may be a so-so or ambiguous title for you. I sometimes start with a title merely because the story seems to have
grown around it without any pretense and also because its words are
comprehensive and terse enough to cover what will be said in the story.
"Three Writers" is such a story: without its emphasis on "Three" I
somehow do not think I would have finally been fair enough to give
Hamilton Ferris his full human value—when I had finally realised I
must establish this, there was no possibility of going back or of ever
changing the title. But sometimes—I have never figured the incidence of
how and when—I end what I know is a story at least relatively close to
my visualized ideal, without any title having suggested itself, and sit
there at the end smiling pleasantly at this new intelligent child and
wishing it had a name.

Sooner or later, in a case of this latter kind, I know I am going to trudge
mentally through a vast, shadowy storehouse of titles in search of the
one that, out of them all, has special meaning for this story. I know I do
not want it to spell out precisely what goes on—"How Mrs. Bemedjian
Become an Expert Belly Dancer and Kept Her Little Family Together"—
and I am sure I do not want it overpoeticized—"Warm Music in a Cold
Year." (There is nothing wrong with that latter title, and I may even use
it sometime, but it happens to telegraph a little too much and at the
same time to be applicable to too many other stories.) I have, through
thirty extremely odd and richly satisfactory story years, accumulated a
list of titles which I do not even think I have written down anywhere,
and I will now discover myself ransacking among them at leisure, making pertinent noises to myself—H-m-m-m-ph," "Doesn't sound *too*
bad," "No, no, it sounds like a tune on an off-key pianola."

Some of these titles could be called all-purpose serapes, in which almost any story could be wrapped for the time being; which means they are usually too broad and stagy for actual use at the head of a story. "Twenty Minutes Till Sunset" is one such utilitarian set of words; it could cover everything from a tragic duel toward the end of the French Revolution to an encounter in a roadside diner in the Big Bend country of Texas. "A Talent for Delight" is another one, but I have used it once and could never visualize it adorning any other story, no matter how neatly and fully it describes what a new story is and means. "The Amanuensis," applied to a story about a beloved and wasp-tongued teacher and her triumph over a school library board determined to remove *The Wizard of Oz* from its shelves, simply sits there and droops; the gap between the thrust and fullness of the story and the abstract title is a chilly one and could be bridged only with difficulty by the running reader who wants a concrete warm flash of mystery at the very start. Through some painfully attractive titles I wend my way, stopping from time to time to reflect that it may soon be time to consult the *Oxford Dictionary of English Verse*, where so many titles have leaped from the page to fit themselves to appropriate stories that the source seems inexhaustible. I find myself dreaming half-titles and juggling names of characters—and as I work, I can sense that I am creeping up on a sort of revelation which was concealed from me at the first because it is somehow so simple, so overwhelmingly right I failed to let it burst over me. And wonder of all wonders, sometimes the real title is there, in a group of words I have read fifty times while going over the story—a title intact, not saying too much but implying everything. (Such a title was "Summer Candles"— two words which summed up the hope and remembrance and poignancy of the young men and women who lived the story and remembered it; it was there all the while, and before I found it I had nearly despaired of finding it at all.)

As you go on title-searching—now and then knowing from the beginning that the working title will be the final one, because nothing else will do; and again, waiting for the true title to show through—this matter of the right title probably won't get much easier. You will become more skillful at swifly separating the dross from the plausible, the pretender from the possibility—but there will never appear a title wizard, spreading a cloak like Merlin's, who will murmur "Here's your title" in your ear and fly away. A fine title is not always the simplest title—neither is it the most directly stated. Neither is it always picturesque—but it is always deeply related to the story, a blood relative of it. When it is achieved, the ring of the inevitable sounds through it, embracing each word of the story as though they had been born together.

Last Words: Short Story to Novel

The decline, fall, and failure of the short story as a medium of enchantment, instruction, entertainment, has been regularly announced and deplored by theorists throughout time. It is not, indeed, a medium that fits any specific category—only one whose potential has never waned and whose varied styles, moods, and amazing flexibility baffle those codifiers of behavior who seem to wish it would stand still, go away, or be absorbed into some other form and stop being so stubbornly alive. It is not my place here (and I wouldn't make it my place even if I thought it was) to defend the story—it has never asked for defense, only for appreciative readers and for enough lovers to keep it from growing static in the archives of history. This book has, indeed, attempted what I have wanted to do for a long time—to encourage and abet the young or starting writer in knowing what he or she is getting into; to indicate as if on an animated prose map the immense depth and scope of the marketable short story—and to bulwark those whose special, specific talent leans toward the creation of stories as a desirable lifetime's work in itself. I do not believe outstanding stories are written merely to justify a writer's own exercise of his or her talent—they need to be read by as many appreciative readers as possible and paid for as highly as any market can afford. They begin in utmost privacy and grow to universal size.

This is not to deprecate or lower the novel by comparison; both prose forms, infinite in variation, can plainly be considered gifts from God. But certain writers—those who were overtaken, early, by the wonder inherent in the story—have devoted most of their careers to the story; and many of these same writers preceded their novels by an acute understanding of the art of storytelling which made those novels sharper, stronger, truer, than they might have been without the craftmanship learned from the making of stories. At the opening I said that writing the successful, artful story *cannot* be taught; that it can be guided and that its mastery springs from the individual. I hold to that. I also believe that the demands of the commercial story whet and improve the art of the novel, so that without the many stories written for money (and out of great delight and exploration) by Scott Fitzgerald, we would not have *The Great Gatsby* as it stands today—and without his more than apprenticeship in the story, Erskine Caldwell would never have learned the foreshortened power of his strongest novels.

If you will read, and you *must* read hungrily all your days to achieve a fraction of what you are capable, the novels of Eudora Welty, Erskine Caldwell, Truman Capote, and other writers who began with the short story, against the novels of those who set out to be novelists without training themselves in the shorter form, you will find a tonal difference, a qualitative freshness of approach in the storywriters. This has little to do with style, preference of subject, or scope—it has everything to do with concision coupled with strength.

The professional short storymaker is one of the last of the world's nonspecialists—a person who realizes that the frontiers of the story are endless, just as the frontiers of science are endless, and who takes singular pride in expanding his or her own boundaries during a full career. The ideal attitude of such a writer is: "Indeed, I write for money; I am worth whatever I can command; and I cannot write *badly* for money, because that is the cardinal and only sin."

Last Words: Filling the Space

The painter Georges Rouault claimed that his great concern was to make his picture perfectly fill its space.

This is not a fanciful statement—it is hardheaded and clear. A painting, a musical composition, and a story have limits. Within the limits, what goes on is truly accommodated, or spills over the edges and goes shooting out in a surplus, or is limited and appears scraplike in comparison to the chosen boundary. When a story fills its space, the reader feels it, as it is felt when looking at a Rouault or a Matisse. The reader experiences from a satisfactory story a sense of balance in the most profound human affairs——a stay against confusion. An emotion of completion, of fulfillment, is there—as it was in the writer while working.

Rouault's concern runs side by side with the established Chinese theory of *K'ai-ho*—the unity of coherence. A Chinese writer of the eighteenth century, Shen Tsung-ch'ien, said: "There is nothing that is not K'ai-ho...if you analyze a large K'ai-ho, within it there is more K'ai-ho. Even down to one tree and one rock, there is nothing that does not have both expanding and winding up. Where things grow and expand there is K'ai; where they are gathered up, that is ho. When you expand (K'ai) you should think of gathering up (ho) and then there will be structure; when you gather up (ho) you should think of expanding (K'ai) and then you will have inexpressible effortlessness and an air of inexhaustible spirit. In using the brush and laying out the composition, there is not one moment when you can depart from K'ai-ho."

I do not know if Shen Tsung-ch'ien wrote stories. He was admirably equipped to. His eloquence applies to the internal balance of any story which aims at affinity with mankind—not toward perfection, which isn't reachable by people, but at the wrestling which holds the story in tense cords and keeps it from spilling over its invisible frame.

Creativity, of all kinds, has a tendency to explode. It is likely to detonate with a flash and leave in its wake the debris of what might have been. It's also likely to fume and rant and expound endless theory when it could have been channeled into what medieval craftsmen called "the Power of the Hand."

It is with the Power of Your Hand that you make stories.

They improve as your hand grows in power. Filling a waiting space has been an art, a craft, and a trade for generations—and as you train yourself to fit your story to the envisioned space, you draw closer with each working session to your own comprehension of K'ai-ho.

To "inexpressible effortlessness and an air of inexhaustible spirit."

moral (in stories), 79
Munro, H.H. ("Saki"), 32
Murdoch, Iris, 182

Nabokov, Vladimir, 112
narrator, use of, *see* viewpoint,
    first person offset
naturalism, misleading, *see* style,
    artificiality needful in
nooses, see participles, dangling
notebook, 71-73
novel
    contrasted with short story, 7,
        41, 70, 93, 235-236

O'Connor, Flannery, 35, 126
O'Flaherty, Liam, 99
O'Hara, John, 15, 19, 86, 99, 113,
    135
originality, 98-99

pacing, *see* plot
Pancake, Breece D'J, 99
parentheses, *see* style
participles, dangling, *see* style
plot
    conflict in, 51-57
    difference in, between novel and
        short story, 7, 41, 70
    endings
        inorganic
            trick, "dirigible," 73-75;
            see also Porter, William Syd-
            ney
            "happy," 135
        organic, 73-75, 135, 229-232
    flashbacks in, 131-133
    formulas in, 70-71, 76-77, 133-
        135; *see also* stereotype
    mechanical devices for (Plotto),
        59
    mood in, and as a form of, 75-76;
        see also mood story
    notebooks for, 71-73
    outlining, 59-62

plausibility in, 73-75, 77
revelation in, 52-56
selecting events for, 69-70
structure unified to, 77-79; *see al-*
    so unity
Poe, Edgar Allan, 44-45
Porter, William Sydney (O. Henry)
    trick endings of, 56, 71, 103, 127
Priestly, J.B., 139
professional attitudes, *see* writers,
    professional

question marks, *see* style
quotation marks, *see* style

readability, 7-9
readers
    family members and friends as,
        168
    other writers as, *see* writers'
        groups
reading
    aloud, 101-102, 119, 170
    as a way of learning how to
        write, 2-3
Remus, Uncle, *see* Harris, Joel
    Chandler
reviews, little or literary, *see* maga-
    zines
revision, *see* draft, second; *see also*
    draft, final
Robbins, Harold, 134
Rouault, Georges, 236

"Saki," *see* Munro, H.H.
Salinger, J.D., 7, 43, 79, 99, 112-113
Saroyan, William, 51-52, 135, 140,
    174
Scott, Sir Walter, 7
second draft, *see* draft, second
semicolon, *see* style
senses, 19-30, *see also* imagery
sentences
    declarative, overrated, 221-222;
        see also style

Other Books of Interest

General Writing Books

Beginning Writer's Answer Book, edited by Polking and Bloss $14.95
Getting the Words Right: How to Revise, Edit and Rewrite, by Theodore A. Rees Cheney $13.95
If I Can Write, You Can Write, by Charlie Shedd $12.95
International Writers' & Artists' Yearbook (paper) $11.95
Knowing Where to Look: The Ultimate Guide to Research, by Lois Horowitz $16.95
Make Every Word Count, by Gary Provost (paper) $7.95
Teach Yourself to Write, by Evelyn A. Stenbock $12.95
Writer's Encyclopedia, edited by Kirk Polking $19.95
Writer's Market, edited by Paula Deimling $19.95
Writer's Resource Guide, edited by Bernadine Clark $16.95
Writing for the Joy of It, by Leonard Knott $11.95
Writing From the Inside Out, by Charlotte Edwards (paper) $9.95
Complete Guide to Writing Nonfiction, by the American Society of Journalists & Authors $24.95
The Craft of Interviewing, by John Brady $9.95
Complete Handbook for Freelance Writers, by Kay Cassill $14.95

Fiction Writing

Fiction Is Folks: How to Create Unforgettable Characters, by Robert Newton Peck $11.95
Fiction Writer's Help Book, by Maxine Rock $12.95
Fiction Writer's Market, edited by Jean Fredette $17.95
Handbook of Short Story Writing, by Dickson and Smythe (paper) $6.95
How to Write Best-Selling Fiction, by Dean R. Koontz $13.95
How to Write Short Stories that Sell, by Louise Boggess (paper) $7.95
Secrets of Successful Fiction, by Robert Newton Peck $8.95
Writing Romance Fiction—For Love And Money, by Helene Schellenberg Barnhart $14.95
Writing the Novel: From Plot to Print, by Lawrence Block $10.95

Special Interest Writing Books

The Children's Picture Book: How to Write It, How to Sell It, by Ellen E. M. Roberts $17.95
Complete Book of Scriptwriting, by J. Michael Straczynski $14.95
The Craft of Lyric Writing, by Sheila Davis $16.95
Guide to Greeting Card Writing, edited by Larry Sandman (paper) $7.95
How to Write a Play, by Raymond Hull $13.95
How to Write and Sell Your Personal Experiences, by Lois Duncan $10.95
How to Write and Sell (Your Sense of) Humor, by Gene Perret $12.95
How to Write the Story of Your Life, by Frank P. Thomas $12.95
Mystery Writer's Handbook, by The Mystery Writers of America (paper) $8.95
On Being a Poet, by Judson Jerome $14.95
Poet's Handbook, by Judson Jerome $11.95
Travel Writer's Handbook, by Louise Zobel (paper) $8.95
TV Scriptwriter's Handbook, by Alfred Brenner $12.95
Writing and Selling Science Fiction, by Science Fiction Writers of America (paper) $7.95
Writing for Children & Teenagers, by Lee Wyndham $11.95
Writing to Inspire, by Gentz, Roddy, et al $14.95

To order directly from the publisher, include $1.50 postage and handling for 1 book and 50¢ for each additional book. Allow 30 days for delivery.

Writer's Digest Books, Department B
9933 Alliance Road, Cincinnati OH 45242
Prices subject to change without notice.